I0819556

BORDERLANDS

BORDERLANDS

RECIPES AND STORIES FROM THE RIO GRANDE TO THE PACIFIC

Hank Shaw

H|H

To the proud people of the border, the fronterizos, who straddle two worlds and bring out the best in both, day in and day out.

Saludos!

Published by H&H Books
huntgathercook.com
All H&H books may be purchased for business or promotional use, or for special sales. For information, email hank@huntgathercook.com

Design and layout: Laura Shaw Design
Food and prop styling: Hank Shaw and Holly A. Heyser
Editorial: Lisa Ekus
Icons: Allison Meierding
Photo credits: pages 9 and 292, Miguel Angel Fuentes; page 62, Cinthia Martinez; page 63 (bottom) and 155 (top), Francisco Chavira; page 83, Mike Ortiz; pages 128 and 202, Shutterstock; pages 25, 34, 38–42, 45, 47, 53, 55, 63, 66, 69, 71, 73, 76, 79, 81, 89, 91, 98, 100, 102, 105, 117, 120, 123, 136, 139, 144, 148, 153, 165, 168, 171, 174, 180, 190, 196, 200, 204, 207, 212, 226, 232, 235, 237, 239, 241, 244, 247, 249–50, 253, 260, 264, 269, 271, 274, 278, 281, 284, Holly A. Heyser

ISBN-10: 2025902945
ISBN-13: 978-09-9694-4830

1 2 3 4 5 6 7 8 9 10

Printed in the USA

Library of Congress Cataloging-in-Publication Data is available.

CONTENTS

FOREWORD

I first met Hank Shaw the way a lot of people do: through his writing. Back in 2010, my wife and I had just moved to Roseville, California, and I was deep into cooking, obsessing over ingredients, and, frankly, trying to figure out what the hell I was doing with my life. I stumbled across this blog, Hunter Angler Gardener Cook, and suddenly I'm reading a guy who's talking about curing wild duck prosciutto and making nettle pasta and pickling anything he could get his hands on; and doing it all with the tone of a dead-serious reporter turned food researcher. I thought to myself, "I need to be friends with this guy."

Turns out, he was local. So I did the only thing that made sense: I reached out cold and tried to become his friend. I emailed him; attended his first book's release dinner at Grange Restaurant in July of 2011 where I tried sturgeon for the first time, and followed up again. And again. And again. It's fair to say he was a little . . . reserved at first. The man is a planner, someone who maps things out in advance and sticks to the map. I'm more of the "hey, that road looks interesting, let's take it" type. But eventually, after a few shared meals, some drinks, and what I can only describe as a slow-burn friendship, we got close. Nixtaco became his watering hole. Fast forward to now, Hank is the kind of friend with whom we'd spend holidays and who knows he has a bed at my house whenever he visits Sacramento.

Hank used to work as a political reporter, underpaid by his own accounts, and would for years live off the fish and seafood he could catch himself. He escaped political writing into food and has since become, in my not-so-humble opinion, the foremost authority on wild food in the United States. His blog won a James Beard Award in 2013 (after being nominated twice before that), and if you've ever heard him talk about foraging, fishing, or hunting, you know the man doesn't just read about things—he does them. Then he breaks them down into perfectly calibrated prose and recipes that actually work.

He knows where (and when) the mushrooms are in the Sierras (and the Mexican desert's sky islands), when the fish are biting, and which duck makes for the best rillettes. He's the guy who plans his entire year around what nature's giving and when. That freezer in his house? It's a map of his travels.

But what really sets Hank apart isn't just the encyclopedic knowledge, it's the storytelling. He has this way of weaving personal experience with fact, of grounding hard research in soft dirt. And nowhere is that clearer than in *Borderlands*. One of the things that struck me most is how he managed to capture the spirit of the people who live in this liminal space between the U.S. and Mexico. People like me, who grew up in Monterrey with Sunday carne asadas and family gatherings that blurred the lines between celebration and weekly ritual. People who know that food isn't just about sustenance, it's about identity. People like Mario from Juarez, who loves Colitas de Pavo. Culture and story. Hank gets that. He gets us.

When Hank first told me he was working on a Mexican cookbook, I was thrilled. Then he asked me to help write it. I said yes immediately. We came up with a sort-of plan, traveled together to Monterrey, my hometown, and I showed him around, introduced him to the flavors I grew up with and shared a curated list of recipes I felt belonged in any book that wanted to do justice to the northern Mexican borderlands. I even wrote a few things. But life got busy, as it does, and my other projects pulled me away. Hank, of course, kept going. He went on to travel the entire U.S.–Mexico border, gathering stories, tasting food, and documenting it all, the way only he can.

The result is *Borderlands*. It's not just a cookbook, it's a living, breathing document exemplifying traditions of a region that defies easy definition. Mexican food isn't a monolith. It's many things, shaped by geography, culture, and personal flair. What's a machaca in one place might be something entirely different a few miles away, and yes, flour tortillas are real; as real as nixtamal tortillas. Hank's seemingly academic dissertation on the matter tackles that debate like a culinary anthropologist with a bone to pick.

Hank doesn't just list recipes. He explains why they exist the way they do, who makes them, and what corners of the world came together to shape them. He brings order to a cuisine often misunderstood as chaotic or inconsistent. It's not chaos, it's nuance. It's regional pride. It's the flavors of La Frontera.

The best part? These recipes work. They're functional. This book is written for the cook who wants to try Machito in Minnesota, who wants to make border-style flour tortillas without having to track down Sonoran wheat or barter for beef tallow. They're practical without compromising authenticity. They're tested. They're thoughtful. And yes, they're delicious.

I'm endlessly proud of this book, even if I only had a hand in shaping its early beginnings. Hank carried the torch and ran with it, and what he has made is more than I ever imagined. *Borderlands* is going to be the go-to book for anyone serious about understanding the cuisine of the US–Mexico border. And I say that not just as a chef, but as a northeastern Mexican kid who once dreamed of becoming one.

So, *querido lector*, get ready. What you hold in your hands isn't just a cookbook. It's a journey through smoke and salsas, flour and fire, tradition and innovation. It's Hank's love letter to the borderlands.

¡Buen provecho!

—PATRICIO WISE, chef/owner of
Nixtaco Mexican Kitchen, Roseville, CA
Recipient of a Michelin Bib
Gourmand Award, 2022–2024

KING RANCH

INTRODUCTION

You hold in your hands my love letter to a region: its people, its food, its environment, and all the plants, animals, and fungi that live within it.

I've been traveling along the border of the United States and Mexico for decades, first as a tourist, then as a hunter and angler, and ultimately as a researcher fascinated—obsessed, even—with the people and foods of this astonishing part of the world. I've set foot on nearly every mile of the US side of the border, from the beaches of San Diego to the beaches of South Padre Island, and most of the thousands of miles of desert that lie in between. I've traveled extensively on the Mexican side of the border, too, visiting each of the states along la frontera, several enough times where I feel as at home there as I do in the country of my birth.

In that time, I've eaten thousands of tacos, hundreds of burritos, and untold meals grand and humble. I've chatted up ranchers and cabbies—in both English and in Spanish—bartenders and servers, grandmothers, old guys on the corner, and random people I've just met on the street.

I've felt my skin redden and parch in the convection oven of a Sonoran summer, and have huddled in my truck against the chill of the Chihuahuan Desert in December. I've sweat through my clothes in the steaming tropical heat of Brownsville and, well, felt the tranquility of walking the beach at dawn in San Diego.

The borderlands are a liminal space between two nations that can be uncomfortable neighbors. Mexico is, as of this writing, the United States' largest trading partner, yet political rhetoric on both sides of the border can make our nations' relationship seem far less friendly than it really is.

Leaving politics aside, the geography of the region is incredibly varied and its environments are deceptively rich. Snow-capped peaks in Arizona, New Mexico, and Chihuahua, dunefields that echo the Sahara in northern Baja, tranquil beaches on both the Pacific and Gulf shores, tropical scrubland in Tamaulipas and South Texas, and everywhere, desert. The borderlands contain three great deserts: the Mojave, the Sonora, and the Chihuahua.

Spend time along the border and you will soon see that the people there are neither fully Mexican nor fully American—whatever that means to you. They are fronterizos, the people of both worlds, sliding in and out of mores and predilections and desires as easily as they slide between English and Spanish, often in mid-sentence. It is not uncommon to hear fronterizos speak twangy English, but accentless, perfect Spanish. Or vice versa: I've heard people speak in heavily Mexican Spanish, then effortlessly slide into accentless English in a heartbeat.

La frontera calls to me so strongly because I've lived my own life in a similar space. Never truly a member of any group, shifting depending on need, requirement, and environment, I deeply identify with the multifaceted nature of the denizens of the borderlands. I feel at home among them.

When I was a child, I was mesmerized by the movie *Lawrence of Arabia*. I still am. There is a line in the movie when Alec Guinness's character eyes Peter O'Toole, and says, "You are one of those desert-loving Englishmen." I feel that in my soul. I love the desert. Its clarity, its decisiveness. The sound of the cactus wren, the white-winged dove, and the Gambel's quail. I love its silence, too, which can surround you so fully that the ringing in your ears threatens to overwhelm you. The ozone-like smell of creosote bushes after a rain. The scent of desert flowers, so seeming strange in such a harsh place.

Each of these landscapes sports a vast array of edible wild plants, mushrooms, and game animals that, if you know what you're doing, will feed you so well you might grow fat.

The primary keepers of that natural knowledge are the Indigenous peoples who live there, some for thousands of years, some as more recent arrivals. The Zuni, Kumeyaay, Tohono O'Odham, Pueblo, Seri, Mayo, Yaqui, Tigua, Kikapü, Apache, Tarahumara, Hopi, Navajo, and Comanche are only the most well known. Through personal experience, conversations with elders, and study, I've come to know the edible wild plants of the borderlands as well as my home regions—maybe even better. The breadth of wondrous wild flavors these plants and mushrooms add to the tables of the region would require its own book, and a thick one at that, but I'll introduce you to my favorites in these pages.

Readers of my previous books know that game and fish are my chief specialties, and you will not be disappointed here. I've hunted every state along the border, and fished both coasts. From Coues deer to quail, nilgai, ducks, and doves, and even the noisy-but-tasty chachalaca, the borderlands offer unique game animals that enhance our meals. The fishing on both the Gulf Coast and San Diego is world class: tuna, yellowtail, snapper, grouper, snook, seabass, and sea trout are some of the finest fish you can catch. And nowhere is the shellfish better than Baja: clams, oysters, lobsters, and crabs of all varieties.

Leavening all this are the singular cuisines of the borderlands. The food of la frontera is a hybrid between Mexican cuisine and Southern sensibilities. The majority of the Anglo population in American border states were originally from the South, and, to some eyes, Texas remains Southern; I'd say Texas is its own thing, not quite Southern, not quite Southwest. So all along the border, you'll see amalgams like green chile cornbread and apple pie—yes, green chile in apple pie is amazing!—biscuits served alongside pozole, the addition of a flour-and-fat roux in the green and red chile sauces of New Mexico.

Flour tortillas and beef are king here, except on the coasts, where seafood reigns. To be sure, corn remains vital to the identities of many in the borderlands, primarily Indigenous groups, and corn tortillas, often made with blue corn, are highlights of both New Mexican and Chihuahuan cuisine. Pork dishes exist, but chicken is relatively rare in the traditional food of the borderlands. Mostly now you see it in modern chain restaurants as well as some dishes that are straight out of the South.

Chiles, sweet corn, beans, squash are all prominent here, and parts of the borderlands, notably California's Imperial Valley and the Rio Grande Valley of South Texas, are some of the richest vegetable growing regions in the United States, as is southern Sonora in Mexico.

It's this cornucopia, farmed and wild, that keeps me coming back. The flavors are big, the dishes uncomplicated (for the most part), and the ingredients are varied and wonderful. Underlying it all is the whiff of smoke. Char and smoke connect the borderlands more closely than Interstate 10. From a California barbecue, which is mostly grilling, to a Sonoran carne asada or a Chihuahuan

A basket made by the Kumeyaay people in Baja California.

discada, to a real-deal, slow-and-low Texas barbecue, smoke and fire rule the region.

So settle in for a ride, an admittedly idiosyncratic ride, through recipes wild and farmed, American and Mexican, esoteric and commonplace and everything in between. Buen provecho, y'all!

A NOTE ON THE RECIPES

All the recipes in this book have been tested by regular humans, not chefs. I do this because clarity is vital, especially when dealing with hard-to-get ingredients like wild foods. You can't simply walk down to the supermarket to get venison tenderloin or another bag of that precious spice mix you brought back from Tampico. If this is your one chance with an ingredient, I want that chance to succeed.

These recipes are developed for an American kitchen, using as authentic a set of ingredients as I can get here in the States. In most cases, this isn't an issue because Latin markets are everywhere in the US and Canada. Fun parlor trick? Google "Latin market near me" and you might be surprised to find one a few miles away. Or closer.

However, where I can, I will also include substitutions. I'd rather you make a recipe with a few alterations than not make it at all.

There also exists a ton of variations surrounding these recipes within Mexico and the border states. Unlike the often dogmatic cuisines of Italy and France, for example, Mexican cuisine hinges on the sazón, the personal flair, of each cook. So while yes, there was an original tacos gobernador invented in Sinaloa, that basic structure has been joyously played with by countless cooks all over Mexico. So long as it has cheese, fish or seafood, and chiles, it's a gobernador. Whether you like x version or y is up to you.

Innovation and fun in the service of flavor is the essence of modern border cooking. Birria comes from Jalisco, but the birria taco is a *very* Tijuana thing, likely first served by Tapatios who moved there. And if I had a peso for every version of ceviche or aguachile I've seen in Mexico, I could eat at Mexico City's Michelin-starred restaurant Pujol. Twice.

So, in these cases, the recipe that appears in this book is one I like best. It's either someone's, and that someone is credited in the headnotes, or it's an amalgam of the many recipes I've heard, read, and eaten over the years. Yes, you'll see my own sazón within these pages.

Most of the recipes in these pages I have eaten "on location." A few I've learned from borderlands folks living elsewhere, a few are my own inventions, and a few are so good I felt compelled to put them in the book, even though I've not yet eaten them in situ. I am keeping this final category of recipes to a minimum because I'd like this book to reflect my travels more than my aspirations.

Each chapter forced me to make crushing decisions about what recipes to include and what to drop. The individual cuisines of places such as New Mexico or Texas or Sonora are so vast that it's impossible to fully do justice to them here. Each could fill a huge cookbook by itself—and they do. I am sorry if your favorite dish isn't in here. Hopefully you'll find plenty of other recipes as fascinating, and as memorable, as I do!

HOW TO USE THIS BOOK

Borderlands departs from the structure in my other books, which are, more or less, in standard cookbook format. All of us who put this book together felt so strongly about its nature—the place, the journey—that that's how we decided to organize it: as a journey.

Consequently, it must start in Sacramento, where I lived for nineteen years and where I conceived of this book. After that, I take you to the mouth of the Rio Grande and we go east to west along the border, threading our way through both Mexico and the United States. The recipes are organized according to that journey, so you'll see a recipe that is very Sonoran in the Sonora chapter—or, if it's a case where variations of the recipe exist all over the region, the version I like best will be placed where I found it. Asado de puerco is a great example of this: Some form of it can be found from Baja to Tamaulipas, but I really like the rendition I had in Nuevo Leon.

So you won't find all the beef dishes in one place, or all the mushroom recipes in another. I know this can pose a challenge, so that's why we included a very thorough index to help you out. If you pick up this book to cook, say, some borderlands-style venison, look to the index.

Along those lines, lots of these dishes can be, and are, made with multiple meats or fish or whatever. In these cases, I will provide a few icons of alternates in the margin of the recipe, similar to what I did in my book *Pheasant, Quail, Cottontail.*

You will see some recipes, primarily baking or charcuterie, where I switch to grams. I do this because in these special cases, precision is vital. An example is the Mesquite Chocolate Chip Cookies (page 216): You can get wildly different results depending on how you pack the flour in a cup, but the weight measurements will be consistent every time.

▸ The Rio Grande at St. Elena Canyon in Big Bend National Park, Texas.

The mouth of the Rio Grande at Las Palomas Wildlife Area in Boca Chica, Texas.

PART 1

BASICS

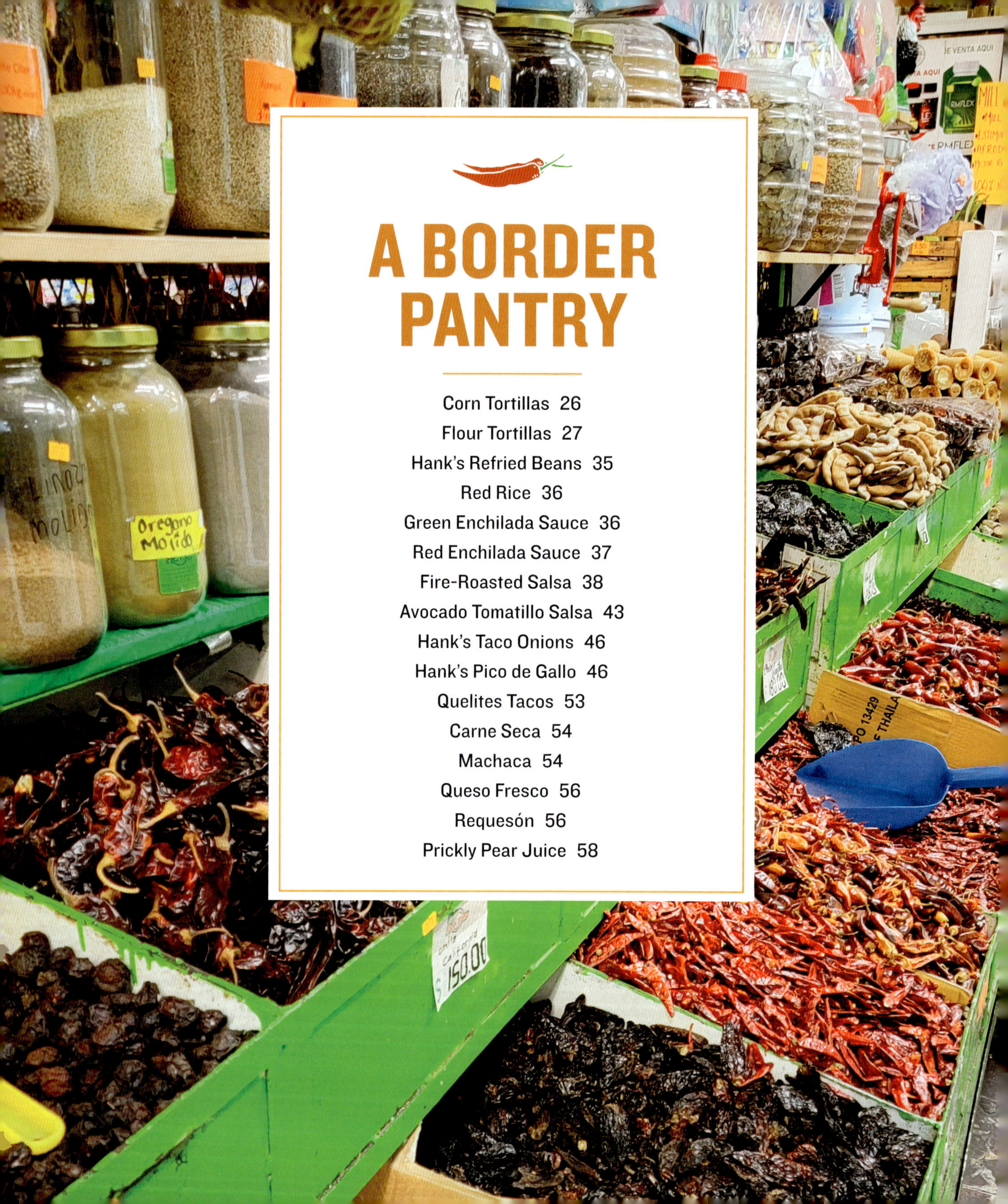

A BORDER PANTRY

With some exceptions, the pantry of the borderlands is similar to yours. Eggs, flour, baking soda, spices, herbs, etc. But a host of premade and convenience foods exists that makes life easier. They range from appalling to sublime. Here are a few I always have in my kitchen.

CHILES

There is a saying in Mexico that a day without chile is like a day without sunshine, and I wholeheartedly believe that. Chiles in all forms—red, green, fresh, frozen, dried, and canned—are vital to border cuisine.

Let's start with fresh. The workhorse chiles along the border are all green. Jalapeños are the most famous, but the smaller and zippier serranos are almost as universal. You will see poblanos, mostly east of El Paso. From El Paso west, the Anaheim takes over. It's called green chile or chilaca depending on where you go, and the green chiles from Hatch, New Mexico are legendary—although they're not the only good ones along the border.

Frozen peeled and seeded roasted green chiles are excellent. You can find them along the border, but also via mail order. If you can roast and put up your own, this is a great option.

Another green(ish) chile you see mostly in Sonora and Baja is the chile güero, which is very close to the Hungarian wax chiles we see in US supermarkets. Mostly I see these pickled or served stuffed as Toritos (page 278).

Yes, you can find fully ripe red jalapeños in border markets, as well as the wild chiles (see page 31), but for the most part, red chiles are dried.

Dozens of varieties of dried chiles exist along the border, all red except for the chile pasado, which I write more about on page 181. By far the most common are guajillos in the east, dried red New Mexican or California—these are the ripe Hatch chiles—in the west, and ancho chiles everywhere. All are fairly large and not terribly spicy, although there are exceptions.

Small, fiery chile de árbol chiles are common, too, and are used for a salsa that can range from zippy to lethal.

You can definitely find other chiles in the region, but for the most part they are there to cater to the cuisines of other parts of the world. I haven't seen too many traditional border recipes with habaneros or any of the myriad chiles of central Mexico.

Two types of chiles are commonly canned: jalapeños and green chiles. The canned green chiles come stemmed, seeded, roasted, and peeled, and they're . . . OK. I don't love them, but they'll do in a pinch. If you have the option, buy the whole ones in the large cans and chop them yourself. And rinse them. Canned green chiles seem to have a weird metallic twang going on unless they're washed.

Canned jalapeños will either be pickled or sold as chipotles in adobo. Yes, a chipotle is a fully ripe, smoke-dried jalapeño. Canned chipotles in adobo are a mainstay of the border kitchen, so have some on hand always. It is possible to find dried chipotles along the border, but they are less common. The larger, tobacco-colored chipotle meco is considered superior to the smaller, darker morita chipotles, which are the ones you'll find in the can.

HERBS AND SPICES

By far the most important herb or spice in your border kitchen is Mexican oregano, *Lippia graveolens*, which also grows in West Texas and a few places on the New Mexico–Chihuahua border. It shows up everywhere. The bean company Rancho Gordo sells this kind online. There are several kinds, notably *Poliomintha longiflora*, that possess a beguiling, floral-fruity aroma. Mexican oreganos are not even in the same genus as European oregano, but if you absolutely cannot find Mexican oregano anywhere in your town, it's OK to use. But I'd buy the real stuff . . .

◂ A market stall in Tijuana, Baja California.

Epazote is important, too. A strange-smelling cousin of lambsquarters and spinach, epazote is commonly used in cooking beans to add flavor and, allegedly, reduce flatulence. Buy it fresh if you can at Latin markets. Or grow it yourself and dry it on your own. Or find some—I once saw a wild epazote growing in a sidewalk crack in Las Cruces, New Mexico. Commercial dried epazote is often so old it's brown and sad.

Allspice plays a role in the border kitchen, as do cinnamon and cumin. In fact, cumin is the dominant spice from El Paso east, all along the border. There is some thought that 19th century immigrants from the Eastern Mediterranean brought this flavor to Mexico, but many very old Spanish dishes use it, too.

In terms of fresh herbs, cilantro is the undisputed queen of all Mexican herbage. I have a theory on why it's so ubiquitous: A native herb, culantro, *Eryngium foetidum*, has been used along the Gulf for millennia, and it tastes very similar to cilantro, which is native to the Old World.

I see chives and green onions with some frequency, and parsley occasionally, but that's about it. The border is a hot, dry place, and tender herbs wither easily.

BEANS AND PULSES

You can't cook border food without beans. And for the most part, that means pinto beans. They are the king of beans in the region, although they're not my favorite. Two other beans fill out the border's Big Three: bayo beans and tepary beans. I mostly use bayo beans, which are smaller and meatier than pintos. Bayo beans are common in Nuevo Leon, but I've bought them in Tijuana, too.

The two most important indigenous beans are the tepary, which grows wild in Arizona and Sonora, and the New Mexican Anasazi bean. The tepary bean is drought and heat tolerant, small and very meaty. I've grown them for years, and love them. They come in many colors. One tip on cooking tepary beans is that they take

Bayo beans

significantly longer to get tender than regular beans. Allow yourself an extra hour when cooking them. Anasazi beans cook like pintos, but I think they're prettier.

Many of these beans you can buy in good supermarkets, although I prefer specialty online stores such as Rancho Gordo or Masienda.

A few other beans play a role along the border. Canario beans, which as you might imagine are yellow, are common and cook up creamy white. They're sometimes called peruano beans. In California, there is a bean called a pinquito, a very small, pink pinto bean. I love these. Cowpeas, such as black-eyed peas, are not native to the region, but are widely grown, especially in Arizona and Sonora. There are very old varieties in that part of the world, ranging from bright red to black and mottled.

Black beans, other than black teparies, are not common on the border.

Generally speaking, if you're planning on making refried beans, pintos are fine—as are Anasazi or any brown bean. But if you plan on making pot beans, where you'll be eating them whole, try to get the other varieties, such as bayo or tepary.

I'm going to add pepitas here, even though they're not a bean, they're a seed. Husked squash or pumpkin seeds, pepitas are used widely in border cooking, and I'll tell you here first, make one of the best toppings on a taco in the world. They add salty crunch to soft, comforting guisados, stews so thick you can serve them as tacos, an example of which is the Carne Guisada (page 97). Have them around for snacking and as your secret weapon for tacos.

CORN AND FLOUR

Tortillas are not made with the sort of cornmeal most Americans are familiar with. To make a corn tortilla, you need masa harina, which is corn that has been treated with an alkaline solution to make nixtamal, and then dried and ground. The industry standard is the Maseca brand, but it's flavorless and chemically treated. Avoid it if at all possible. I love the masa harina from Masienda, which sells online, and Bob's Red Mill makes a good masa harina, too.

Keep an eye on the packaging: Some companies will sell a masa harina in a rougher grind for tamales. That makes a bad tortilla; tortillas require a finer grind.

As for flour, ideally you'll want Sonoran flour, which makes the best flour tortillas. This will be sold as harina para tortillas in Latin markets. All-purpose is OK, but never use bread flour. Arizona's Hayden Mills makes a fantastic Sonoran flour, and White Lily flour works well, too. Soft wheat is the key.

PRODUCE

The Holy Trinity of border produce are ripe Roma tomatoes, white onions, jalapeños and cilantro. OK, that's four, but you get my point. Oh, and limes. Can't live without them. So it's less like a Holy Trinity and more like a mariachi quintet.

Any lime will do, but the best are those little Key limes. If you can get them, use them. They'll make your food taste more like your last vacation to Cabo.

White onions are the rule along the border, but I see yellow ones occasionally. White onions are less sulfurous and brighter tasting—better for eating raw—although they won't keep as long as yellow storage onions. Red onions are typically used as a garnish, often soaked in lime juice.

For grilling, there's a sort of hybrid green onion–white onion mix called a Cambray onion—it's basically a small white onion with healthy greens attached—that is a staple of a Sonoran carne asada. You can find them in Latin markets.

Roma tomatoes are the standard because they can be grilled or seared easily, and are pastier than beefsteaks. Many times when you buy them in supermarkets they'll be wan and unripe, so letting them sit on the counter a few days should help. Never refrigerate tomatoes.

If you are going to crush the tomatoes anyway, it can be better to buy quality canned whole peeled tomatoes. And some companies do sell fire-roasted tomatoes, which are good in a pinch.

Jalapeños will mostly be unripe green ones, and in the US they range wildly in terms of heat. Generally speaking, they will be hotter in Latin markets—the only place you'll likely find red ripe jalapeños, too—and larger and milder in regular supermarkets. One tip: Look for striations on the skin of a jalapeño. That means the chile was stressed while growing, which means it'll be hotter.

Tomatillos, a tomato cousin, are indispensable. You'll find them wrapped in their paper husk. The best are milpa tomatillos, a wild variety that is tiny compared to the "improved" supermarket kind. Latin markets often sell the milpa tomatillos, but the regular kind is now a staple in supermarkets all over the United States.

Garlic is an everyday item, too, so have plenty.

Squash you'll find both in summer and winter forms. Winter squash, calabazas, are often a dessert item, and I have a Candied Squash recipe (page 252). Sweet potatoes often appear interchangeably. Summer squash show up in sautés and are grilled.

Nopales, cactus paddles of the *Opuntia* genus, are a common vegetable along the border. You

Clockwise, a cheese shop in Chihuahua, Mexico; a bowl of chacales; a meat market in Brownsville, Texas.

can buy them spines on, but, better to buy them de-spined and whole. Yes, you can buy bags of de-spined and diced nopales, but I prefer the whole paddles because they will always be fresher than the precut ones.

DAIRY

The border is big on dairy, despite the heat. Arguably Mexico's greatest dairy region is in Chihuahua, where Mennonite settlers arrived in the early 1900s and set up communities indistinguishable from those in the United States and Canada . . . except they speak Spanish. Neighboring New Mexico is a top 10 dairy state, too.

Cheese is white or ivory in New Mexico and in Mexico. The yellow cheese you may associate with border cooking is from Texas, and was historically longhorn, a variant on Colby cheese. Border cheese is mostly melty, with Colby, jack or cheddar as the most common on the US side of the border, and queso Chihuahua, queso Oaxaca, and queso asadero as the main melty cheeses on the Mexican side.

Nuevo Leon loves its panela, which holds its shape on a grill like halloumi, and everywhere there is both queso fresco—farmer cheese—and queso añejo or cotija, which is a drier, salted version that resembles feta or ricotta salata.

Sour cream rules in the United States, and a thinner crema agria is dominant on the Mexican side. You can switch back and forth. If you want that pretty drizzle that Mexican crema gives, you will want to stir in a little cream or whole milk into regular sour cream.

MEAT

For a border kitchen, the only two staple meat products you might want to have lying around the house are chorizo and machaca. Mexican chorizo comes in various forms, in beef or pork, and the exact spicing changes from place to place, but it's always red and always rather soft—Mexican chorizo is rarely eaten in casings, and is usually crumbled and cooked and added to things. I have a Baja California–style recipe on page 277.

Chorizo will be at every Latin market on either side of the border. Chorizo de San Manuel in Edinburg, Texas makes some of the best. Try to not buy chorizo at fancy supermarkets that make their own sausage (unless you live in an area where the people making it are likely Mexican) because it's never quite right—I think the problem is that these sausage makers learned their skills in the German tradition, and those links are very different. I don't have a preference for beef over pork.

The other meat staple would be machaca or carne seca. Carne seca, dried meat, is jerky. Usually spiced with salt and chiles, carne seca is the basis for machaca, although it is used as is in recipes like Caldillo de Carne Seca (page 146). Machaca is pulverized carne seca. Sometimes you see it as jerky bits, but in Sonora, Arizona, and in Nuevo Leon, machaca is so annihilated and fluffy it resembles meat cotton candy. This is used in eggs and in burritos and stews and a whole lot of other dishes. I have instructions on how to make it on page 54.

Don't use the more baroquely flavored jerkies for carne seca. As for machaca, good luck. You can definitely buy it online, and it's all over Latin markets along the border, but when I lived in Sacramento, no one in the Mexican markets had even heard of it, let alone carried it.

LARD

Yes, lard. Pork lard, and sometimes beef tallow. Fresh pork lard is vital to border cooking. This is not the shelf-stable, white hydrogenated crap. Latin markets sell it in quart containers at the meat counter. Good lard is liquid at room temperature and is a pretty beige, not white. Buy it. Trust me. It's lower in saturated fat than butter. And it will keep for months in the fridge, and forever in the freezer.

Beef tallow is used in Arizona and Sonora, mostly for making the best flour tortillas you've ever eaten. If you're old enough to remember before 1990, when McDonald's fries were cooked in beef tallow, you know . . .

OTHER FUN STUFF

In New Mexico, Nuevo Leon, Coahuila, and Chihuahua, you'll see dried corn called chacales or chicos. There's a difference, but they are broadly interchangeable. See page 192 for a recipe that uses them.

Chocolate in large tablets, almost always mixed with spices, is used for drinking, moles, and for sweets.

Brown sugar is primarily sold in cones called piloncillo, and you grate off what you need. Dark brown sugar is a good substitute. In Coahuila and Nuevo Leon, there's a special variety with pecans embedded in the cone that, when grated over a flour tortilla, rolled, and heated up, is one of the great simple treats of this world.

You will see some global ingredients in border cuisine, notably Worcestershire, called salsa inglesa, soy sauce, and Maggi seasoning. Soy sauce appears mostly in Sonora and in Baja, where there is a venerable Chinese immigrant community based in Mexicali. Maggi was invented in Switzerland, but is primarily of German origin. There is a huge German influence along the border: You can hear it in the music and drink it in the beer.

HOW TO MAKE TORTILLAS

MAKING TORTILLAS

Most of you will probably not make your own tortillas, and that's OK. Most people along the borderlands don't, either. But then they have access to excellent tortillas made by locals who do it for a living. If that's you, have at it. But for most of the United States and Canada, good tortillas range from difficult to impossible to source. I've seen some things . . . dreadful things: Flimsy corn tortillas that basically dissolve before you can eat a taco, flour tortillas that are basically Indian naan they're so thick. Or flour "tortillas" that lack fat in the dough, making them, well . . . not tortillas.

What follows are some basic instructions for making flour (page 27) and corn tortillas (page 26). Both are important to the borderlands, and flour tortillas especially have a few regional variations that are so good they need to be in this book. They'll follow the master recipe below.

Tortilla Presses

Get the best you can afford, and weight matters. I love my Masienda tortilla press because it's heavy and large enough for both corn and flour tortillas. Barring that, get an iron one, which will be black. Avoid the flimsy aluminum presses. The wooden ones are quaint, but clunky and weird to store.

Comals

A comal is a Mexican flattop, a typically round pan with low, sloped sides. You really want a comal or something like it if you're going to make tortillas more than once, and you can use it for more than tortillas, too. I use mine as a flattop to char vegetables and meats, too. A cast iron griddle works, and if your stovetop has a flattop, use that. A heavy sauté pan is a decent option because they usually have sloped sides. You want those sloped sides to be able to flip and remove the tortillas easily. The straight sides of a cast iron frying pan hinder that.

BLUE CORN

Blue corn exists in southern Mexico, but it is most prominent in Chihuahua and neighboring New Mexico. It is the dominant corn among the various pueblo groups in New Mexico, and among the Hopi of Arizona. Another variant is grown by the Tarahumaras in Chihuahua that's a bit taller than the stubby Hopi corn.

What's the big deal? Other than that it's pretty, blue corn is higher in protein than yellow or white corn, and it contains antioxidant anthocyanins. The starches in blue corn are easier to digest, with a lower glycemic level, than those of other corns. And in my experience, a blue corn tortilla has a softer feel than those made from other corns. My friend Patricio Wise, who owns several Mexican restaurants in Northern California, prefers blue corn for his house-made tortillas for that reason.

Another thing about blue corn is that the plants are deep-rooted, grow fast and stocky, and are drought tolerant. This makes them an excellent corn to grow as the Southwest continues to dry out. I grew it in Sacramento, and it loved the climate there. They do need soil temperatures of 70°F or above to germinate, though.

You can buy blue corn products everywhere, but if you want to make masa things with it, like tortillas, sopes, tamales, or the like, your best bet is the company Masienda. Masienda sells blue corn masa harina—nixtamalized corn flour—online.

Corn Tortillas

PREP TIME: 30 MINUTES | COOK TIME: 30 MINUTES | MAKES ABOUT 2 DOZEN SMALL TORTILLAS

The best corn tortillas are made from nixtamal, freshly treated corn that has been ground fine in one smooth overnight process. I am not going to ask you to do that, because home grinding of corn fine enough for good tortillas is not easy (ask me how I know). It's a lot easier to grind for tamales, which is a coarser grind.

That leaves masa harina, premade tortilla dough that has been dried into flour. Buy quality masa harina in blue or white for borderlands corn tortillas, but yellow is fine if that's what's available. Again, the Maseca brand is terrible. See the Sources section for quality purveyors.

Masa harina absorbs a lot of water, so you will want to use twice as much water as masa—by weight. Yes, you should weigh your ingredients here, at least as a newbie. If you can't, go 1:1 by volume. It's close enough. Knead the dough well, and then let it sit a few minutes to absorb the water. The dough will feel overly sticky at first.

240 grams masa harina, about 2 cups

480 grams warm water, about 2 cups

Knead the masa harina and water together into a cohesive ball, then let it rest a bit to let the corn absorb the water. Break off bits the size of a walnut, about 30 grams, and roll into balls. Set these balls inside a plastic produce bag or something similarly lightweight.

Get another produce bag and cut it into two sheets of thin plastic. I find that this thin plastic works far better than using a thicker plastic bag. Place one sheet of plastic on each side of your tortilla press. Set a masa ball on it, slightly closer to the inside, hinge side of the press than the lever side. Cover with the second sheet of plastic and press firmly, but don't take all your aggressions out on it. You want a tortilla about 1⁄16 inch thick, slightly thicker for tacos that are wet, like a guisado.

Sometimes you'll get a thick end and a thin end. Flip the tortilla, still in between the plastic sheets, and gently press the second side. That helps even things out.

Have your comal hot—like 500°F. Remove the top plastic and set it aside. Lay the exposed part of the tortilla in your palm and use the other hand to gently lift off the second piece of plastic. Carefully lay the tortilla on the hot comal. You will need the courage of your convictions to do this because the wet dough will set almost instantly when it hits the metal. If you've messed up and there is a little buckle in the tortilla, leave it for the moment.

Let your tortilla cook for about 30 seconds. Use a thin metal spatula to flip it, and flatten it out now. If your comal is seasoned well and you are practiced, you won't need the spatula. Cook the tortilla on the second side another 30 seconds. Flip one more time and cook a final 30 seconds, or until the tortilla puffs up completely, whichever comes first; they don't always puff up.

Set each tortilla into a warmer lined with paper towels, or wrap them in a terrycloth towel. When you're done making them and are ready to serve, flip the stack of tortillas so the oldest one is the first to get eaten.

TIP: The side that has been cooked only once is the side that should get the stuff on it. The twice-cooked side is the outer side, and will be slightly tougher to hold any juices in. This is true for both flour and corn tortillas.

Once made, corn tortillas don't keep well—if you're using them for tacos. Leftover tortillas have an entire cuisine of their own. Tortilla chips, enchiladas, tostadas, to name a few. You can also let your tortillas cool completely, separate them from each other (important!) and then restack and wrap them tightly in plastic before freezing. They'll keep this way a couple months. Thaw slowly before reheating.

Flour Tortillas

PREP TIME: 90 MINUTES | COOK TIME: 20 MINUTES | MAKES ABOUT A DOZEN TORTILLAS

Flour tortillas are way more borderlands, are way more complicated and varied, and to many who live there, way better than corn. I love both kinds, but yeah, a perfect Arizonan or Sonoran flour tortilla is the tortilla I will eat for my deathbed taco (page 74).

You will want soft wheat flour for flour tortillas. In a Latin market you'll see harina para tortillas. In American markets, look for White Lily flour or Hayden Mills. When in doubt, use all-purpose. Do not use bread flour.

The basic flour tortilla is flour, a fat, a pinch of salt, and hot water. In Texas and parts of New Mexico they will add baking powder. I never do, because I am biased and prefer Sonoran style, which are thinner and more awesome. I will admit that the thicker Texas/New Mexico style is better for a wet taco, like a guisado. They're also better for sopping up the juices in a stew. What's more, the thicker ones are easier to make. So both have their place.

The fat is almost always fresh pork lard, but I've seen oil a lot. Butter is for a dessert tortilla, and beef fat is for a Sonoran-style taco tortilla—they're amazing, but need to be eaten hot or they get leathery. Bacon fat rocks, too. If you have access to schmalz, chicken fat, or duck fat, they might be the best of all. You need your fat to be soft before adding it to the flour.

My method is unorthodox, but it works. This recipe can be scaled up indefinitely.

250 grams Sonoran or all-purpose flour (about 2 heaping cups)

3 grams salt (½ teaspoon)

40 grams lard, bacon fat, duck fat, vegetable shortening, or butter (a full quarter-cup)

210 grams hot water (⅞ cup)

Mix the flour and salt together in a large bowl. Add the fat to the bowl and with your fingers, work it until the mixture resembles a coarse meal. Add the hot water and mix well into a soft dough.

Squeeze small balls off the larger dough ball, each about the size of golf ball, about 40 grams. Roll into a ball and set them one by one in a plastic produce bag. Continue until you've used the rest of the dough. Close the bag and let this sit for 1 hour.

Line your tortilla press with thin plastic cut from a produce bag. Have your comal medium-hot, about 400°F. (I use a laser thermometer, but you can set your comal over medium-high heat.) Take a dough ball and set it in the press, slightly closer to the hinge side. Set the other piece of plastic over it and press down a little. Now crank the press down hard. If you want, flip and press the other side, too.

Lift the plastic off, and set the tortilla in your hand. Carefully lift off the other piece of plastic and set the tortilla on the comal. In some cases, it's going to want to spring back—in this case, hold the tortilla by its edge (they're far stronger than corn tortillas), like pizza dough, and let it hang a little, then set it on the comal.

Cooking time is a little shorter than with corn tortillas, so go for 30 seconds on the first side, then 20 seconds for each of the next two flips. Flour tortillas almost always puff up a lot. It's fun to watch.

Set each finished tortilla in a warmer, and when you're ready to serve, flip the stack so the oldest is first to get used.

Flour tortillas keep better than corn ones, and will keep in the fridge a few days. Like corn tortillas, you can let them cool completely, separate them, then restack and wrap in plastic and freeze.

Tips and Variations

There are some variations for flour tortillas you'll see along the borderlands.

- Add ½ to 1 teaspoon baking powder to the flour at the start, then reduce the lard by 1 tablespoon. This makes a breadier, poofier Texas-style tortilla.
- Sub in other wheat flours. My all-time favorite is the roasted wheat flour you can get from the San Xavier Co-op in Tucson. Alas, no online sales. A little whole wheat or other wheat flour is a nice change.
- Sub in a little non-gluten flour. I've seen both acorn flour and mesquite flour tortillas. Use no more than 25 percent in the whole mix or you will risk the tortillas falling apart.
- Add requesón or fresh ricotta to the mix right after the fat. Use up to 50 percent of the weight of flour, but I recommend 25 percent of the weight of the flour.
- Go with butter and hot milk instead of lard and hot water. This makes a marvelous breakfast tortilla. Definitely do this for tortillas slathered with more butter and then cinnamon sugar.

FLOUR TORTILLAS ARE REAL TORTILLAS

Let me state this plainly: Flour tortillas are authentic. They are a real thing. They have a long history in the border regions. And they are every bit as delicious as the finest corn tortilla.

Anyone can prefer one type of tortilla over the other. I love them both, and will switch tortillas depending on the filling.

Let's start with the germ of truth in the flour haters' claim. Yes, corn tortillas have a far longer history in Mexico than flour tortillas. Why? Because wheat is a Eurasian crop brought to Mexico after Hernán Cortés arrived in 1519. Montezuma ate corn tortillas, not flour.

"In the United States, the great Mexican food evangelists see flour tortillas as a gabacho or a white appropriation of Mexican food, which is totally not the case," says Gustavo Arellano, a historian of Mexican and border food.

No one really knows when flour tortillas were introduced to the borderlands, but similar flatbreads exist in both the North African (Moorish) and Sephardic Jewish traditions. As it happens, Spain only threw out the Moors a few years before Cortés arrived, ending seven centuries of Arab domination of the region. And as it also happens, a large number of Sephardic Jews settled in northern Mexico, especially around Nuevo Leon.

What's more, corn doesn't grow as well along most of the border as it does in the south of Mexico or further north in the US. Wheat thrives along the border. Careful readers (and anyone who keeps kosher) will note that adding lard to a flour tortilla is a no-go for a Jewish or Muslim person, but there have always been other fats available, such as olive oil, beef and poultry fat. (Side note: Flour tortillas made with chicken fat are ethereal. Please make them if you get a chance.)

If you look at the flatbreads of the world, many are so similar to flour tortillas you'd be forgiven for making connections that may well be convergent food evolution: Add fat to flour, then water, and knead, and you have a delicious, easy-to-cook flat bread. It's not rocket science.

Then again, those connections might be real. Mexico was settled by all sorts of flatbread-eating peoples, from the Chinese and Indians who came with the galleon trade to Persians and Arabs and Jewish people. And let's not forget that Indigenous peoples are known for their flatbreads, too. You know, like the corn tortilla.

Several styles of flour tortilla exist today. My favorite is the ultrathin Sonoran-style tortilla, which can often be translucent. To me, this is the ultimate flour tortilla. It's beautiful, delicate, and can be breathtakingly delicious, especially when made with beef fat.

Move east and you get to New Mexican—and Chihuahuan-style flour tortillas, which are thicker and less fatty because it gets really cold in New Mexico, snow even. And during these months, New Mexicans make thick, hearty guisados, stews like green chile stew and carne adovada. You want a stouter tortilla for something this robust.

Farther east and you get the Texas tortilla, which, interestingly, stays in Texas. Neighboring Nuevo Leon and Coahuila tend toward thinner flour tortillas, albeit not as delicate as a Sonoran. Texas tortillas almost always are puffy, largely because they're normally made with less fat and added baking powder—something rarely used in Sonora or Arizona.

I've seen many variations on the flour tortilla, usually in the form of fat. Most common is pork lard or vegetable oil. I prefer lard. Beef fat is very Sonoran, and makes a superior flour tortilla. The Mennonites of Chihuahua sometimes use requesón, a ricotta-like fresh cheese. Sometimes you'll see whole wheat in there, and I've seen acorn flour in Sonoran tortillas on occasion.

Bottom line: Wheat has been grown along the border for 500 years. It's integral to the cuisine.

WILD CHILES

Nowhere are wild chiles more important to the cuisine than along the border. Chances are you will find salsa like the one on page 204, on many a border table and, in Arizona and Sonora, little dishes of dried ripe chiles in case you want to spice up whatever you've ordered.

Botanically, both pequins and chiltepins are the same plant, *Capsicum annuum* var. *glabriusculum*, and if we're all being honest, their shapes are so variable that this should be obvious: I've seen bullet-shaped chiltepins and round pequins. However, lively arguments ensue over whether the bullet-shaped pequin or the globular chiltepin is the better chile.

They're both great, and both zippy. The special heat of the chiltepin and the pequin is like a firecracker: a big blast of heat that lights you up, then dissipates relatively quickly. They're addicting, and both surpassingly good at cutting the heaviness of gut bombs like a chimichanga or too many chilorio tacos.

Depending on the variety, wild chiles range from 30,000 to 60,000 Scoville units, so just under that of an old-school habanero.

If you are a forager, you can find wild chiles tucked in with larger shrubs in Arizona, New Mexico, and Texas. I once saw a huge plant in an alley in Austin, Texas. Look for them in canyons and other places that get a little shade.

Both peppers can be cultivated. I've grown one or more plants for more than a decade, because there really is no substitute for these peppers. One now lives on my windowsill in Minnesota. Sure, you can get the heat elsewhere, but the flavor of both chiles is floral—before it punches you in the mouth.

Most people buy their wild chiles. You can buy dried ripe chiltepins along roadsides in Sonora and Chihuahua in September through December. Bagged ripe, dry pequins are a common sight in Latin markets all over North America.

Many times you'll see dark little ironwood sculptures for sale alongside the chiles. Often carved by the Seri, an Indigenous group who live near the Sea of Cortez in Sonora, they are little mortars and pestles meant to crush a chiltepin without getting the capsaicin on your fingers. Unless you want to play pepper roulette with your fingertips, you might think about buying one.

A word on gloves and chiles: I never wear them, and I've only gotten "chile hand," where my hands burn for hours from the capsaicin, once—after chopping a 30-pound case of jalapeños. But if your hands are more sensitive, a pair of nitrile gloves might be a sound idea.

Occasionally you will find fresh chiltepins and pequins in the produce section of a Latin market. If you do, buy them.

I like to salt down excess fresh pequins and chiltepins—bury them in salt—and keep a jar of them in the fridge. This is a great way to scratch your wild chile itch in winter.

GROW YOUR OWN

A tip on if you ever want to grow your own: Brew some chamomile tea, drink it, then brew a second cup with the same tea bag. Use that tea, cooled down, to soak your wild chile seeds in overnight. In the wild, most chile seeds germinate only after being eaten by a bird, which then leaves undigested seeds in its droppings. There's something about chamomile that strips the seeds of a protective coating that prevents them from germinating. Even so, they'll take upwards of three weeks or more to germinate, and that first year is slow. But these plants are perennials if you can keep them away from a hard frost (they'll tolerate barely freezing temperatures).

◀ Roasted green chiles in Hatch, New Mexico.

HOW TO ROAST CHILES

Roasting green chiles, and sometimes red ones, is an important skill for a borderlands cook. Roasting adds flavor, and the process of removing the skins makes them far more digestible. If you've ever experienced the, er, "ring of fire" after eating chiles, chances are the culprits were the skins and seeds.

There are lots of ways to go about it. Best of all is on a grill over a mesquite fire. It's absolutely worth it to buy a case of green chiles in late August or September, set up a mesquite fire, and have at it. Make a day of the operation, and freeze the chiles later—being sure to mark them "mesquite roasted" because then you'll remember your treasure.

Alas, this is not always possible. Next best is a chile roaster: a rotating cage with propane blasters that does the job very quickly. Awesome device if you're a chile head like me, but it's a one-trick pony.

The next best option would be a gas burner. I set chiles directly on the stovetop grates with the burners going full blast, turning them with tongs. This method is far superior to broiling or roasting in the oven because in those cases, you are thoroughly cooking the chiles, and you really want the skins off but the chiles themselves fairly sturdy still.

Another option I typically only use for chiles güeros, also known as Hungarian wax chiles, is to fry them. This is a fraught activity because they'll pop and spit. I was making toritos in Nuevo Leon with my friend Patricio and a chile popped hot oil on him. "Ay, chingada!" He was not happy. But frying works well for thin-skinned chiles.

What chiles do we do this for? The top two would be Anaheim (Hatch) style green chiles, and poblanos. These are the chiles of chiles rellenos, and rajas, and, and, and . . . roasted green chiles are all over this book.

There's also the chiles güeros, for toritos (page 278), and yes, you can roast jalapeños, serranos, even habaneros, although they're rarely skinned afterwards. Obviously bell peppers can be roasted, and roasted red bell peppers, while more of a Spanish thing than a borderlands thing, are excellent.

You can roast red Hatch chiles, but the problem is that the skins get thinner and so does the flesh, so skinning red ones can be a mess. Not worth it.

Procedure

- Blacken the skins of your chiles in any of the ways described above.
- Cover them somehow. I prefer a large bowl with a plate or pot lid on top. You need the peppers to steam for about 15 to 30 minutes. I've used plastic and paper bags, and they work . . . unless an ember from the scorched chiles melts the plastic or sets the bag alight.
- Pull one out and use a butter knife to scrape off as much of the skin as you can. Do not use running water, as this steals flavor. Set the chile aside as you do the rest. You will need to clean your work surface frequently.
- When they're all skinned, use a knife to remove the tops of the chiles, ideally taking the stem and the seed ball with it. After you do this, either find a slit in the pepper or make one with a knife and open it up flat.
- Use the butter knife to scrape out all the seeds. Be fastidious with this. Seeds are not digestible.
- Repeat this with all the chiles and you're good.

You'll want to save some of the charred bits here and there, as well as the juices that collect. This is bonus flavor you really want in your food.

Once roasted, chiles can keep for a week in the fridge. I like to either vacuum seal them and freeze, or dehydrate into Chiles Pasados (page 181).

HOW TO REHYDRATE CHILES

Dried chiles, red and green, are essential to border cooking. In most cases, you'll need to rehydrate them before using. Here are a few ways to go about it.

In most cases, I prefer to stem and seed my chiles before rehydrating. It's a little easier to deal with dried seeds and stems than it is to try to remove a zillion wet seeds from a floppy chile.

If you are in a hurry, pour boiling water over your dried chiles and cover the bowl or pot. Let them steep about 20 minutes. I tend to discard the soaking water because it is often bitter.

TOASTING AND FRYING

Rehydrating is the end point for most recipes, but if you have time and want to add flavor to your dish, you'll want to toast or fry your dried chiles before rehydrating. To toast, get a comal or frying pan hot and have your dried chiles ready on one side, a separate bowl on the other.

With tongs and a spatula, set a chile on the hot metal, and press it down with the spatula. The moment it blisters, flip the chile and toast the other side. You will want to moderate the heat so you get toasting, not charring. If your chiles are blackening instantly, turn the heat down. Usually it's about 20 to 30 seconds per side.

Another option is to fry them. Get maybe ½ inch of vegetable oil hot in a pot and drop in a few dried chiles at a time, pressing them down with the spatula until they blister and inflate. Move to the separate bowl with tongs. This process can take only seconds per chile.

In either case, your chile sauce, mole, or whatever will taste better than if you rehydrated the chiles without an initial cooking step.

HOW TO COOK NOPALES

Cooking nopales without slime is the end goal of, well, I'd say almost everyone who cooks the paddles of the prickly pear cactus. I get it. Nopales are a vegetable with twin barriers: First, you need to clean nopales to remove the spines. Then you need to remove the slime they exude, especially once the nopales hit water. Think okra with a runny nose.

Once you get there, however, they are fantastic. Crunchy, tart, like lemony green beans. Nopales are good pickled, dried and reconstituted for soups and stews, grilled, added to salsas, etc.

But that slime! It's called babas in Spanish. Fortunately, there are many ways to remove it.

Raw

When you eat raw nopales, you will want to toss them in fine sea salt for about 10 minutes first. Roughly a tablespoon or two per large paddle. Dice or slice the nopales how you plan to eat them in a salad, then put them in a bowl and toss with the salt.

Move to a colander for 10 to 20 minutes to drain, then rinse under cold water, vigorously rubbing the nopales to remove all the slime. You're good to go for your Cactus Salad (page 88).

Cooked

A few tricks for de-sliming cooked nopales:

- First, the old abuelas' tale about putting the husk of tomatillos in the water when you boil nopales *actually works*. I have no idea how, but it does. I boil however many nopales, diced or whatever, as I plan to eat, in salty water with the husks of about 3 to 6 large tomatillos, for about 10 minutes. Drain and proceed.
- **BAKING SODA.** Adding a healthy pinch of baking soda near the end of boiling works pretty well. Boil your nopales in salty water for 10 minutes, as in the previous method, but add the baking soda in the last 3 to 5 minutes. Be careful, though, because it can make the water froth over—so make sure you have some room in your pot for the water to expand.

- **GRILL THEM.** If you crosshatch a nopal, just scoring the skin, not actually cutting through the paddle, and grill it, the babas will seep out and evaporate over the fire. Grilled nopales are fantastic.
- **BAKE THEM.** This is a Rick Bayless trick. Preheat an oven to 375°F. Dice your nopales and toss with a little salt, as much as you'd want to season them (so a lot less than when you prep them raw). Arrange in one layer on a baking sheet and bake about 20 to 30 minutes. The slime will ooze out and dry up.
- **SAUTÉ THEM.** Doing this requires some faith and a little patience. If you have a stir-fry or sauté with nopales, all will go well, until the babas flows. There will be a moment when everything in your pan is snotty and nasty. Hang in there. It cooks away. Once it does, you're good to go.
- **DRY THEM.** Yep. I learned this trick by accident. I happened to know that cholla buds (see page 224) are much better dried, then rehydrated. It eliminates the slime in that vegetable. Wonder if it would work with nopales? The answer is yes, it does.

Drying nopales is also a fantastic way to preserve your prickly pear cactus paddles for the long term. Sure, you can buy Mexican-grown ones all year long, but if you have them in your yard or you forage for them, the young paddles only come out once a year. Old paddles develop a woody center and are far less palatable. I add previously dried nopales into stews and soups all the time.

◀ Roasting nopales over charcoal.

Hank's Refried Beans

PREP TIME: 15 MINUTES | COOK TIME: 2 HOURS | SERVES 6 TO 8

I wasn't going to include a recipe for refried beans in this book because, well, there are thousands. But refried beans are so vital to border cooking, and I've eaten so much crappy refried beans, that I thought it'd be worth it. I start with dry beans because I am a sucker for the kinds of beans you can't buy in cans. Your Big Three in the border regions are pinto beans, bayo beans, and tepary beans. There are many others, and variants of these, and they will all give you a lovely refried bean. By all means use canned pinto beans if you are pressed for time.

Err on overcooking your beans because no one likes chalky refried beans. Also err on less salt rather than more, especially if you are using bacon fat instead of lard. Oh, and yes, the best refried beans are made with animal fat. That said, you can make vegetarian refried beans with the oil of your choice, but I never do this unless I'm cooking for vegetarians. The flavor is better with lard or bacon fat.

You can mash your beans with a potato masher, a food processor, blender, or a dedicated wooden bean masher if you're really, really into refried beans. My preference is to make my refried beans thin and blend them smooth, then cook them in lard until thickened to my preference. You might prefer chunkier refried beans, in which case use the potato masher.

Refried beans keep for a couple weeks in the fridge, so it's great to make a big batch and have them ready.

1½ cups dry beans

2 bay leaves, 1 avocado leaf, or 1 sprig epazote

Salt

½ cup lard or bacon fat, divided

½ white or yellow onion, chopped

2 cloves garlic, smashed

1 teaspoon Mexican oregano

1 rehydrated guajillo, New Mexican, or colorado chile, or 2 tablespoons adobo sauce from canned chipotles in adobo

Black pepper

Simmer the beans, partially covered, in plenty of water with the bay leaf or avocado leaf or epazote. When they are tender—eat 5 beans when you think they're ready, and if all 5 are tender, you're good—add a healthy pinch of salt. At this point, you can turn off the heat, cover the pot, and let the beans come to room temperature. You can do this step up to 3 days in advance.

When you're ready, heat 1 tablespoon of the lard or bacon fat in a large pan and brown the onions over medium-high heat. Add the beans and a bit of their cooking liquid (save the rest), the garlic cloves, and the Mexican oregano. If you're using the rehydrated chile, chop it, then add to the pan. Or add the adobo, if using that.

Simmer everything 5 minutes or so, add a few grinds of fresh black pepper, then turn off the heat. Move all this into a blender or a food processor and purée. You might need more of the cooking liquid with a blender.

Wipe out the pan and melt the rest of the lard over medium heat. Pour in the purée and stir constantly until the purée has absorbed the fat. Keep stirring, it'll happen. Drop the heat to low and cook this until it's as thick as you like, stirring occasionally.

Red Rice

PREP TIME: 20 MINUTES | COOK TIME: 25 MINUTES

SERVES 4 TO 6

Red rice is the staple rice dish all over the borderlands. There are endless variations to what's called "Spanish rice" from California to Brownsville, Tampico to La Paz. This is the way I like to make mine. It's good to have some made and ready if you are cooking from this book, because this rice ends up in burritos and as a side dish to many of the guisados I feature here. It will keep a week in the fridge. It's not good cold. Reheat it.

I use regular long-grain rice here, but basmati or jasmine will work, too.

- 2 tablespoons lard or vegetable oil
- ½ white onion, minced
- 2 cloves garlic, minced
- 1 heaping cup white rice
- 1 heaping tablespoon tomato paste
- 1 to 2 tablespoons enchilada sauce or red adobo from a can of chipotles in adobo
- ½ cup chicken broth
- 1 cup water
- Salt
- Minced cilantro (optional)

Heat the lard or oil over medium-high heat in a medium pot. Sauté the onion, stirring often, until it browns a little on the edges. Add the garlic and rice and cook, stirring almost constantly, for about 2 minutes. Stir in the tomato paste, then the chile sauce, then add the broth and water. Add a pinch of salt. Mix well, bring to a simmer, cover, and drop the heat to low.

Cook gently for about 15 to 20 minutes, then turn the heat off and let the rice steam by itself another few minutes. Stir well before serving. If you like, mix in a little minced cilantro.

Green Enchilada Sauce

PREP TIME: 30 MINUTES | COOK TIME: 20 MINUTES

MAKES 3 PINTS

This is the other basic sauce you'll use in enchiladas, although it's good in a lot of other things, too. Keep in mind that this is, more or less, a New Mexico version, thus the flour. You can skip the flour for a lighter, cleaner sauce, but I prefer the roux for Southwestern enchiladas. My friend Lane Warner, chef at La Fonda in Santa Fe, is a huge duck hunter and loves this sauce over grilled teal ducks. It's also fantastic over venison or pork or potatoes.

You'll want either a mixture of mild and hot chiles, or use medium-heat green chiles.

Once made, it will keep in the fridge for a few weeks. If specks of white mold appear, skim them off. If black mold appears, throw it out.

- 3 tablespoons lard or cooking oil
- 1 large onion, chopped
- 4 cloves garlic, chopped
- 3 tablespoons flour
- 2 cups chopped roasted green chiles (about a dozen)
- 1 teaspoon epazote (optional)
- 1 teaspoon ground cumin
- ½ teaspoon ground coriander
- 2½ cups chicken or other broth
- Salt (smoked salt if you have it)
- Black pepper

Heat the lard in a large pan over medium-high heat and cook the onions until soft but not browned. Add the garlic and cook another minute, then add the flour and stir well. Cook this until the flour turns the color of coffee-with-cream, about 5 minutes. Add the remaining ingredients and stir well to combine. Let this simmer about 20 minutes. Add salt and pepper to taste.

I prefer this sauce smooth, so I purée it in a blender, but it's nice chunky as a pour-over sauce for duck, turkey, pork, or chicken.

Once made, it will keep in the fridge for about a month.

Red Enchilada Sauce

PREP TIME: 30 MINUTES | COOK TIME: 20 MINUTES
MAKES 3 PINTS

This is a basic red chile sauce that you can use for enchiladas, the Sonoran Carne con Chile recipe (page 240), added to beans, refried or whole, or to sauce tamales. You can even use it as a salsa for chips if you wanted to.

The color and flavor of the sauce will change depending on the chiles you use. Traditional would be red New Mexican (Anaheim) chiles, called chile colorado in Spanish. Guajillos are a good option, as are other dried chiles like ancho or pasilla, which will give you a darker sauce.

Once made, it will keep in the fridge for a few months. Once opened, if specks of white mold appear, skim them off. If black mold appears, throw it out.

½ pound dried chiles (see headnote for varieties)
1 white onion, chopped
3 cloves garlic, chopped
2 teaspoons dried Mexican oregano
1 pint tomato sauce or tomato purée
Water and salt
4 tablespoons lard or vegetable oil

Stem and seed the chiles and put them in a bowl. Pour boiling water into the bowl to cover the chiles, then cover the bowl with a plate or something. Let the chiles rehydrate for 15 to 20 minutes while you chop the onions and garlic.

Put all the ingredients except for the lard or oil into a blender and purée. You want to add enough water so the sauce flows like cream, so thicker than water. Add salt to taste.

Heat the lard or oil in a pan over medium-high heat and pour in the sauce. It will spatter, so stir constantly until it calms down. Turn the heat to medium-low and cook, stirring often, for 15 to 20 minutes.

Pour into jars and seal.

Fire-Roasted Salsa

PREP TIME: 30 MINUTES | COOK TIME: 25 MINUTES
SERVES 6 TO 8

This roasted salsa is the perfect accompaniment for anything grilled. Make this salsa before you put the meat on the grill. Then you can enjoy it with chips as your meat grills, and then put more on your tacos.

I like to grind my roasted salsa with a basalt mortar and pestle called a molcajete, which gives it a far better texture than if I blast it in a food processor or blender. But it's fine in either.

This salsa is also fine if you have a gas grill, or no grill at all. You can make it in winter using your broiler or a comal. A cast iron frying pan works, too.

Once made, your roasted salsa will keep a week or so in the fridge, and if you add some citric acid to it, about a teaspoon per pint, you can water-bath can it for winter.

A FEW TIPS BEFORE YOU BEGIN

- If you are using a grill, get the grates very hot and scrape them well. Food sticks to dirty grates.
- Use plum tomatoes, like Romas or San Marzanos. They grill or broil more easily than regular tomatoes. Also, if you have to buy crappy supermarket tomatoes, buy them several days before you make this salsa and sit them on the kitchen table. They will improve dramatically.
- Peel your tomatoes after grilling or searing. The peels should pull right off and they're hard to digest, anyway.
- Keep your garlic in its skin. This gives it some protection from the searing heat. Also, put the garlic cloves around the edges of the grill or broiler.
- Always make sure you have some of the root attached to your quartered onion. This keeps the layers together. Also, if you are using a molcajete, chop your onions after they've been charred. You'll thank me later.
- Set your charred chiles in a plastic produce bag to steam after you've blackened the skins. Then use the back of a knife to scrape off the skins. Do not rinse them with water, as this removes a ton of flavor. Slice off the tops, open them up and use the knife to scrape away seeds.
- If you are using a large molcajete for your roasted salsa, start the grinding process with salt and your garlic, then add onions, then chiles, then finally tomatoes and herbs.

4 to 6 plum tomatoes, cut in half
1 or 2 white onions, cut in quarters
3 or 4 unpeeled cloves garlic
1 to 4 serrano or jalapeño chiles (see Tips below)
1 teaspoon salt
1 teaspoon dried Mexican oregano (optional)
3 tablespoons chopped cilantro or other herb

Place your onions and tomatoes cut side down on the grill. Place the chiles and garlic cloves on the grill, too. If you are broiling, arrange everything on a baking sheet, cut side up.

Let the onions and tomatoes grill a solid 5 minutes before trying to move them. You want significant blackening. Turn the garlic cloves as the peel blackens, and rotate the chiles so their skins blacken. Remove the vegetables when several sides of the garlic have some char, when the skins of the chiles are well blackened, when both cut sides of the onion quarters are charred, and when the cut faces of the tomatoes are well blackened. You will want to use a thin metal spatula to do this. If you are broiling, simply wait until you get good char on most of the vegetables.

Put the chiles into a plastic bag to steam. Chop the onion coarsely. Peel the garlic, and if the cloves are large, chop into a few pieces. Remove the skins from the tomatoes. After 10 minutes or so, peel the chiles with the back of a butter knife, then open them up and scrape away their seeds. Chop them coarsely.

If you are grinding your salsa in a molcajete, add half the salt, the oregano, and the garlic and pound to a paste. Add the onion bit by bit, grinding and pounding all the way. Next come the chiles, then the tomatoes. Finally, grind the chopped herbs into the salsa. If you are not using a molcajete, simply put everything into a food processor and blitz it a few times, starting with half the salt, adding more if needed. You want this salsa to have some texture. Add salt if you need it, and you are good to go.

Tips and Variations

- I like to add tiny chiltepin or pequin chiles instead of the serranos. If you have those, simply grind them in with the salt and garlic.
- Other tomatoes work, but they are juicier. For a green version, substitute tomatillos that have been husked and halved.
- Not all roasted salsa has herbs in it, but mine always does. I will use whatever looks good in my garden: cilantro, pipicha, papalo, fresh Mexican oregano, even pitiona, which is an unusual herb from Oaxaca. For most people, cilantro is the ticket. Hate cilantro? Use chives.

Avocado Tomatillo Salsa

PREP TIME: 30 MINUTES | COOK TIME: 15 MINUTES | SERVES 6

Avocado tomatillo salsa is neither guacamole nor salsa verde. It's the best of both worlds. Tart from the tomatillos, creamy from the avocado, and as picante or mild as you want it. It can be smooth or chunky, and either completely raw or a mix of raw and cooked ingredients.

You'll either toss everything in a blender and call it a day or roast the tomatillos and chiles and add that to the raw ingredients in the blender. If you want a more textured salsa, crush everything in a molcajete or mortar and pestle, or chop fine and muddle it all up in a steel bowl with a spoon.

You can use alternate herbs instead of cilantro, such as pipicha, parsley, or even epazote. Each will give you a different flavor. If you have access to culantro, that will taste close to cilantro.

Once made, this salsa will keep a few days in the fridge. Cover the salsa with plastic wrap, pressing it right on top of the salsa to keep the avocado from discoloring. Serve at room temperature or a little cooler.

5 large tomatillos or a dozen small ones, husked and halved

2 Hatch, Anaheim, or poblano chiles

1 or 2 unpeeled cloves garlic (see Tips)

⅓ cup chopped cilantro

6 green onions, coarsely chopped

2 or 3 avocados, pitted and skins removed

Salt

Freshly squeezed lime juice

Preheat the oven to 425°F as you are husking the tomatillos and chopping the other ingredients. Don't mess with the avocados yet.

When the oven is hot, put the halved tomatillos and the chiles on a baking sheet and roast until the tomatillos have some blackening and the chile skins are well blackened on all sides. The tomatillos may take less time than the chiles. If you want roasted garlic, add this with the chiles and tomatillos and remove when partially blackened. All this should take about 20 minutes or so, but check after 10 minutes.

ALTERNATE METHOD: You can char the chiles directly on a gas flame or grill.

When things are well charred, put the tomatillos in a blender, peel the garlic and put the cloves in the blender. Remove the skins, stems, and seeds of the chiles and put the chiles in the blender, too. Add the cilantro, green onions, and avocado to the blender, along with some salt and about 1 tablespoon lime juice.

Purée together the tomatillos, chiles, green onions, avocados, garlic, and cilantro. Add salt and lime juice to taste.

Tips and Variations

- You want avocados that are fully ripe, even with a few blemishes.
- Tomatillos can be of whatever variety, either the big supermarket ones or my favorite, the little tomatillos de milpa.
- Ditto for the green chiles. I prefer hot Hatch chiles, roasted by hand. Poblanos are my second choice. But any roasted green chile will do, even canned ones. Or skip them and use jalapeños, serranos, or even green chiltepins or pequins if you are a hot head.
- Roasting the garlic with the tomatillos and chiles mellows it out, so if you don't like raw garlic, do it. Roasting will let you use more garlic, too.
- I like this with green onions, but you can use chopped white onion if that's what you have.
- You can make this a raw salsa by skipping all the cooking steps and simply puréeing everything in the blender. This takes seconds and is great for making this salsa on a hot day.

TACO JAZZ: HOW TO MAKE GREAT TACOS EVERY TIME

"In order to produce a taco that is amazing, you have to understand how a taco is built. And I'm not talking about diagrams and case studies about a taco. I'm just saying you have to eat a lot of tacos to know how a good taco feels in your mouth."

—ENRIQUE OLVERA, chef of Mexico City's Pujol, one of the world's best restaurants

I can't say it any better than Chef Olvera. That said, I am going to try to walk you through it, skipping the diagrams.

Start by stopping what you're doing for a moment. Turn off the radio or whatever other noise or stimulation you might have going on right now. Sit with yourself a moment, and think about all the great tacos you have eaten in your life. And chances are, if you are reading this book, that number is more than one.

This mystical Perfect Taco could be beef or pork, mushrooms or greens, fish or seafood or chicken or grasshoppers. But what it has is a focus, a main thing, a reason for being.

That reason is held up, like a newborn, by the soft embrace of the tortilla. While I recognize that there may be someone somewhere for whom the 1970s hard-shelled tortillas, à la Ortega or early Taco Bell, is the pinnacle of tacodom, know you are the exception that proves the rule. For the overwhelming majority of humans, the greatest tacos are on soft corn or flour tortillas.

Note that either flour or corn is an acceptable answer here. Different tacos are best on different tortillas, but even that is a matter of taste. Corn is not "more authentic" than flour, just different. More on that on page 29.

Whatever it's made from, that tortilla must be well made. A beautiful filling atop a crappy, disintegrating tortilla is a sin against God and nature. Don't let that aggression stand, man. Beyond that, anything goes, but all must be in balance: sweet, sour, spicy, salty, savory, crunchy, colorful, hot, and cool, everything. Think about those memorable tacos you've eaten. Every one of them was a masterpiece of balance.

Let's look at a simple, familiar example, the carne asada taco. At its core, this is grilled steak on a flour tortilla. Rich, savory, maybe even fatty. The most basic toppings would be white onions soaked in lime juice and minced cilantro. Sour, crunchy, herbal, floral, bitter. Stop it right there and you're in a good place. Add a bright red salsa and you add a touch of sweet, a spicy kick, and more acidity. See the colors in your mind? Taste that balance? It's a wondrous package of simple perfection.

I'd advise you to keep your tacos simple. Remember that main thing, the meat, fish, mushroom, whatever, that is the reason for the taco to exist. Make or buy quality tortillas. Don't skimp here. Add to this a few elements that build the whole in terms of color and spice, texture and temperature.

One insanely simple touch I started doing years ago was to add roasted pepitas, the shelled, green pumpkin seeds that are increasingly common in stores, to any "green" taco, and roasted, salted sunflower seeds to "red" tacos. These add visual interest, saltiness, fat, and most importantly, crunch to tacos that need it—and in these cases I am mostly talking about guisados in taco form, like if you made tacos with the Chilorio on page 283 or the Carne Guisada on page 97. That one tiny touch elevates the taco seamlessly. There are other ways to do this, too.

In the borderlands, much of the freestyling you see within tacos happens with the salsas that go on at the very end. Every self-respecting taquero will be most proud of his or her salsas; Chef Maria Mazon from Tucson happens to be one of the best salseras there is, and she is, justifiably, proud of her creations.

Salsas are the tie, or the scarf, to the business suit. A carne asada taco may be the workaday business suit of tacos, stolid and sturdy and predictable, but the salsa you choose to put on top, like a man's tie or a woman's scarf, is where you can show individuality and personality.

One other note about tacos: Serve them and eat them. Don't wait. Tacos die on the plate. Their beauty and taste are ephemeral. This is why the greatest tacos are served quickly and are usually eaten standing. One bite for discovery, one bite for bliss, one bite for regret because it's gone . . . until you sidle up to the taqueria and ask for "dos mas, porfa."

Hank's Taco Onions

PREP TIME: 10 MINUTES
SERVES 6 TO 8 AS A TACO TOPPING

This is the standard taco topping I use for almost every taco in this book. It's a slight modification of what you see all over the borderlands. Make these about an hour before serving the tacos, and they will keep a day or two in the fridge.

1 large white onion
Pinch of salt
Pinch of dried Mexican oregano
⅓ cup freshly squeezed lime juice

Mince the onion and toss with the remaining ingredients, making sure to crush the dried oregano into a powder with your hands. Let this sit for at least 15 minutes before serving.

Hank's Pico de Gallo

PREP TIME: 20 MINUTES | SERVES 4 TO 6

Another absolute standard all over the border is pico de gallo, which to many Americans is synonymous with salsa. This is my version, and it appears a lot in this book. You'll note that I chop things a bit more finely than most versions: This makes a salsa that is easier to eat and which lays down on a taco or other dish more easily.

Once made, pico de gallo will keep a couple days in the fridge, but it deteriorates after that.

1 small clove garlic, minced
1 small white onion, minced
½ teaspoon dried Mexican oregano
4 Roma tomatoes, seeded and diced small
1 to 3 jalapeños, stemmed, seeded, and diced small
⅓ cup freshly squeezed lime juice, ideally from Key limes
Salt
½ to ¾ cup chopped cilantro

Set the garlic and onion in a bowl. Mix in the oregano, then add the tomatoes and jalapeños, the lime juice, then salt to taste. At this stage, you can let things sit for up to a day in the fridge, or several hours on the counter. When ready to serve, stir in the cilantro.

You can play with the herb. I've used chives, pipicha, papaloquelite, and pitiona—all very Mexican herbs—in place of cilantro. And if you have culantro available, go for it.

"Echarle mucha crema a sus tacos"

A person who "adds a lot of sour cream to their tacos" is a person who brags and exaggerates about his or her abilities.

SPIRITS OF THE BORDER

Oaxaca has its mezcal, Jalisco tequila and raicilla. And the north? Well, the borderlands have several excellent local spirits, as well as the best wine and arguably the best beer in either country.

BEER

You'll be familiar with some of the classic beers. After all, Mexico is the world's largest exporter of beer. Tecate comes from Baja, Carta Blanca from Nuevo Leon, Pacifico from Sinaloa. Most of these beers are part of mega brewing empires now, but regional loyalties still exist. Tecate in Baja or Sonora is everywhere, as is Carta Blanca in Monterrey. On the US side, only Texas has a similar macro-brew industry, with Lone Star and Shiner beers getting special attention.

Microbreweries are everywhere along the border, on both sides. Buqui Bichi in Sonora is excellent and now has two taprooms in Arizona. Equally good is the Agua Mala Brewery in Ensenada. Zopilote Brewing in Loreto, Baja, makes great beers, and there are others dotted all across the region. On the US side, San Diego is arguably the greatest brewing town in America. They perfected a style of IPA beer that the rest of the world still chases. I've had great beer even in small towns from San Diego to Brownsville. A few standouts are Ice Box Brewing in Hatch, New Mexico; Aurellia's in El Paso, and Barrio Brewery in Tucson.

In broader terms, the beer styles in the entire region—except for San Diego—are German, Pilsners and lagers of all colors. The reason is tied to

The Valle de Guadalupe, Baja, Mexico.

German immigration to the area more than a century ago. It's also hot along the border, and a light, crisp Pilsner or lager is what you want when the mercury tops 110°F.

WINE

While wines are made in several places along the border, such as Coahuila and the Texas Hill Country, and even in parts of New Mexico and Arizona, the only substantial wine region along the border is Mexico's Valle de Guadalupe in Baja. A quick drive across the border from San Diego, the Valle has developed into a world-class wine appellation. The wines there range from standard Bordeaux varietals to specialty grapes like nebbiolo, which grow well on the Pacific coast.

Generally speaking, however, the borderlands are a beer and hard liquor area. The Valle is the exception.

LIQUOR

Three main varieties of agave spirit exist on the border: bacanora, lechuguilla, and sotol, which is not technically an agave spirit; it's made from plants in the genus *Dasylirion,* a cousin of agave. (Oddly, there is one spot in the Mexican state of Tamaulipas that can legally make tequila—tequila is like bourbon in that to carry the name, it must be distilled in specific areas, in this case mostly Jalisco.)

All three are mezcals in the broad sense in that they are all distilled similarly, served young and unoaked, and can be fierce, sporting alcohol levels higher than 50 percent on the regular. This is so fierce in fact that bacanora distilling wasn't legalized in Mexico until 1992.

Spiky leaves of the agave are chopped off the plants, which are then pit-roasted, sometimes for days, to turn starches to sugar, which is then fermented in open vats. The distilling process can be idiosyncratic in the same way that moonshining is in the United States so every mezcalero's product will be different, and often change year to year.

All three drinks are enjoying a surge in popularity and are in demand in the United States. I've seen them in cities all over the States, and most liquor stores will carry at least sotol. Los Magos is a well-known brand out of Chihuahua, and there is at least one Texas sotol, from a company called Desert Door. Both of these sotols are grassy, floral, and very drinkable.

Another good option is the spirits from Los Sotoleros, which sells small batch sotols and lechugillas, A general rule is to look on a bottle's label to see if there's an individual maker's name on it and a list of data on the making of that bottle, such as the type of still and the specific agaves or sotol varieties used in the distillation. Many will have individual bottle numbers on them.

INDIGENOUS DRINKS

Three native drinks exist along la frontera, and a fourth has become very popular: pulque, tesguino, tepache, and more recently, brews from mesquite bean syrup.

Pulque is essentially agave beer. It's the beginning stage of making mezcal, and is normally a cloudy, low-alcohol drink that has been enjoyed by millions since before Europeans arrived in 1519. For decades the Mexican government discouraged its consumption, in no small part because it can be made at home, and the big beer brewers held (and hold) political and economic sway in Mexico City. Pulque ranges from sweet and zippy to appallingly sour. It does not keep well, and it often sold out of big kegs or plastic jugs. Pulque can be found in the United States, but it's rare.

Tesguino is essentially corn beer, and it has a tradition that predates European contact as well. Historically a ceremonial drink, I've made it a few times, and it can be good—but like pulque, tesguino doesn't keep well. I don't know of any commercial source. Ditto for another ceremonial wine made from the sweet juice of the saguaro cactus. Both Arizona's saguaro and the fruits of the prickly pear and pitahaya cacti can be and have been fermented by Indigenous peoples for centuries. They can make a heady drink, but unless made with modern winemaking methods, both will turn to vinegar quickly. Not a bad thing, because they make a tasty pink vinegar.

Tepache is made by fermenting the rinds and core of a pineapple, often with cinnamon and clove and ginger. I like to add some brown sugar, and piloncillo is the rule in Mexico. It's a fantastic summer drink, low in alcohol and fun to drink over ice with some mint when it's hot. I have seen any number of commercially made tepaches, including some without alcohol. I have a recipe for tepache on page 86.

Finally, the beans from the mesquite tree have enough sugar in them to brew a syrup that can then be fermented. I've done this (see page 222), and used that sweet liquid as part of a wort in an English-style ale. It's quite good and makes a fun brown ale.

VENISON ALONG THE BORDERLANDS

It is not uncommon to see venison served all along the borderlands, usually white-tailed deer in the east, mule deer in the west, as well as the little whitetail variant Coues deer in Sonora and parts of Chihuahua. By far the most common way I've seen it has been as carne seca (jerky) or its shredded form, machaca. Dried and salted, venison makes superior jerky and machaca because it's so lean—fatty jerky can go rancid.

Deer hunting is far more common in northern Mexico than in most other Mexican regions, and is something close to religion in Texas. It actually *is* religion among the Mayo and Yaqui people of Sonora. Their deer dancers are a huge part of their annual festival cycle.

Other than dried, venison tamales and enchiladas are the norm. Some hunters will have whole deer turned into tamales, which are then frozen and eaten all year. Venison enchiladas and chicken-fried venison are ranch favorites in Texas, and I've seen venison subbed in for beef almost wherever it appears: gallina pinta, carne asada, carne guisada, discada, and the like.

It is among the various Indigenous groups of the borderlands where venison is most prominent, at least historically. Any number of venison-specific recipes dot the recipe books written by anthropologists covering these groups. I've recreated several in this book.

On a mechanical level, you can assume that unless I state otherwise, you can use beef or venison of any kind—deer, elk, pronghorn, moose, nilgai, etc.—interchangeably. I mostly used venison in my test kitchen, and my recipe testers mostly used beef.

OTHER WILD GAME

Other species of wild game show up here and there on the border, mostly in home recipes, but occasionally in restaurants or food stalls. True wild game is illegal to sell in the United States, but the closest thing to it is at Broken Arrow Ranch in Texas, which sells nilgai—an exotic Indian antelope species imported to Texas a century ago—as well as feral hogs.

I've eaten wild quail in Baja, and feral hogs are surreptitiously served wherever they are found, often as carnitas.

The range of game animals along the border is vast, and every one of them appears in some form on people's tables. Doves start the annual hunting season in sweltering September, and the annual Labor Day dove hunt is sacred in places like the Rio Grande Valley in Texas and Yuma in Arizona (see Yuma Dove Hunt on page 210). Dove hunting is so important on the border that I've included a couple dove recipes in this book. You'll find far more in my book *Pheasant, Quail, Cottontail.*

Four species of quail abound in the region, from bobwhites in Texas and Tamaulipas to scaled quail in West Texas and New Mexico, Gambel's and Mearns quail in Sonora and Arizona, and the Valley quail in California and Baja. Wild quail meat is a touch darker, and the birds are larger than most farmed quail, which are an imported Asian species. This, plus the occasional piece of bird shot, is the giveaway if you're wondering if that grilled quail you're enjoying was wild or farmed.

Rabbits and jackrabbits appear in many cookbooks covering the Indigenous peoples of the area, and many recipes you might recognize with beef or pork show up as jackrabbit recipes in these books. Jackrabbit is a lean, dark meat, and that of just one of the antelope jackrabbits of the Sonoran Desert—yes, there really is a jackalope, although no antlers!—can feed a family. If you have a jackrabbit, use it in any recipe where you see the deer icon.

A few other big game species are hunted along the borderlands, including the desert bighorn sheep, pronghorn antelope, elk, and even bison in Arizona. Several exotic species roam the region, too, notably nilgai in South Texas, aoudad sheep in West Texas and New Mexico, and oryx in New Mexico. All can be treated like beef or deer in the recipes in this book.

Javelina are small, pig-like animals whose northern range coincides with the border. Collared peccary is their official name, and contrary to popular belief, they are not rodents. They are New World pigs, but their ancestry diverged from the pig we all know and love millions of years ago. It's a great example of convergent evolution. Once fun fact about javelina is that they are vegetarian (hogs are omnivores), so javelina do not carry the trichinae parasite. They are prized game animals in Arizona, New Mexico, and in Mexico, but are, for reasons known only to Texans, despised in the Lone Star State. In recipes, javelina can be substituted for pork seamlessly.

A few more obscure animals are eaten here and there along the border, although I've not personally seen them cooked. The anthropological cookbooks all have recipes for things like raccoon, opossum, coati, chachalaca, and the like. I've cooked and eaten both coati and chachalaca, and they were very good—chachalaca especially so; it's like a fatty wild chicken. A noisy one.

QUELITES

Quelites are wild greens in Mexican Spanish, and there are a lot of them—all worth your time to get to know. Many we consider weeds here in the United States, and some may be living in your yard right now.

Pronounced "keh-LEE-tays," quelites are widely eaten all along the border. I have a series of cookbooks from Mexico that feature the common cuisine in each of their 32 states, and quelites feature in every one of them. Other than perhaps the Greeks, no culture I know of makes more use of wild edible greens.

This is, no doubt, because their use long predates the arrival of the Spanish in 1519. The word quelite is of Nahuatl origin, which is the language of the Aztecs and their neighbors in central Mexico. It means, as you might guess, edible herb.

So what are we talking about? Mostly edible weeds many of you are already familiar with: purslane, pigweed, and lambsquarters. But there are many others, some common, a few obscure. I'll walk you through them: names, uses, as well as how to get quelites seeds if you want to grow them in your yard.

For starters, it's safe to say that you will likely see purslane somewhere near you, often in your garden beds, whether you like it or not. It is a warm weather plant, and is totally edible, so much so that cultivated forms exist. I've grown them and prefer the wild variety.

Lambsquarters is another common one you may or may not already have in your yard. One of

Wild amaranth growing in California.

the many *Chenopodium* species, it is a wild spinach. Several wild varieties grow in the US, and it is a very common roadside and garden weed. If you want to grow it, I recommend the cultivated variety huauzontles because the leaves are larger.

Wild lambsquarters in most of the US is usually *Chenopodium album*, known as quelites cenizo in Spanish, and the huauzontles are *C. nuttalliae.* Incidentally, in central Mexico it's the young seed heads that are mostly eaten with huauzontles, battered and fried like fritters. (Use the Baja Fish Taco batter on page 273 if you want to do this.) Latin names aside, you should definitely be familiar with at least one chenopod: quinoa. Epazote is also in this family.

Their cousins are the *Atriplex* clan, the saltbushes and oraches. My absolute, all-time favorite quelites are the species *Atriplex hortensis.* I know them as Chamisal quelites, named for the area of New Mexico they are from.

Now, pigweed. Lots of plants go by this name, but here I am referring to amaranth, which is any one of the zillions of *Amaranthus* species. Some are used as grain—they have lots of little seeds, and the grain varieties will have larger ones. But here I am talking about the varieties used for their large leaves. The one I really like is actually Asian, and it's called white leaf amaranth, *Amaranthus mangostanus*. In Spanish, you'll see amaranth is quintoniles.

I can almost guarantee you that some species of pigweed grows near you. One spontaneously appeared in my brand-new Minnesota garden beds within weeks of their completion.

Another common cooking green along the border is called chichiquelites, and you may know it as garden huckleberry or wonderberry, *Solanum melanocerasum*. It grows all over the US. Unlike belladonna, which is European and toxic, this nightshade has edible berries that taste like their tomato cousins. The greens are cooked and eaten all over the border, especially among Indigenous peoples.

One other wild green you are also probably familiar with: watercress. Yep, it grows in high mountain streams in Mexico, as it does here in the United States, and it is a welcome addition to any plate of greens. Hell, you can find it in many supermarkets here. One word of caution if you are foraging for watercress: Unless you are at very high elevations, you will want to cook it. Otherwise, you risk a rip-roaring case of "beaver fever," a.k.a. giardia.

Everything I've mentioned so far is a spinach substitute. But that's only to put you in the right frame of mind. In reality, every one of these quelites is superior in every way to spinach. They are denser, meatier, more nutritious, easier to grow, shrink less when cooked, and all are perfectly OK with 100°F. Take that, spinach! The only thing spinach has on any of them is leaf size, and if you grow those Chamisal quelites, their leaves are up to three times *larger* than those of spinach.

But quelites go way beyond leafy greens.

HERBS

There is a whole class of quelites that are herbs. We've already mentioned epazote, which many of you will be familiar with. But there are others, and if you grow them you will be on your way to being able to get those mysteriously authentic touches you will want in your own cooking.

Most common of them would be papalo and pipicha. Related, they are pungent herbs that can be used in place of cilantro—they are different, but you'd use them in the same way. I prefer pipicha, *Porophyllum linaria*. It's wispy and aromatic and tender. A little citrus, a little mint, a hint of . . . ozone? It is vaguely similar to cilantro, which is a European herb, but only in a galactic sense. One bonus? It reseeds itself well.

I reckon that culantro, *Eryngium foetidum*, counts as quelites, too, because it is native to the Americas. It is why you see cilantro in everything in Latin America. Culantro, while not botanically related, has almost the exact same flavor as cilantro. Only culantro likes hot weather, while cilantro does not. You want both in a year-round Latin kitchen.

I've seen culantro in supermarkets in South Florida, and you can buy culantro seeds. Beware: Culantro needs heat and time to germinate. It can take three weeks before you see seedlings.

Another seasoning quelite would be hoja santa, *Piper auritum*. It grows wild in the Gulf region, and it was a perennial in my Sacramento garden. Also called root beer plant, it has giant leaves often used to wrap things. It is indispensable in mole verde.

Other than simply sautéed as a side dish like spinach, the uses of quelites are numerous. I've seen them used as a taco filling, in tamales and empanadas, and in various guisados.

Quelites Tacos

PREP TIME: 25 MINUTES | COOK TIME: 15 MINUTES | SERVES 4 TO 6

3 tablespoons vegetable oil or lard

1 white onion, minced

4 cloves garlic, minced

1 or 2 poblano or Anaheim chiles, roasted, peeled, seeded, and chopped

Salt

1 pound wild greens, spinach, or something similar

1 teaspoon dried Mexican oregano

8 to 12 corn tortillas

Queso fresco or anejo, crumbled, for serving

Roasted pepitas, for serving (optional)

Lime wedges, for serving

Heat the oil in a large sauté pan over medium-high heat. Add the minced onion and sauté until it begins to brown at the edges, about 4 to 6 minutes. Add the minced garlic and roasted, chopped chiles, and cook 1 minute, stirring often. Salt everything well.

While this is cooking, chop the wild greens coarsely. Add them to the pan and stir well. They should start popping. Keep them moving, stirring constantly, and as they wilt add the Mexican oregano. Taste for salt: You want it slightly undersalted because the cheese will be salty. Everything's done when the greens have all wilted. Turn off the heat.

Heat up some corn tortillas—flour doesn't seem right for this taco—and build your tacos. Top with the cheese and maybe some roasted pumpkin seeds for crunch, then serve with lime wedges.

Carne Seca

PREP TIME: 15 MINUTES | COOK TIME: 4 HOURS
SERVES 8

Carne seca is Spanish for jerky, and is an important part of the cuisine on the border. It's super easy to make. All it is is sliced meat, salt, spices, and one of the following: blazing sun, a dehydrator, or a smoker. What meat? Normally beef, but I see carne seca de venado—venison jerky—all the time in Baja, and when I am in southern Arizona. I've seen it done with pork, goat, and mutton, too.

I use a hind leg roast. You could use backstrap, but it seems like a waste. For beef, you want top round, sirloin, or eye of round. Any meat largely free of connective tissue works best.

Basically the process is this: You take a big piece of meat and slice it thin. I like to do this when it is partially frozen. In Mexico, they are impressive with a knife and slice long, thin sheets of meat from larger cuts the same way the Chinese do with daikon radish, which is to say a continuous cut round and round. I'm not that good, so I cut my venison the way I would for any jerky; with or against the grain, up to you.

You then moisten your meat with lime juice. Not a ton of it, just enough to get the spices and salt to stick. You then mix fine-grained salt and ground chiles together, and massage that into the meat. You can use whatever ground dried chiles make you happy. Don't want any heat? Use paprika. Or skip it. Lots of carne seca has only salt. Let all these ingredients get to know each other in the fridge for a day or three.

Now, time to secar your carne, or dry your meat. Traditionally in Arizona and Sonora you'd drape it over a clothesline and let the desert sun do its thing. I could do this in Sacramento in the summer, but not so much in Minnesota, where I live now. Equally traditional is to dry your meat over a smoky fire.

I prefer this, so I use my smoker set at 165°F for a few hours. Mesquite or oak are the woods you want.

Your carne seca is ready when you think it is. Leave it leathery and pliable if you are going to eat it within a week or two. Dry it brittle for long keeping, and if you are going to make machaca later.

2 pounds venison, beef, or other red meat
Juice of 3 or 4 limes
2 tablespoons fine-grained salt
1 to 2 tablespoons ground dried chiles or paprika

Slice the meat to about ⅛ to ¼ inch thick. Remove any excess fat. You can pound it thinner if you'd like. I do this if the carne seca is going to be machaca.

Moisten the meat with the lime juice. Mix the salt and chiles together and coat every slice of venison with it. Press the mixture into the meat firmly. Let this set in the fridge for at least 8 hours and up to 3 days.

Lay the meat out in one layer on the grates of a smoker or dehydrator. Smoke at 165°F or dehydrate at 145°F until the meat is dry, about 4 hours. Pull it when it's pliable if you want to eat it within a week or two, or dry it brittle if you want it to keep for a long time or make machaca.

Machaca

PREP TIME: 20 MINUTES | SERVES 10

You can make machaca as fine or as coarse as you want. Generally speaking, the fine stuff, which looks like meat cotton candy, is put in eggs, and the coarser stuff goes into stews, like Caldillo de Carne Seca (page 146).

1 pound carne seca
6 cloves garlic
1 tablespoon dried Mexican oregano

Break the carne seca into smallish pieces with your hands or scissors, then add the garlic and oregano and blitz it for about 3 to 5 minutes in a food processor. You may have to give the machine some breaks in case it gets too hot.

Lay out the finished machaca on a baking sheet for the rest of the day to fully dry some more, then it will be stable at room temperature in dry places. If you are in a humid place, keep your machaca in the fridge, where it will last months.

Queso Fresco

PREP TIME: 5 MINUTES | COOK TIME: 25 MINUTES
MAKES ABOUT ½ POUND

This farmer cheese is not unlike the simple, fresh farmer's cheeses all over the world. I use queso fresco on tacos, with eggs, in burritos, and on top of beans. It's a crumbly cheese, and if you press and salt it for several days, it can become queso añejo, which is not unlike cotija or Italian ricotta salata.

1 gallon whole milk
1 cup white or cider vinegar
Salt

Heat the milk slowly over medium-low heat, stirring often to avoid scorching. When the milk hits 170°F, which is the barest simmer, take it off the heat and pour in the vinegar and 1 teaspoon salt. Stir this to combine, then let the pot sit undisturbed for about 45 minutes.

Meanwhile, line a large sieve or colander with cheesecloth. Make sure the cheesecloth drapes over the sides because you're going to tie it into a bundle. Set this over a large bowl.

Ladle the curds into the cheesecloth-lined sieve, catching the whey, which you can use in Caldo de Queso (page 206) or as the hot water for flour tortillas. Let the curds sit in the cheesecloth for 30 minutes. Carefully fold in any more salt you want.

Bring the bundle up and squeeze out excess liquid. Tie this off and set it back in the sieve to drain a bit more for another 20 minutes.

It's now ready, but I like to pack the cheese into cheese molds and let that set in the fridge overnight. You can pack it into any suitable container or shape it the way you like while it's in the cheesecloth.

Eat your queso fresco within a week. Or double the salt and squeeze it tighter to remove even more liquid, and it'll set up as queso añejo.

Requesón

PREP TIME: 5 MINUTES | COOK TIME: 1 HOUR
REST TIME: 30 MINUTES | MAKES 2 TO 3 CUPS CHEESE

This is the border's answer to ricotta cheese. It's a bit more acidic, but is so delicious and so easy I thought I'd include it here. You'll see it as a taco filling all over Mexico, and the Mennonites of Chihuahua put it in flour tortillas, which is divine. Mix some with sautéed quelites and some pepitas and you have a memorable vegetarian taco.

1 gallon whole milk
½ cup white or apple cider vinegar
2 teaspoons salt, fine-grained if possible

Heat the milk and vinegar in a large pot over medium-low heat. Take your time with this part. You want it to come up to the steaming point (155°F to 165°F) slowly, then hold there for about 45 minutes. Take the pot off the heat and let the mixture sit another 10 to 15 minutes undisturbed.

Set cheesecloth in a sieve set over a bowl. Carefully ladle the curds into this. The whey can be used in Caldo de Queso (page 206) or as the hot water for making flour tortillas. Let the curds sit until they cool, about 30 to 45 minutes.

Move the requesón to a bowl and fold in the salt. Chill and use within a week.

▶ Prickly pear fruit

Prickly Pear Juice

PREP TIME: 45 MINUTES | COOK TIME: 20 MINUTES | MAKES ABOUT A GALLON

Called agua de tuna in Spanish, prickly pear juice is arguably the best thing to make with these cactus fruit; tuna is the Spanish word for the fruit. Aguas frescas are popular all across the borderlands, from San Diego to the Gulf. Here's how to go about making a prickly pear agua fresca without getting all the spines stuck in your hands.

Obviously, you need to start with prickly pears. Interestingly, species of this cactus live in every American state outside of New England, as well as many Canadian provinces. Every species will have a slightly different flavor, but they are mostly a combination of bubblegum and watermelon, with almost no tartness. More on that in a bit.

Almost all species are defended by two sets of spines: the ones you can see, and the glochids, which are hairlike and almost invisible . . . until it's too late. There are a number of ways to deal with them. Start by knocking off the big spines with some twigs or a brush before you even pick the fruit. You can also use a torch to singe them on the plant, too, but be careful about starting fires. You then use tongs or a stiff leather glove to twist off the fruit. I sometimes use a knife to slice them off at the base.

To get your prickly pear juice, you *can* peel the fruit—carefully—with a knife and proceed, but that leaves some flavor and tartness on the cutting board; most of the tartness in any prickly pear fruit is in the skin. I rarely do that, but you can.

With my method, you drop the fruit into a pot, barely cover with water, and bring to a boil. Let it cool, then mash the now softened fruit with a potato masher and run the whole shebang through a food mill.

Tip: Freeze your prickly pears first, as this makes them even softer. Strain the mash through a sieve and you are good to go. No glochids.

Now, about that tartness thing. I add Fruit Fresh, which is citric acid (it's often in the canning section of the supermarket), but lime juice is a good alternative. Add to your taste.

Similarly, add sugar to taste. I don't end up adding much at all, because I don't love overly sweet things. You do you. Add ice, and, well, sotol, bacanora, mezcal, or tequila, and you are good to go! Or skip the booze and make agua de tuna. Or make the cactus sorbet (page 289).

Once made, it will keep a few weeks in the fridge. Left on the counter, it will ferment in a day or two.

3 pounds prickly pears
Water to cover
Sugar, agave syrup, or honey
Citric acid or freshly squeezed lime juice

Remove the spines from the fruit, as noted in the text above. Put the fruit in a pot and barely cover with water. Bring to a boil. Turn off the heat, and when it cools enough to work with, mash everything with a potato masher.

Run the mash through a food mill, or if you don't have one, push it through a colander with a rubber spatula. You need to get rid of the many seeds. Once that's done, strain the mash through a fine sieve, pushing it through with a rubber spatula. If you want a very clear juice, run that one more time through a sieve with a paper towel set inside it, and do not push it through—let it drip through over the course of an hour or two.

Add sugar, plus citric acid or lime juice to taste. Enjoy over ice.

KEY TO ICONS

In so many cases, either the original recipes or just common sense allows for many different kinds of meat or fish to be used, depending on your preference or what you have available. So rather than write recipes for, say, chicken enchiladas and beef enchiladas, when everything but the meat is the same in the recipe, I've provided a visual key for all the various proteins that will work in any given recipe. Feel free to experiment beyond my suggestions!

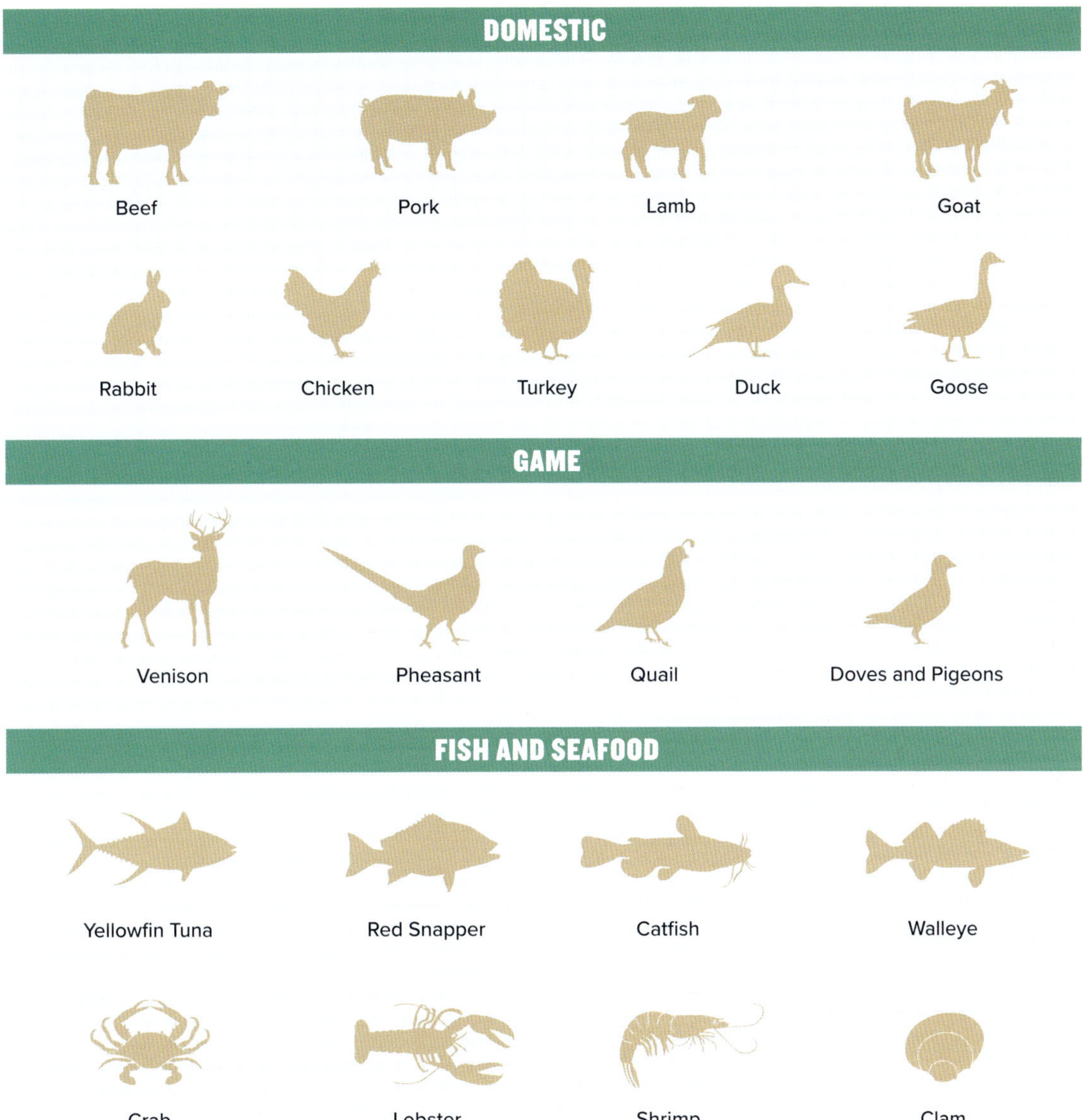

Manuel
Salorjo

PART 2

THE JOURNEY

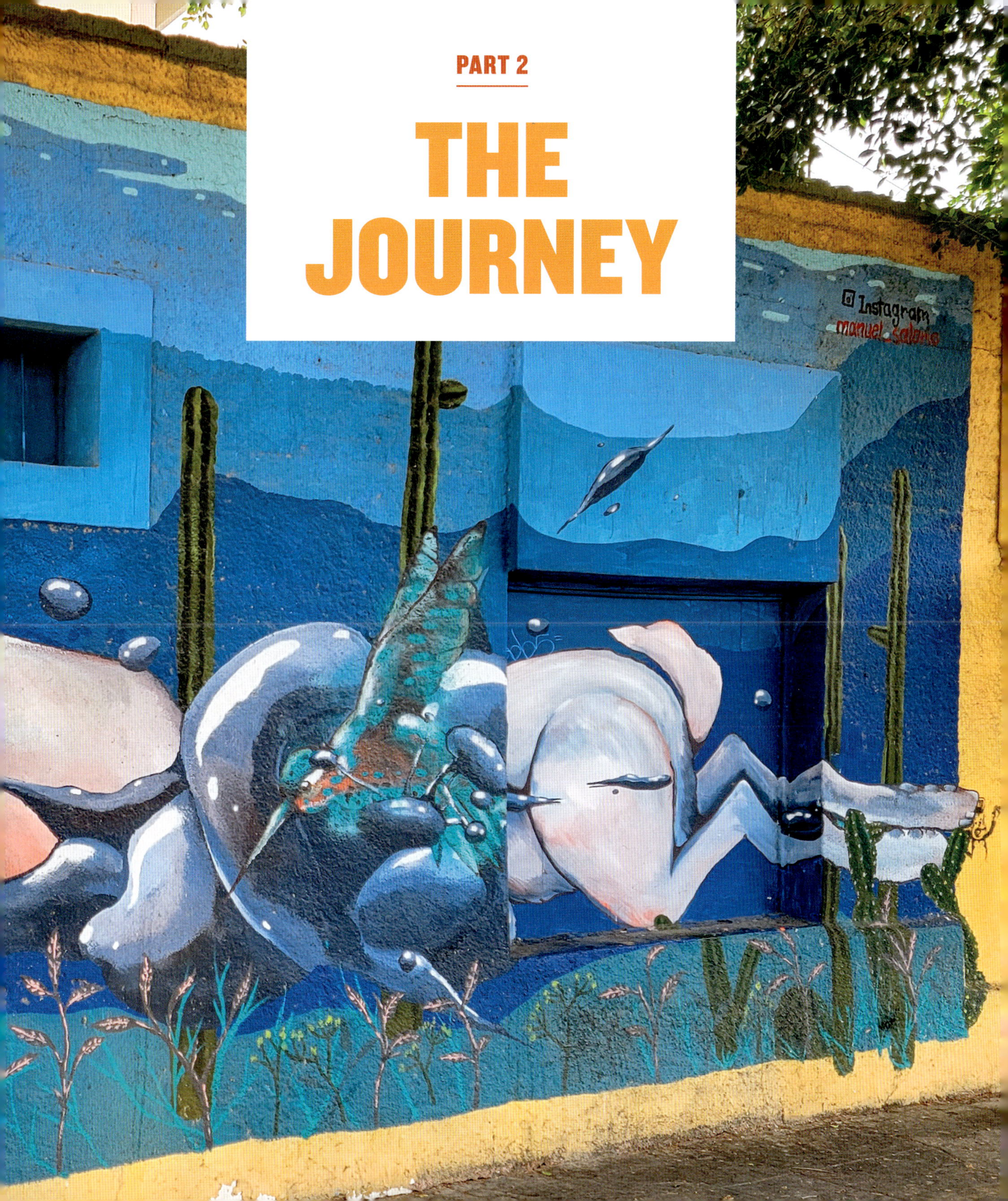

SACRAMENTO

WHERE IT ALL BEGAN

I started traveling along the border long before I moved to Sacramento in 2004, but those were only tentative steps. The journey really began once I settled in California, a state where Mexican influences permeate the culture—after all, Alta California was a Mexican state prior to the Mexican-American War of the mid-1800s. My partner at the time, Holly Heyser, is a California native and for her Mexican food is, largely, just food. Nothing exotic or special about it. Breakfast? Burritos. Cold out? Mole or pozole. Taco Night on the regular. From her lead I branched out.

Soon after I moved to Sacramento, I met Patricio Wise and Cinthia Martinez, both from Monterrey in Nuevo Leon. Pato, as he's called by friends, soon introduced me to a Mexican cuisine unlike that of Sacramento, whose Mexican-American population hails largely from Jalisco and Michoacan. And soon after that, "Los Wises" opened Nixtaco in Roseville, California. Nixtaco became my watering hole, the headquarters of all my initial explorations. I am happy to say that since those early days, their restaurant has received international acclaim in the form of a Michelin Bib Gourmand award, given to restaurants with Michelin-quality food but casual surroundings. If there is a spiritual home to this book, it's Nixtaco.

What you find in this chapter are my borderlands beginnings: foods Pato and Cinthia introduced me to, including a few of their own recipes, as well as border favorites I first enjoyed in Sacramento—and even a couple of my own recipes I developed after trips to the borderlands.

These are the recipes that stoked the fire.

Tacos de lengua in my old backyard in Sacramento, hoja santa plants in the background.

Patrico Wise and Cinthia Martinez, owners of Nixtaco in Roseville, California.

MACHACA CON HUEVOS (Machacado)

PREP TIME: 20 MINUTES, IF YOU HAVE COOKED POTATOES | COOK TIME: 15 MINUTES | SERVES 4 TO 6

I was getting bored with my usual chorizo, egg, potato, and cheese breakfast burritos at Adalberto's in Sacramento when I noticed this other dish in the breakfast section: machaca. Huh? Why not? And so a love affair was born. Machaca is shredded jerky, carne seca. And this dish is by far the most common: I've eaten it from Sacramento to San Diego to Brownsville, and everywhere in between.

The best machaca con huevos tacos (or burritos) are made with real machaca, the kind on page 54. But in Sacramento, where the tradition isn't so borderlands, they use shredded brisket that's slightly dried. To me, that's not machaca, but it's still good.

What follows is my favorite breakfast taco or burrito. *Oh, and I still love you, chorizo!* Feel free to sub that for the machaca.

- 3 tablespoons lard, bacon fat, butter, or vegetable oil
- ½ white onion, minced
- 1 or 2 seeded and chopped jalapeños (optional)
- ½ pound potatoes, peeled, cooked, and diced
- Salt and black pepper
- ¼ pound machaca, chopped, or ½ pound Mexican chorizo, crumbled
- 6 eggs, lightly beaten
- ¼ pound melty cheese, like queso Oaxaca, Jack, Cheddar, or mozzarella
- 8 to 12 flour tortillas
- Salsa of your choice, for serving

Heat the lard in a large pan over medium-high heat. Add the onions, jalapeños, and potatoes and sauté until they brown a little. Salt them as they cook. Add the machaca. Stir to combine and cook for a few minutes undisturbed to get some browning. Stir and add the eggs, cheese, more salt, and some pepper. Mix well to combine and drop the heat to medium. Cook until the eggs set and the cheese melts.

Divide into portions and fill warm flour tortillas with the mixture. A little salsa is a nice touch.

"Barriga llena, corazón contento"

Full belly, happy heart

TACOS DE LENGUA

PREP TIME: 30 MINUTES, MOSTLY TO PREP TACOS | COOK TIME: 3 HOURS, MOSTLY TO BRAISE TONGUE | SERVES 8 TO 10

Let's blast right out of the gate with a recipe that might seem challenging, but really isn't. Tongue tacos are a staple at every taco truck in Sacramento, and they're made in varying ways. All are good. I'll provide two methods for cooking the tongue here, one easy, one better.

Keep in mind that a tongue is a tongue, so while beef tongue is most common, I've used tongues from elk, bison, nilgai, deer, even antelope and hogs. Lamb tongues are a great option, too, and are usually cheap when you find them. Feeling squinchy? Remember ***a tongue is just meat***. It's not really an "organ", like kidneys or tripe. Fear not: We chop the tongue at the end, so you don't get that sensation of food that tastes you back.

The only barrier here is that you really should peel the skin off the tongue after braising. Not *everyone* does along the border, but most do. Be sure to do this while the tongue or tongues are still hot, or it'll be a chore. You can do this braising step up to a couple days in advance.

- 2 to 3 pounds tongue (normal weight of 1 beef tongue)
- 1 large onion, chopped
- 5 cloves garlic, peeled and crushed
- 2 bay leaves
- 1 tablespoon black peppercorns, cracked
- 2 tablespoons salt
- 1 sprig epazote (optional)
- 3 tablespoons lard or vegetable oil
- 16 to 20 corn tortillas
- Fire-Roasted Salsa (page 38)
- Hank's Taco Onions (page 46)
- Diced or sliced avocado (optional)
- Chopped cilantro, radish, and serrano chiles, for garnishes

SIMMER THE TONGUE: Put the tongue or tongues in a large pot and cover with water by 2 inches. Bring the water to a simmer and add the onion, garlic, bay, black peppercorns, epazote, and salt. Simmer the tongue until the sharp point of a thin knife will pierce it easily, about 2 to 3 hours.

PREP THE TONGUE: When the meat is tender, set it on a cutting board to cool somewhat. When it's barely cool enough to handle, peel off the skin and discard. You can do all this up to a few days ahead if you want. Wrap the peeled tongue in plastic, or store it in the braising liquid, then refrigerate.

When you're ready to make the tacos, cut the tongue into large pieces. Sear in the lard until they're nicely browned, then chop coarsely. Serve on warm corn tortillas with salsa, onions, avocado, cilantro, and other garnishes.

ALTERNATE METHOD: Once the tongues are peeled and tender, finish them by coating with a little lard or oil, then grilling them whole over wood or charcoal, *then* chopping and serving.

The Fire-Roasted Salsa and Hank's Taco Onions are a perfect accompaniment, along with some chopped cilantro. Avocados, radish, and some extra chiles are great, too.

CHICHARRON EN SALSA VERDE

PREP TIME: 15 MINUTES | COOK TIME: 20 MINUTES | SERVES 6

There is so much to say about chicharron en salsa verde . . . For starters, it is a near universal dish all over the borderlands and all of Mexico—something rare. Pato first served it to me even before he opened Nixtaco.

Yes, there are fancy versions of chicharron en salsa verde that use fresh pork belly. I've eaten them, and they are great. But in most places, the actual dish is made from cracklins, the leavings after you render lard. This leads to some confusion because chicharron is a term also used for pork rinds, those light-as-air crunchy bits of fried pork skin. I've seen some recipes that use them, but if you do, the texture gets flabby and flaccid. Not a fan.

But make it with cracklins, ideally with the skin still on them, and you have a magical dish. There's a bit of meat, some crispy fat, and a wisp of that puffed skin from a proper chicharron. All of which is simmered in a spicy tomatillo and green chile sauce.

It is a quintessential taco filling, but you'll see it in burritos, sopes, tortas, you name it. What's more, it's cheap, so it's a filling in the classic tacos de canasta, the "basket tacos" beloved by Mexican students in the way American students love Taco Bell.

Virtually every recipe for chicharron en salsa verde is made with pork cracklins. But there is one other option I stumbled on: cracklins from rendering duck fat. Duck skin is, to me, too sturdy to make a nice cracklin. But simmered in salsa verde? Game changer.

Top your tacos with cilantro, Hank's Taco Onions (page 46), and some queso fresco or cotija cheese.

The stew will keep in the fridge for a week or so, and it can be frozen.

Side note: You will see chicharron en salsa roja in Nuevo Leon. If you want to do that recipe, use my Red Enchilada Sauce (page 37) to simmer the cracklins.

- 1 recipe Tomatillo Salsa Verde (page 70)
- 1 pound cracklins (see sidebar on page 70) from pork, duck, or goose, cut or broken into bite-sized pieces
- 8 or more corn tortillas
- 4 tablespoons chopped cilantro
- Hank's Taco Onions (page 46)
- Cotija cheese, crumbled, for garnish

Pour your salsa over the cracklins in a pot, cover the pot, and bring to a simmer for 20 minutes. You might need to add a little water or stock to keep it from sticking. You want the mixture to be stiff enough to not soak and melt the tortilla. You can cook your cracklins for more than 20 minutes if you want a softer texture.

Heat up your tortillas and make your tacos. Top with cilantro, the onions soaked in lime juice, and cotija cheese.

NOTE: You can use 1 pound pork belly if you can't find cracklins. Cut it into batons and fry them crispy. Save the fat!

Tomatillo Salsa Verde

PREP TIME: 30 MINUTES | COOK TIME: 1 HOUR | SERVES 20

Make this salsa in large batches and store it in the fridge. It will keep a month or more that way.

- 1 to 2 pounds husked tomatillos, preferably the little milpa tomatillos
- 4 cups sliced white or yellow onions
- 6 unpeeled cloves garlic
- 1½ cups chopped roasted, peeled, and seeded poblano or Anaheim chiles (about 4 chiles)
- ½ cup chopped peeled and seeded jalapeños (about 3 to 5)
- 2 teaspoons cumin
- 1 tablespoon dried oregano, preferably Mexican
- 1 tablespoon kosher salt
- 2 tablespoons chopped epazote (optional)
- ¼ cup chopped cilantro
- Freshly squeezed lime juice
- Fruit Fresh or other source citric acid (only if canning)

Arrange the tomatillos, sliced onions, and the garlic cloves on a baking sheet (or two) and set under the broiler until they are a bit charred.

Once you have all the chiles prepped, peel the garlic and put it and everything else into a food processor and pulse to make a rough salsa. You're done if you don't want to can your salsa.

Canning

If you are canning, add 1 teaspoon Fruit Fresh (citric acid) to each pint jar; the jars should be sterilized beforehand. Pack the salsa into the jars and use a knife or chopstick to remove as many air pockets as you can find. Leave about 1 inch headspace. Seal the jars and process in a boiling water bath for 15 minutes.

When the jars are ready, lift out of the boiling water and let them rest until their lids plink. Once they've cooled to room temperature, the salsa will keep in the pantry for more than a year.

CRACKLINS PRIMER

It's worth knowing how to make cracklins not only for this recipe, but to have the best lard in the world. Fresh rendered lard is lower in saturated fat than butter, lasts months, and best of all, has a tan—the process of making cracklins heats the pork fat to its smoking point, so it browns enough to add a distinctive flavor.

First, buy pork belly. I'd start with a pound or two. You can remove the skin or not. I leave it. Cut the belly into batons about ½ inch thick and wide by 2 inches long. The skin is tough, so have a sharp knife. Arrange the batons in a pot and turn the heat to medium-high. As soon as you hear them sizzling, stir. Keep stirring and sizzling away until quite a lot of fat has rendered out. The more fat, the less you need to stir. As things progress, drop the heat to medium.

Eventually, the cracklins will bubble less in their fat. At this stage, if you have a meat thermometer, measure the fat temperature. Now you want to raise that temperature to about 325°F. When you get there, the skin on the batons will start to puff out like a pork rind. Now is the time to ladle them out onto a paper towel.

Remove the pot from the heat and let it cool. Pour the lard into a container and use it for any of the recipes in this book, then make some Chicharron en Salsa Verde!

PATRICIO'S SALSA NEGRA

PREP TIME: 20 MINUTES | SERVES 10

I'd never heard of salsa negra until I volunteered to help Patricio cook at his restaurant's New Year's Eve party. This inky sauce lurked in a squeeze bottle, to be used on a poblano soup (page 126). "Don't use too much," Patricio said. "It's very strong."

I tasted it. Dark, nutty, loaded with chiles and garlic and sesame, this sauce lingered on my tastebuds. It wasn't picante spicy, but it was exotic. Like a mole, almost. But somehow cleaner tasting. What's in it? "Secreto," he said, only half joking.

Patricio ultimately did give me the recipe, and I urge you to make it. Most of the ingredients are easily found, save one. Pato's Salsa Negra relies on black garlic. If you have a Trader Joe's around, they sell it, and you can also buy black garlic online. What is it? Slow-fermented garlic that is murky, garlicky, and sweet. It lasts forever in the pantry.

Patricio says this salsa is good on anything, and I believe him. I first put it on some slow-cooked goose legs with cilantro rice and toasted pumpkin seeds. As expected, it was amazing. Since a little of the sauce goes a long way, and because it lasts a long time in the fridge—several weeks—have some fun experimenting with it.

If you want the exact sauce they use at Nixtaco, follow this recipe by the gram. If you're okay with a little variation, use the volumetric measurements.

- ¾ cup sunflower, canola, or vegetable oil (175 grams)
- 2 teaspoons lime juice (about 1 Key lime)
- 1 teaspoon smoked salt (3 grams)
- 1 tablespoon dry roasted peanuts (5 grams)
- 1 tablespoon coriander seeds (4 grams), toasted
- 1 pasilla or guajillo chile, stemmed, seeded, and torn up
- 1 ancho chile, stemmed, seeded, and torn up
- 1 tablespoon ground cumin (4 grams)
- 1 teaspoon chipotle powder (2 grams), or 1 chipotle in adobo
- 2 tablespoons sesame seeds (13 grams), toasted
- ½ teaspoon garlic powder (1.5 grams)
- 3 cloves black garlic

Purée all the ingredients on high in a blender until smooth. Store in an airtight container in the fridge for months.

MUSHROOM TACOS

PREP TIME: 35 MINUTES | COOK TIME: 40 MINUTES | SERVES 4 TO 6

This recipe isn't exactly from the Nixtaco menu, but it is inspired by it. The restaurant offers an amazing mushroom taco, which, in my opinion, absolutely must be served on a flour tortilla. It is the vegetarian companion to the very meaty Deathbed Taco in this chapter.

Any mushroom will work, but wild ones make this even better. I've eaten wild mushroom tacos in both New Mexico and Chihuahua, where the Tarahumara gather all sorts of mushrooms; I ate a taco a bit like this that was filled with lobster mushrooms. I used morels in the picture. Save this taco for when you have fresh mushrooms—or thawed sautéed mushrooms, which are almost as good. I would not make this with dried mushrooms.

The mushroom filling will keep a few days in the fridge, and can be reheated in a pan when you're ready.

Filling

1 pound fresh mushrooms, chopped

½ white onion, chopped

3 tablespoons lard, bacon fat or oil

Salt

3 cloves garlic, minced

A pinch of dried Mexican oregano

Black pepper to taste

To Finish

½ pound shredded melty cheese such as asadero, Oaxaca, mozzarella, or "Mexican blend"

Flour tortillas

Chopped cilantro

½ red onion

¼ cup freshly squeezed lime juice

Lime wedges, to serve

Serrano Crema (optional)

1 or 2 serrano chiles, seeded and minced

2 cups Mexican crema, or 1½ cups sour cream and ½ cup cream

Salt

Soak the red onion in the lime juice with a pinch of salt.

If you're making the serrano crema, blitz the crema and the serranos in a blender on high until completely puréed. If you want to get fancy, push the mixture through a fine-meshed sieve. Set it aside for now.

To make the filling, add the mushrooms and onion to a large sauté pan, and turn the heat to high. Toss the contents of the pan to keep the mushrooms and onion moving as it heats up. As soon as it starts to sizzle, sprinkle some salt over everything. Shake the pan from time to time. At some point the mushrooms will give up their water. Add the lard or oil now and toss to coat.

Add the minced garlic and oregano and mix well. Let all this cook, undisturbed, a few minutes to develop some browning. Stir and mix well one more time, then let it brown once more. Turn off the heat and cover the pan.

To make the tacos, set about 2 tablespoons shredded cheese on a hot comal, griddle or flattop, set over medium-high heat. As it begins to melt, set a flour tortilla on it and press this down with your hand or a spatula until the melted cheese barely reaches the edges of the tortilla.

Let this cook until the cheese releases. Usually this is about 1 to 3 minutes, and it's better to let the cheese sit a little too long than too short. You want it pretty and brown and crispy. When it releases, or when you decide to scrape it off the comal with a spatula, flip the tortilla over, top it with some of the mushroom mixture, some of the lime-soaked onion, a bit of cilantro, and a drizzle of the serrano crema. Serve with lime wedges.

NOTE: If you're not using the serrano crema, you may want to add hot sauce. The Monterrey Salsa (page 75) is a great option, and Patricio's Salsa Negra (page 71) will take it to another level of luxury.

DEATHBED TACO

PREP TIME: 25 MINUTES | COOK TIME: 40 MINUTES | SERVES 4 TO 8

Here it is. My deathbed taco. And again, I have Patricio to thank for it. A few years ago on my birthday, I was at Nixtaco and he decided to make a special taco to celebrate. It was smoky, grilled, well-aged ribeye on a flour tortilla with a costra, topped with roasted bone marrow and Monterrey pequin salsa, with extra pequins and some onions and cilantro.

The combination is otherworldly. Chewy, almost translucent tortilla. Crispy, rich melted cheese. Smoky, perfectly cooked ribeye of the highest quality. Dollops of ultrarich roasted bone marrow, or as we like to call it, beef butter. All that richness meets its match with the bracing Monterrey salsa, plus a few extra pequins because I like it hot. Some crunchy, bright white onions and a sprinkling of cilantro round everything out.

There are a lot of components, but none is overly technical or difficult. If you want to scale back on the richness, use venison backstrap in place of ribeye. Do not skip the bone marrow. The one trick to this recipe is timing: Most of it must be cooked and served within an hour or so. I'd expect nothing less for my last taco.

Canoe cut marrow bones will be at most butcher shops in the frozen section, or you can ask them to saw you some on site.

- 2 marrow bones, canoe cut (4 halves)
- Salt and pepper
- 1 or 2 ribeye steaks
- 8 to 16 flour tortillas
- 1 pound shredded melty cheese, such as queso Chihuahua, asadero, or "Mexican blend"
- 1 recipe Hank's Taco Onions (page 46)
- 1 recipe Monterrey Salsa (page 75)
- Chopped cilantro, to serve
- Lime wedges, to serve

Preheat the oven to 450°F. Set the marrow bones marrow side up on a baking sheet lined with foil. Sprinkle salt over the marrow and set them in the oven for 20 minutes. Keep an eye on them at 15 minutes. If the marrow is bubbling and liquidy, they're ready. Move them to the stovetop and turn off the oven.

Meanwhile, salt the steaks well on both sides and let them come to room temperature for 30 minutes to 1 hour. Grill the steaks over mesquite wood or charcoal until medium-rare. Grind black pepper over them as they rest.

Warm the flour tortillas and set in a tortilla warmer, or tuck them into a kitchen towel and fold it over to keep them warm and pliable.

Start making the costras. Depending on how large your comal or flattop is, set about 2 tablespoons shredded cheese on the hot metal, and as it melts, press one of the flour tortillas on it until the melting cheese underneath just about reaches the edges of the tortilla. Let this brown a few minutes. The cheese will release if your comal is well seasoned, but a thin metal spatula can come in handy if not. Do all the tortillas and set them in the turned-off oven. Set the bone marrow in there, too.

Chop the ribeyes into pieces that you'd want to eat in a taco, so about the size of your thumbnail. Hit them with a little more salt.

To assemble, scoop some ribeye onto the costra side of the tortilla, then spoon some marrow on top, then some of the lime-soaked onions, then the Monterrey salsa, then finish with the cilantro. Eat and die happy.

Monterrey Salsa

PREP TIME: 10 MINUTES | SERVES 4 TO 6 AS A TACO SALSA

Here's a far simpler salsa that is still one of my favorites. In fact, it's required on the Deathbed Taco, opposite. Ideally you'd have fresh green chiles pequins, the wild, bullet-shaped chile that is beloved in both Texas and its neighboring Mexican states. At its most basic, this salsa is just pequins, salt, and water. True hardcore pequin enthusiasts say this is the way. I prefer a bit more, so I grind pequins with salt and garlic, then add lime juice. But that's as far as I go. This is a minimalist salsa designed for rich, fatty, beefy dishes.

This is a molcajete salsa. You can't really achieve the same effect with anything other than a Western mortar and pestle. Like Italian pesto, it needs to be pounded, not buzzed in a food processor.

If you can't find chile pequins, green habaneros are a decent substitute, as are green Thai chiles or green árbols. If all else fails, chop a serrano and put that in the molcajete.

6 to 12 chiles pequins, stems removed

1 teaspoon salt

1 large clove garlic

At least ½ cup lime juice

Put the pequins, salt, and garlic in a molcajete or mortar. Grind into a paste, then stir in the lime juice. A little of this salsa goes a long way.

THE MAGICAL COSTRA

Like tacos? How about grilled cheese? Well a costra is grilled cheese on a taco. Patricio is very fond of this addition to his tacos, and he and his sous chef Ryan Visker taught me how. Perfecting a costra takes practice, as I learned the hard way.

We were all cooking at a Heritage Fire event in California's Napa Valley, using a huge slab of steel as a comal. We had just seasoned it, and there were still some sticky spots. We got into the weeds as the crowds discovered how good our tacos were, and I chipped in to help start them off with the costra. Well, it didn't go well. I didn't let the cheese caramelize enough, and the tacos were sticking to the steel. Ryan had started giving me pointers when a nearby chef, a Texan from Dallas legendary for trash talking, started heckling me. As a proud New Jersey native, I told him to kick rocks with sandals (what I said was far more vulgar), but I soon got the hang of it, thanks to Ryan, and we all settled down after that.

The story is relevant because you need to basically use The Force to determine when the cheese is ready, although slightly rotating the tortilla to see if the cheese has released off the hot comal will help until you achieve Jedi status. You can use a thin metal spatula to sweep up the tortilla, but Mexican moms will laugh at you. It took me a little while to get it, but it is oh-so worth it!

Any shredded, melty cheese works, even those shredded "Mexican blend" cheeses, which are actually excellent because they are drier than, say, queso asadero, queso Oaxaca, or queso Chihuahua, which are other excellent options.

CHORIZO BURGER

PREP TIME: 45 MINUTES | COOK TIME: 30 MINUTES | SERVES 4 TO 6

I've seen chorizo burgers in Southern California and once in New Mexico, but this, to the best of my knowledge, is not something you'd see in Mexico. It is, however, delicious: chorizo, mixed with the ground meat of your choice, plus the toppings and the green chile mayo combine for a seriously awesome burger.

The meat mix will keep for a few days in the fridge, as will the mayo. So you can get this all prepped the day before guests come over and be all ready and stress-free when you need to assemble your burgers.

Toppings

- 3 tablespoons vegetable oil
- 2 large onions, minced
- 4 roasted green chiles, Anaheim or poblano, peeled, seeded, and sliced

Green Chile Mayo

- 2 cups mayonnaise
- ½ cup chopped cilantro
- 2 roasted green chiles, peeled and seeded
- Salt

Burgers

- 1 pound ground venison, beef, turkey, or bison
- 5½ ounces Mexican chorizo, loose, not cased, or ¼ pound if it's the stuff in a tube
- 1 tablespoon vegetable oil

To Assemble

- 4 to 6 burger buns
- 4 to 6 slices pepper Jack cheese
- Lettuce leaves

Start by heating the 3 tablespoons vegetable oil in a pan over medium-high heat. Add the minced onion and let this cook, stirring often, until the onion has nicely browned. Turn off the heat and set aside when it's ready.

If you are starting with fresh peppers, you will need to roast, peel, and seed them. See page 32 a good tutorial on that, or you can use canned or frozen roasted chiles.

Add all the ingredients for the mayo and purée in a blender. Add salt to taste. You will have some left over, so keep it in a container in the fridge, where it will last a couple weeks.

Mix the ground meats together and knead well so they combine cohesively. Form into balls and slightly flatten them. If you are grilling, just form normal patties and grill. What follows is for a stovetop smashburger.

Get a comal or griddle or large frying pan hot. Add the vegetable oil. Set one of the balls of meat in the center of the oil, and use it to spread the oil around a little. Slick the underside of a bacon press or another pan with some oil. Press the meat into a patty of about ½ inch thick, more or less. Hold the pressure for about 30 seconds, then slide the bacon press off the patty to the side. Don't lift straight up or the patty will break. Salt the patty lightly as it cooks.

Let the meat cook for about 90 seconds more, then flip. Salt the other side. Add some onions to the middle of the patty and top with a slice of roasted chile and then a slice of cheese. I like to put a metal bowl or pot lid over the burger now to melt the cheese. Let this sit for another minute to 2 minutes, depending on how well cooked you like your burgers. While this is happening, lay the lettuce leaves on your buns and top with a little of the mayo.

To build the burger, set the patty on the bun, then top with some more lettuce, and some more mayo. Serve at once.

NOTE: If you are making a lot of these, set a cooling rack over a baking sheet in the oven and turn the oven to 200°F. You can put the buns in there, too, to stay warm.

VENISON TAMALES

PREP TIME: 2 HOURS | COOK TIME: 1 HOUR | MAKES 30 TO 40 TAMALES

I got this recipe from Patricio and Cinthia. These venison tamales are a tradition in their family whenever someone comes home with a deer. They would bring the meat to a lady who specializes in making these tamales, and would often get an entire deer made into them. They are that good.

Keep in mind that there are lots of different kinds of tamales in Mexico. These are from Nuevo Leon, so are tamales norteño, thin tamales wrapped in corn husks. You could of course make yours fatter or wrap them in banana leaves, instead.

I use shoulder, shank, or neck meat for these tamales, but any part will work. The core of this recipe is shredded braised meat—don't forget to save the braising liquid. Beef, lamb, goat, or honestly basically anything works here: turkey or pheasant legs, rabbit, hare, pork, waterfowl, you name it. It just needs to be shreddable.

For those of you who are averse to spicy foods, I use mostly guajillo chiles, which are not even as hot as a jalapeño. Any dried chile will work, and anchos are the mildest of all.

The sauce on top of the tamales is my Tomatillo Salsa Verde (page 70), either the Green (page 36) or Red Enchilada Sauce (page 37) works well, too.

Make quite a lot of these when you do, as they are something of a production. But tamales freeze very well, and you can pop them right from the freezer into a steamer for an easy weeknight meal. Or better yet, reheat them on the comal, slowly, turning them frequently, until the husks are charred. That smoky corn aroma permeates the tamal, making them far better than even fresh.

Fresh masa for tamales is always available in Latin markets, usually behind the counter, but sometimes you can find bags of it either refrigerated or frozen. I'll give you instructions for making masa from masa harina at the end; it's not as good, but it'll do.

Masa

1 tablespoon baking powder

2¼ pounds fresh masa (see Note)

10½ ounces fresh rendered lard

6 cloves garlic, chopped

4 guajillo or ancho chiles, seeded and torn up

⅓ cup braising liquid from venison

2 teaspoons salt

Filling

2 pounds shredded braised venison (about 4 cups)

6 ancho chiles, seeded and torn up

6 guajillo chiles, seeded and torn up

5 cloves garlic, chopped

2 cups braising liquid from venison

1 teaspoon dried Mexican oregano

1 teaspoon ground cumin

1 bunch epazote, chopped (optional)

30 to 40 corn husks, soaked in hot water

Sauce of your choice (see page 78), to serve

Hank's Taco Onions (page 46), to serve

MAKE THE MASA: Cook the chiles and garlic in the braising liquid until limp, then purée into a paste in a blender. Put the lard, salt, and baking powder in the bowl of a stand mixer and beat until light and fluffy. Add fresh masa bit by bit while the mixer is on low speed. About midway through, add the contents of the blender. Take the masa from the bowl and knead it until it is a cohesive mass. I like to put it in a plastic bag at this point.

MAKE THE FILLING: Sauté the garlic with the torn up chiles in a little lard until fragrant. Cover with water or braising liquid from the venison and simmer until soft, about 10 minutes. Purée in a blender. Mix this with the spices and herbs and the shredded venison.

SPREAD THE DOUGH: Place the corn husk wide side away from you. Smear some masa dough in the center of the husk, about ⅛ inch thick. Leave 2 to 4 inches room on the top and bottom of the husk, and about an inch or so on the sides.

FILL THE TAMALES: Add about a tablespoon of the venison filling to the center of the spread-out dough. Leave enough space around the dough so you'll be able to fold the tamal over.

FOLD THE TAMALES: Fold the tamal over lengthwise, touching the ends of the dough together. Usually the easiest way to do this is to fold the husk over itself. Tuck one end of the husk over the tamal, then roll the husk over to form a cylinder. Fold up the bottom to seal. If you want, tie the tamal with some string or strips of corn husk.

Repeat this with all the remaining masa and filling. If you have extra filling, use it for burritos or tacos.

STEAM THE TAMALES: Set up your steamer. This should be a tall, large pot with a vegetable steamer set inside. it. Pour in enough water to barely touch the base of the steamer. Line the steamer with a few spare corn husks. Tuck each finished tamal, open side up, into the steamer. When they're all in, cover the pot and steam for at least 1 hour, and up to 90 minutes.

SERVE THE TAMALES: When they're ready, unwrap the tamales and serve with a sauce and some onions.

NOTE: If you can't get fresh masa, use masa harina. You'll want 6 cups of masa harina mixed with 5 cups of warm braising liquid from the venison, or warm water.

TUNA CHEWS

I love this recipe, or more accurately this technique, which as far as I know I invented, although there must be people doing it somewhere along the border. It makes so much sense. You need large prickly pear fruits, called tunas in Spanish, which are easily found in Latin markets. I grew them in Sacramento. So yeah, no fish in this recipe. The fruits must be red and ripe; they will not ripen off the plant.

Either singe the spines and barely visible glochid spines off with fire—I rotate the fruit around a gas burner—or wear gloves. I do both, because the juice will stain. Peel all the fruit carefully, taking off just the skin.

Now use a paring knife to carefully slice off pieces of the fruit without cutting into the central seed layer. On large tunas, this will be a good ¼ inch thick. Save the central part with the seeds for Prickly Pear Juice (page 58).

Now dust the largely seed-free slices with Tajín, the chile-lime-salt mix that is so popular I've seen it even in rural supermarkets in places like North Dakota. I'd frankly be shocked if you are in a place that sells fresh prickly pears that doesn't also sell Tajín. But in a pinch, dampen each tuna slice in lime juice, then dust in a 50-50 mix of cayenne and fine salt.

Dehydrate the slices at about 140°F until they are leathery, about 2 to 4 hours. You may need to flip them after 1 hour. Eat as a snack or as a dessert topping. A slice is really nice on top of vanilla or Pine Nut Ice Cream (page 174). They will keep in the fridge for a month or so.

Dried prickly pear fruit is like a sweet and spicy fruit leather.

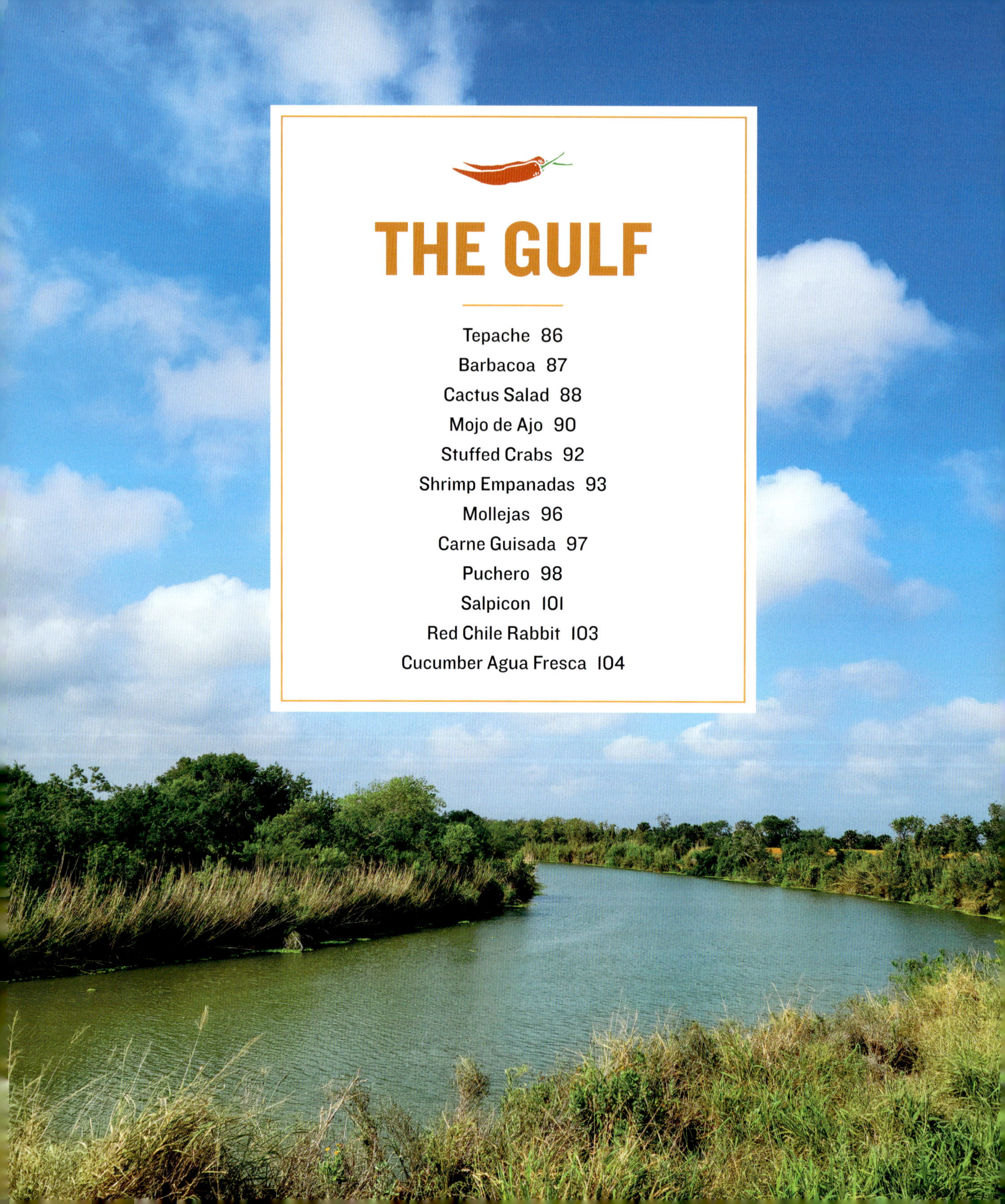

THE GULF

Culture blurs on the coasts. Nowhere along the 1,954-mile border between the US and Mexico do the cultures of both nations meld more than where the Rio Grande drains into the Gulf of Mexico—with the possible exception of where the border meets the Pacific. The Rio Grande Valley (RGV), a sprawling, steamy, 120-mile-long swath of South Texas stretching from the Gulf to Rio Grande City, is at once Mexican and Texican. And its position as the only place where the subtropical United States meets Mexico is unique. The valley is not a desert. It is lush.

The Rio Grande Valley, it should be said, is not an inherently pretty place. It is a patchwork of urban and agricultural, stitched together with highways and those typically Texas flyovers that make the interchanges look like concrete sailor's knots. The air is heavy with humidity. One early morning, walking out to my car, it was already 85°F, the windshield beaded with condensation.

The only hills are those paved interchanges. The pom-pom tops of the palm trees are the tallest things on the landscape, waving their fronds idly like cheerleaders on heroin. Everyone is working. The RGV is a place where immigrants come to work, and locals stay to make money. Oil and gas are big here, as are cotton and sorghum. Citrus, once king here, is waning because of freak frosts that are getting less freaky even as the average temperatures rise. And then there's SpaceX.

Everyone in the valley knows that weekends are for barbacoa. Barbacoa in South Texas is barbecued beef head, known as tacos de cabeza in places like Sonora and Baja. The best places separate the cuts—tongue, face (!), cheeks, brains, palate (!!), sweetbreads, and eye meat (!!!) and you can order one, or mix and match. There is no better place to eat this treasure than Vera's in Brownsville.

Open only on weekends, and really only mornings because they sell out each day, Vera's is an unassuming jewel of a restaurant whose main distinction is that they are the last restaurant in Texas legally allowed to roast their cow heads underground in pits, as is tradition. The smokiness comes through, and the meats are rich, unctuous and tender.

A speckled trout I caught at the mouth of the Rio Grande.

Normally you buy by the pound, grab the fixins' you want—salsas, onions, cilantro—a packet of corn tortillas, and go home to be a hero to your family. It's a meaty version of what my stepfather Frank would do on weekend mornings in New Jersey: Before us kids woke up, he'd go out and get everyone donuts and pastry, a real treat for a Sunday morning, a small kindness never forgotten.

Similarly, when I was at Vera's one early Sunday morning, a line of men—all men—waited to buy hero-sized portions of barbacoa. With one exception (besides me), all were Latino, all working class. Flip-flops, tank-tops and jean shorts were the uniform.

Tacos from Sheko's in Brownsville, Texas, and salsas from Ana Liz Taqueria in Mission, Texas.

It was here where I heard the sweet sound of Spanglish in full chorus. I love the fluid shifting, sometimes midclause, of Spanish and English words, grammar, and syntax. It is the true mark of a fronterizo. I find that bilingual people in the interiors of both the US and Mexico typically separate their sentences, even conversations. Not on the border, and I love this fluidity.

The other main thing the valley brings to the world is the Matamoros-style taco, tiny tacos famous in Matamoros, across the Rio Grande from Brownsville. They're normally made with corn tortillas about four inches across, and are always minimalist, which I love. Meat, maybe beans, white onion, cilantro, salsa of your choice—although almost never pico de gallo.

What I love about this style is that you can mix and match your meats and have a taco party on your plate without eating 5000 calories and feeling bloated and sweaty and burpy. Many places serve this style of taco, and I'd recommend a tour of Southmost Road along the border in Brownsville. But my friend Mike Ortiz likes a neighborhood spot called Sheko's, and it's damn good. I ordered steak, lengua, barbacoa, and sweetbread tacos. So good.

A word on sweetbreads, mollejas in Spanish. Other than beef barbacoa, this is greater South Texas's contribution to taco meats. Nowhere else is this cholesterol-spiking offal delicacy served so widely. I've eaten them everywhere from Del Rio to Laredo to Brownsville, and they're always tender, creamy-chewy (if that makes any sense), with super crispy outsides. I will never not eat mollejas when I am in the Rio Grande Valley. Nunca.

As I ate through the RGV, with good, great, and gross meals, a pattern revealed itself to me. A pattern I now recognize everywhere in the Mexican food universe. There are three main sorts of Mexican restaurants. Old family-run places—often shabby looking, they can range from gems like Vera's to salmonella factories. Because you have to know which is which, these are often the hidden hotspots in a place's food scene.

Fancy, lush, shiny palaces of Mexican cuisine, some so gaudy I call them templos de los nacos (temples of the tacky). I understand why they owners are doing this: An idea exists in the American mind that Mexican food needs to be low-brow, that it doesn't deserve white linen treatment the way French food does. This is obviously false and bigoted. But, in many cases, the food ends up being ham-handed "elevated" versions of humbler food that simply aren't better than at the family places. The third type of restaurant is a hybrid. Usually renovated places owned now by the children of the old school, family-style owners, they are cleaned up, shiny and welcoming to strangers, but not pretentious at all. Sheko's is a perfect example of this, as is Armando's Tacos in Hermosillo, Sonora.

I mentioned that the Rio Grande Valley is not pretty on its surface. That does not mean there is no natural beauty in the region. Far from it. You have to know where to look. And there's nowhere better than Laguna Madre, the mega-lagoon that stretches from Corpus Christi all the way to Las Palomas Wildlife Area at Boca Chica. The mouth of the Rio Grande is on the other side of this lagoon. The laguna is a haven for fish, and is one of the few places you can routinely catch snook in the United States. Redfish, speckled trout, and the other usual suspects in shallow Gulf waters teem there. The duck hunting in winter is epic.

For whatever reason, on all my visits, I'd never seen the mouth of the Rio Grande. I needed to fix that. I wanted to see the border in its natural state. I'd seen it in the West, the iconic iron fence extending like a blade into the Pacific between Tijuana and Chula Vista, California, and I wanted to see its other end. When Mike Ortiz and I turned onto the beach, the tide was coming in, so we'd need to be quick: It runs up against the dunes in higher tides, which would strand us. And Mike did not want to be on the beach after dark. Too dangerous. But we made it, passing a pair of

A gorgeous Huichol-style mural at Nana's restaurant in Westlaco, Texas.

Border Patrol pickups along the way, including one parked right at the mouth.

The mouth of the Rio Grande is smaller than I had imagined. For a river named Grande or Bravo (Mexico calls it the Rio Bravo), its mouth was surprisingly modest. And shallow. A squad of Mexicans were wading in it, casting lines, under the watchful eye of the border truck. Families were picnicking on the far shore.

Mike had brought a couple rods, rigged up with a plastic lure called an Electric Chicken, which seems to work well for speckled trout and snook. He cast a few times while I stripped off my shoes, rolled up my pants, and took a few pictures. "Here," he said, handing me the rod. "So you can say you wet a line at the mouth of the Rio Grande."

I waded out calf deep and hucked the Electric Chicken into the rushing current, jigging it back. It bent double. *Whaaaaat? A fish!* I had a fish on my very first cast! I reeled in a nice speckled trout, who had seemed very fond of the Electric Chicken before it stung him in the cheek. Mike and I were giddy as I released the fish—too far to bring it back and we had no ice—and I decided to quit while I was ahead. I put the rod away, took one last long look at the little river that separated so much, and we drove back to eat more tacos.

A perfect end to a perfect trip.

TEPACHE

PREP TIME: 20 MINUTES | FERMENTING TIME: 2 TO 4 DAYS | SERVES 6 TO 8, AND CAN BE SCALED UP

A thrifty, mildly alcoholic, and refreshing drink made from the rind and core of a pineapple. I've had it many times in the Rio Grande Valley, but you can find tepache all over Mexico. Commercial versions are even becoming more common in the rest of the United States. Tepache is super easy to make, although it takes a few days.

- Rind and core of 1 pineapple, cut into large chunks
- ½ gallon water
- ⅓ cup sugar, white or brown
- 1 cinnamon stick (optional)
- 4 whole cloves (optional)
- 8 allspice berries, crushed (optional)
- A pinch of salt

Combine everything in a large glass or food-safe plastic jar. Put a lid on the jar loosely, or cover with several layers of cheesecloth. Let this sit on the counter for a few days. There is natural yeast on the skin of the pineapple, which will ferment the mixture. It will get fizzy. Stir once or twice a day for 3 days.

Strain the mixture and chill it before drinking. It will keep fermenting even after straining, and will likely turn to vinegar within a week. So drink up!

YUCCA PETALS

The petals of the various yucca flowers are all edible, and are eaten from the Gulf to Southern California, but they are most important to the cuisine of the Gulf area, where they are called chochas, flor de palma, or izote. Each species has a different level of bitterness, but you can mitigate it by nipping off the part of each petal where it met the center of the flower. Do not eat the centers, which are much more bitter.

Add chochas to stews—carne guisada is excellent with them, as are the Caldo de Oso (page 194) and the Caldillo de Carne Seca (page 146). Or add them to eggs, like the Machaca con Huevos (page 64). I've also battered and fried them. If you want to try this, use a light tempura batter. You can pickle chochas for long-term storage, but they are really best fresh.

There is one species, *Yucca baccata*, that bears edible fruits. It grows from West Texas to the Pacific, mostly in the US, but also in Chihuahua. The ripe fruits in autumn will still be green but will have some give to them. The seeds are large and hard like a pawpaw, and can't be eaten out of hand, but are edible once they are roasted and ground into a meal. Slow-roasted, the pulp tastes a bit like sweet potatoes and can be used as a pie filling.

BARBACOA

PREP TIME: 20 MINUTES | COOK TIME: 3 HOURS | SERVES 6

This is not Vera's recipe for barbacoa. That would involve building underground pits, lining them with brick, and using whole cows' heads wrapped in foil to slow-roast all night. That process is magical, and is why you need to get yourself to Vera's before you die. It's *that* good.

This barbacoa recipe is closer to the one I've been using with venison for almost two decades. I get you close with a few cheater ingredients that get you that smokiness, and the end result is amazing.

If you're using venison, you'll want to use the neck, shanks, or shoulders. Or if you want to get sporty, use skinned doe's heads. Most barbacoa in the borderlands is beef, however. You can buy tongue, cheeks (cachete) and sometimes even whole heads in Latin markets. You need a gigantic pot for a whole head, so be warned. You really should have cheeks for this, but you can get away with the point end of a brisket, or maybe a chuck roast. I find that the combo of cheeks and a tongue works great.

Cooking slow and low like this dissolves all that connective tissue, leaving the meat super tender. Venison will still be really lean, so I add about ¼ cup of lard to shredded venison before I serve. Beef doesn't need this.

This recipe can be doubled, and once made, barbacoa will keep a week in the fridge and can be frozen.

SIDE NOTE: Ever since I first published the first version of this recipe, people have misread the ingredients. You want 2 *individual* chipotles in adobo, not 2 cans. Got it? Good.

- 3 to 5 pounds venison or beef (see headnote for cuts)
- 2 chipotles in adobo, canned
- 1 onion, quartered
- 1 head garlic, cloves crushed
- 2 bay leaves or 1 avocado leaf
- 1 tablespoon smoked paprika (optional)
- 1 tablespoon ground cumin
- 5 whole cloves
- 1 tablespoon salt, smoked if possible
- ½ cup cider vinegar
- ¼ cup lard or vegetable oil

Put everything in a slow cooker or Dutch oven, cover with water, and cook, covered, until the meat falls off the bone, which will be between 2 hours for many domestic meats and young deer and 6 hours if you have a very old animal. If you use a slow cooker, set it to "high." If you use a regular pot, put it into the oven set to 300°F.

Pull all the meat from the bones. If you are using a tongue, peel the skin off it. Use a knife to cut against the grain of the meats so that the shreds you're about to make will not be longer than about 2 inches. Shred the meat with forks or your fingers. Tongues don't really shred, so chop that. Add salt, ideally smoked salt, to taste, and you have traditional barbacoa.

If you're cooking venison, stir in the lard. You want the lard to coat the shreds of meat. Pour over some of the juices from the pot and put the meat in a pan for the table. Serve as tacos, in a burrito, or on a bun.

TIP: If you want to up your game, smoke the cheeks or head or deer shoulder or whatever for several hours before it goes into the pot. That gets the smokiness you want. You can do that step a day or two in advance. If you do this, you can use regular paprika and salt.

CACTUS SALAD

PREP TIME: 1 HOUR | SERVES 4

No one eats cactus like borderlands people, and you will see it most often in tacos or as ensalada de nopales, cactus salad. Why bother? Aside from the fact that nopales are super nutritious and are apparently a good thing to eat if you have diabetes, they taste good. Imagine a lemony, crunchy green bean.

Many recipes for ensalada de nopales will have you cook your nopales to remove the slime. This is perfectly OK and if that's how you like your cactus salad, go for it. See page 33 for instructions for that. This is a raw salad, which will have a brighter flavor. I learned the method of removing the slime from raw nopales in the awesome cookbook *Nopalito: A Mexican Kitchen*. Dice the paddle as you want to later eat it, then toss with a fair bit of fine salt—fine salt is important because it draws out the slime better—let it sit, and then rinse, rinse, rinse. Hecho.

After that, toss with the standard "Mexican salad" ingredients (see Pico de Gallo, page 46) plus cotija or queso fresco a chile or six, and lots of cilantro. You can add a touch of olive oil if you want, too.

Cacti in the wild are spiny and awful, but you can buy cleaned nopales in markets.

- 4 nopales paddles, de-spined
- Fine salt
- 4 plum tomatoes, seeded and diced
- ½ white onion, chopped
- ¼ cup freshly squeezed lime juice
- 2 serrano or jalapeño chiles, seeded and minced
- ½ teaspoon dried Mexican oregano (regular oregano is fine)
- 1 tablespoon olive oil
- ¼ cup chopped cilantro
- ½ cup crumbled cotija cheese or queso fresco
- 1 avocado, diced (optional)

Dice the nopales and toss with salt. You want all the cut sides of the nopales to have salt on them. Put them in a colander in the sink and let this drain for 1 hour. When the time has elapsed, rinse the nopales under cold water until they are no longer slimy, which should take maybe 3 to 5 minutes. Pat dry with a kitchen towel and put into a large bowl; it's fine if they are damp, you just don't want them dripping wet.

While the nopales are sitting in the colander, mix the onion with a little salt and the lime juice and let them pickle a bit. This takes the harsh edge off the raw onion. If you want, you can add the minced chiles to the lime juice, too.

When you're ready, mix all the ingredients together and serve. Eat this salad straight away. It will get a bit slimy if you leave it for a day or two.

MOJO DE AJO

PREP TIME: 20 MINUTES | COOK TIME: 15 MINUTES | SERVES 4

Mojo de ajo is the quintessential garlic sauce of Latin America, and many countries have their own version. I love the mojo de ajo at Mariscos Lauro Villar in Brownsville, and this recipe is close to that. Its simplicity made it the perfect sauce for my first snook. Snook, if you've never heard of it, is a semitropical fish known as robalo in Spanish, and is arguably one of the top ten eating fish in North America. Imagine a walleye, only better. Firmer, sweeter, and way, way more fun to catch. I caught my first one in Laguna Madre.

The combination of garlic, something tart (vinegar or citrus), butter or some other flavorful oil, and a fresh herb is, to my mind, the single best way to cook fish or seafood in a way that you can appreciate its natural flavor. I'm not alone in this idea, since you can see this combination repeated all over the world—If you've ever used lemon pepper or garlic salt on fish, it's the same basic idea.

Obviously, you don't need snook to enjoy mojo de ajo. I've had it on a wide variety of fish and seafood; it's especially good on shrimp.

Technically speaking, because butter burns easily, you will want to do one of two things when you're making dinner: Either cook the fish (or whatever) in oil or better yet, clarified butter (ghee), and add whole butter after the fish is cooked; or be very careful to not let your butter blacken as you are cooking your protein.

This is really a pan sauce, and doesn't keep very well, so make it, enjoy it, then make it again.

Fish

1 to 2 pounds skinless fish fillets

Salt and pepper

1 cup flour, for dusting

Clarified butter or oil, for frying

Mojo de Ajo

½ cup butter

6 to 8 cloves garlic, thinly sliced

Crushed, dried, hot chiles, (I use chiltepins)

3 tablespoons minced parsley

2 limes, zested and juiced

Salt and black pepper

Salt and pepper your fish fillets. Let the salt do its thing for 10 minutes or so while you chop parsley and slice garlic, etc. Add enough clarified butter or cooking oil of your choice to a pan and start heating it on medium. Set a cooling rack over a baking sheet in your oven and turn the oven to "warm."

Once the fillets are a little damp from the salt extracting moisture, dust them in flour, pressing it in well. Jack the heat up to high to get the clarified butter or oil between 325°F and 350°F, When the clarified butter is hot, fry the fish until it's golden brown on both sides, about 2 to 4 minutes per side depending on the heat of your fat and the thickness of your fish.

Move the finished fillets to the cooling rack in the oven while you finish the rest.

When the fillets are all done, pour off the clarified butter and wipe the pan out. Add the whole butter and melt it over medium heat. Add the sliced garlic and chiles to taste and cook until the garlic is tan but not brown.

This is the only tricky part: Turn the heat to low and start swirling the pan so the hot butter begins to swirl. Pour in the lime juice little by little until it emulsifies with the butter and garlic. Once it does, add the parsley, lime zest, and a little salt. You can add black pepper, too, if you want.

Return the fillets to the pan and bathe them in the sauce for a moment or two. Move them to plates and divvy up the remaining sauce on each piece of fish. Serve with bread, rice, or potatoes.

Tips and Variations

- You can mix and match the citrus. Use Seville orange juice, or lemons, or yuzu, or whatever. Or use vinegar.
- Ditto for the herb. Parsley, cilantro, culantro for a Cuban touch, pipicha, summer savory, lovage, celery leaves, you name it.
- If you're not a butter fan, use a quality oil of your choice in the mojo, like a good olive oil or an unrefined nut oil.

STUFFED CRABS

PREP TIME: 20 MINUTES | COOK TIME: 45 MINUTES | SERVES 6

The signature dish of Tamaulipas, I've eaten it many times across the border in Brownsville and the Rio Grande Valley. It's essentially a Mexican deviled crab recipe, where you make a tasty stuffing of crabmeat, breadcrumbs, and such, stuff it into a crab shell—always a blue crab—and bake it. It's an addictive appetizer, and I've eaten four at one sitting.

My recipe is an amalgam of those I've eaten and read about, but a special hat tip goes to Cuitláhuac "Don Piquino" Córdova's excellent book, *Sabor a Tamaulipas*.

- 2 tablespoons olive oil
- 1 white onion, minced
- 1 to 3 serrano chiles, seeded and minced
- 3 cloves garlic, minced
- 4 Roma tomatoes, seeded and diced
- 2 tablespoons minced fresh parsley
- ¼ cup minced green olives
- 2 tablespoons small capers
- 1 pound crabmeat
- Juice of 2 limes or 4 Key limes
- 3 eggs, lightly beaten, divided
- ½ cup fine breadcrumbs
- ⅓ cup shredded cheese, such as mozzarella or Jack
- 6 tablespoons butter, divided
- Lime wedges and more parsley, for serving

Heat the olive oil in a large pan over medium high heat and sauté the onion and chiles until they're soft, but not browned. Add the garlic and cook another minute, then stir in the tomatoes, parsley, olives, capers, and crabmeat. Let this cook a few minutes, then turn off the heat. Mix in the lime juice and 1 beaten egg.

Stuff cleaned crab shells (the top shell) with the mixture tightly. Spoon or paint on some of the beaten egg, then sprinkle on the breadcrumbs and some cheese. Top each shell with about a tablespoon of butter. If you don't have crab shells, use ramekins.

Bake at 350°F until the tops brown nicely, about 20 minutes. Serve with some more lime and parsley.

"If brains were lard, he couldn't grease a pan."

Old Texas saying

SHRIMP EMPANADAS

PREP TIME: 1 HOUR | COOK TIME: 20 MINUTES | SERVES 8

The Gulf of Mexico is home to some of the best shrimp in the world, and while I've eaten shrimp empanadas in the Brownsville area, I found inspiration for this rendition of "shrimpenadas" in an obscure recipe from neighboring Tamaulipas. What sets this recipe apart is the dough: It's made from plantains, those starchy banana cousins called platano macho in Spanish. You see plantains used in lots of ways in the Gulf and even more so in the Caribbean. Here they are used, along with masa harina, as an exceptionally tasty crust.

The filling for these shrimp empanadas is very Gulf-Caribbean, too. You see heavy Spanish influence here, and in this recipe that means olives and a classic sofrito of onions, garlic, tomato, olive oil, and chile.

I won't lie: The plantain dough is tricky. Use green plantains that are starting to turn yellow—don't use plantains that are black because they have too much sugar in them. And that's a problem. You cook the plantains until they're soft, then mash them with masa harina to make a dough. It's a lot like making gnocchi dough with mashed potatoes and flour. When choosing a masa harina, go with yellow or white corn.

Plantain empanada dough browns fast because of its sugar. So everything in the filling needs to be cooked because when you fry these shrimp empanadas, they cook up in a flash.

You'll see my exact filling below, but there is no reason you can't use the plantain dough with other fillings, sweet or savory. The only caveat is that the filling needs to be minced fine because the dough is *very* soft, and so hard things can pierce it. The opposite is also true: You can use my regular empanada dough on page 195, which is far more forgiving.

Once made, shrimpenadas will keep a few days in the fridge. I eat them cold, but you can wrap them in foil and reheat in a 350°F oven for 20 minutes or so. You can also refry them for a minute or two. They do not freeze well.

SHRIMP EMPANADAS, continued

Dough

2 large yellow plantains

Salt

¾ cup masa harina

Oil for frying

Filling

2 tablespoons olive oil

½ white onion, minced

1 to 3 serranos or other hot green chile, minced

3 cloves garlic, minced

2 Roma tomatoes, seeded and minced

1 pound shrimp, peeled, deveined, and chopped

½ to 1 cup green or black olives, minced

¼ cup minced cilantro

Salt and black pepper

To form the dough, cut the plantains into 3- or 4-inch pieces, without peeling. Boil the plantains in salty water for about 20 minutes, then peel them. Mash with a potato ricer or a food mill or just really hammer on them—you want no lumps. Mix with the masa harina until you can knead the dough without it being too sticky. You might need more or less than ¾ cup, so start with ½ cup and go from there. Put the dough in a plastic bag for at least 20 minutes to hydrate.

Heat the olive oil in a pan over medium-high heat, then sauté the onions and serranos until soft. Add the garlic and the tomatoes, and cook another minute or two, then add the olives and the shrimp, and cook, stirring often, until the shrimp are cooked. Add the cilantro, taste for salt and pepper, and let this cool completely while the dough is hydrating.

Divide the dough into golf ball–sized balls. You will get anywhere from 8 to 12 depending on the exact size you made them and the size of the plantains. Keep the balls in the plastic bag as you work with them so they stay moist.

Get several cups of vegetable oil hot in a large, wide pan. You want it to reach about 325°F. Set a baking sheet in your oven and put a cooling rack on top of it. Set your oven to 200°F.

Using your tortilla press (lined with two sheets cut from a plastic bag), press out a "tortilla" about ⅛ inch thick—thicker than an actual tortilla, but still pretty thin. Remove the top plastic sheet and spoon about a tablespoon or two of the filling on one half of the dough circle. If you don't have a tortilla press, roll the balls of dough out between two sheets of wax paper or plastic wrap until you have rounds about ⅛ inch thick.

Fold over the other half and gently press it to seal. Carefully lift the empanada off the plastic—it's fragile right now—and use the tines of a fork to crimp the edges. Make a couple of these, then start frying in batches of 2 or 3, making more as you fry.

Fry the empanadas for a couple minutes per side. They will brown in a hurry, so keep an eye on them. I find 2 minutes per side works. Put the finished empanadas on the rack in the oven while you do the rest. *Note that it is very important to let the oil temperature return to 325°F in between batches.*

Keys to Success

- Make sure the oil is hot, but not too hot or the dough can burn. 325°F is the sweet spot.
- If you have leftover filling, it's good on tortillas or in a burrito, or with rice.
- Crab, crawfish tails, or chopped lobster are all good alternatives.
- Black or green olives are equally good.
- If you hate spicy food, use an Anaheim, poblano, or green pepper instead of the serranos.

TEXAS EBONY

Called mahuacata in Spanish, the beans of the Texas ebony tree, *Ebenopsis ebano*, are eaten in both South Texas and throughout Tamaulipas. Both the young and dry beans are tasty. Dried beans are very hard, but once you pop them like giant popcorn—you'll need a lid on your pot!—they are fun to eat after tossing with a little salt and chile. You can also grind the whole beans into a coffee-like beverage; it doesn't have caffeine, alas.

I prefer the young beans. Treat them exactly like fava beans: Boil the whole green pod for 10 to 20 minutes to loosen it. Remove the beans inside, which will have another seed coat like a fava bean. You use your fingernail or a small knife to nick the leathery seed coat and pop out the sweet, tasty bean inside.

They make a masterful vegetarian taco. Once processed, brown some onions, add the beans and garlic, plus some roasted, seeded, and chopped green chiles and serve with the Salsa Verde (page 70), some queso fresco, and a hit of chopped cilantro. If this sounds good to you but you're far from the Rio Grande Valley, use fresh garbanzo or fava beans.

MOLLEJAS

PREP TIME: 15 MINUTES | COOK TIME: 2½ HOURS | SERVES 6

Mollejas are sweetbreads, and they are astoundingly good in tacos. I've eaten them all over South Texas, the Rio Grande Valley, and Nuevo Leon. The best I've ever eaten were at Avila's in Hebbronville, Texas.

There's a trick to making them irresistible: You really do need a charcoal or wood-burning grill and/or a smoker. This style of sweetbreads aren't great unless you have that live fire action. A typical mollejas taco is minimalist: the chopped sweetbreads, usually but not always a flour tortilla (I've seen corn), pico de gallo, and another, hotter salsa. The mollejas are so delicious and so rich that they need something spicy and acidic to balance them.

Any butcher shop should have sweetbreads, usually frozen, and some larger supermarkets carry them as well.

Dry Rub

2 tablespoons salt

1 tablespoon black pepper

1 tablespoon garlic powder

1 tablespoon onion powder

2 teaspoons dried Mexican oregano, crushed fine

1 to 2 teaspoons cayenne

2 pounds cleaned sweetbreads

Beef tallow, lard, bacon fat, or butter (optional)

To make the dry rub, combine the salt, pepper, garlic powder, onion powder, oregano, and cayenne to taste in a small jar and shake well to mix. (You probably won't need all the rub.)

The sweetbreads will be a big blobby thing. Cut this into workable sections that can go on grill grates. If they are thick, butterfly them. Season the sweetbreads well with the dry rub. Let this sit while you fire up the grill.

Ideally you are burning mesquite or mesquite charcoal. Get the grill to about 275°F or 300°F. Set the sweetbreads in the grill over indirect heat and close the grill. Give them maybe 10 to 15 minutes, then flip. Keep doing this until the sweetbreads take on a nice color, maybe 40 minutes total.

You'll want to wrap them now. You can put them in a pan and cover it, or make a foil pouch. If the sweetbreads are not glistening with their own fat, add some. Put them back on the grill and let them cook enclosed like this for 1 hour, or until they are soft and can pull apart. They should not be rubbery.

Finally, put the sweetbreads directly over the coals and char a little. You want a bit of blackening, but not a ton. Set the mollejas on a cutting board, chop and serve in tacos.

CARNE GUISADA

PREP TIME: 30 MINUTES | COOK TIME: 2 HOURS | SERVES 6 TO 8

Carne guisada means meat stew in Spanish, and it comes in as many forms as there are cooks. I've eaten it all over Texas, and in much of Mexico. If you're in the Brownsville area, look for it on menus all over Southmost Road.

My rendition has its origins in caldillo durangueño, the signature dish of the state of Durango in Mexico. It's normally made with chiles pasados (page 181), tomatillos or tomatoes, broth, onions, garlic, and either fresh or dried red meat—beef rump or carne seca that has been rehydrated. Typically caldillo durangueño is a brothy stew, but if you let it cook down it becomes a thicker guisado.

Keep in mind that there is no absolute need to go through the labor of roasting, peeling, seeding, and then drying your poblano or Hatch (Anaheim) chiles to make this recipe. You can of course skip the drying step. But there is a noticeable difference between rehydrated chiles and fresh, and I like to mix the two here. As for your tortilla choices, up to you.

Use a piece of meat that has a definite grain to it. I like the hind leg roasts on a deer, or beef chuck. Slice big chunks across that grain, then keep whittling the pieces down into taco-sized chunks, again against the grain. Doing this speeds up your cooking time and will result in meat you can bite easily without it pulling out of your tortillas.

Once made, the stew will keep in the fridge a week, and it can be both frozen and pressure-canned. I do like this canned, so I can have wonderful tacos on a moment's notice. Pressure-can quarts at a pressure appropriate for your altitude for 90 minutes.

- 3 tablespoons lard or vegetable oil
- 2 pounds venison or beef roast, sliced and cut into small pieces (see above)
- 1 teaspoon ground cumin
- Salt
- 2 large white or yellow onions, quartered
- 4 cloves garlic
- ½ pound tomatillos, husked and halved
- 1 teaspoon dried sage
- 1 quart venison or beef broth
- 8 to 12 poblano, Hatch, chiles pasados, or Anaheim chiles, roasted, peeled, seeded and cut into pieces
- ½ cup chopped fresh cilantro

Heat the lard in a Dutch oven or other large, lidded pot over high heat. When it is barely smoking, add the venison and stir well. Sear the venison well. If it gives off a lot of water, keep searing it until the water boils away. While this is happening, mix in the salt and cumin.

Meanwhile, char the onion, garlic, and tomatillos either under a broiler or on a comal or cast iron frying pan. You want some blackening. Coarsely chop the onion and put it, the tomatillos, and the garlic (peel it first), into a blender with the sage. Purée this, adding broth as needed to get the blender to spin properly.

Add the contents of the blender to the pot and stir well. Pour broth into the blender to get all the good bits left there and pour that in the pot. If by chance you happen to have used chiles pasados and rehydrated them, pour some of the rehydrating water into the pot, too. At the start, everything should be rather thin. Bring this to a simmer and let it cook, stirring occasionally, for 1 hour.

After 1 hour, add the green chiles and continue to simmer until the meat is tender. You can eat this as a stew, or continue to cook it down until thickened, in which case you can eat it as a guisado on tortillas or with rice.

PUCHERO

PREP TIME: 30 MINUTES | COOK TIME: 4 HOURS | SERVES 12

Originally from Spain, puchero is a big, hearty stew made in various versions all over the Spanish-speaking world. I find it far more common along the eastern side of the border than in the West. The word puchero means stew pot, and that's what this is. Endless variations exist. Nothing absolute defines puchero. Most, but not all, versions have garbanzo beans. Most, but not all, do not use other types of dried beans. Most, but not all, use green beans.

Traditionally, you would get a bowl or cup of the broth, and the vegetables and meat in another bowl alongside, very much like French *pot au feu* or Italian *bollito misto*. I'm not a fan of that presentation, but you can serve your puchero that way if you'd like.

Meat can be really anything. I used shanks from a nilgai I hunted in Brownsville. Shanks, shoulder, or neck are what you want here; cheap cuts with lots of connective tissue. Oxtail is another great choice, as are beef shins or lamb shanks. A marrow bone or two is a great addition.

You'll note that the corn is still on the cob. I was skeptical of this at first, and did it only because really all the recipes do. My inner voice said, "Sigh, this is going to make this hard to eat." I was wrong. The cobs add a touch of sweet to the stew, and when you pick up the pieces at the end and gnaw on them, it's like a little dessert. I'm convinced.

Other vegetable options for puchero include sweet potatoes, green chiles, cabbage, rutabaga, onion, garlic, jicama, and occasionally other sorts of beans.

Puchero is almost always garnished with cilantro or mint, plus lime juice.

Once made, the stew will keep for a few days in the fridge. Reheat it gently, however, or the vegetables will turn to mush.

4 pounds beef or venison shank, shoulder, or neck meat

Salt

Seasonings

1 teaspoon oregano, Mexican if possible

1 teaspoon ground cumin

1 teaspoon ground coriander

1 teaspoon ground black pepper

Vegetables

6 cloves garlic, whole and peeled

1 white or yellow onion, sliced

1½ pounds potatoes, cut into chunks

1 pound winter squash, cut into chunks

2 chayotes, cut into chunks (optional)

4 Anaheim or poblano chiles, roasted, seeded, and cut into chunks

3 ears of corn, cut into 1- or 2-inch rounds

½ pound green beans, cut into bite-sized pieces

1 pound cooked garbanzo beans, canned or pre-cooked

½ cup chopped cilantro

Lime wedges to serve

Salt the meat well before you chop all the vegetables. When those are done, put the meat in a large pot and add about 1 gallon of water, more or less. Bring this to a boil and skim off the froth that floats to the surface. Drop the heat to a simmer and add the onions, garlic, oregano, cumin, coriander, and pepper. Simmer, partially covered, for 3 hours.

The meats should be tender by now; check after 2 hours. Remove the meats and strip off the meat, chopping it into bite-sized pieces. Discard any bones. If there is marrow in the bones, scoop it out and add it to the stew; you can break it up if you want. Add in the potatoes, winter squash, and chayotes. Let these simmer 20 minutes.

Add the green chiles, corn, garbanzo beans, and green beans and cook another 10 minutes. Add the cilantro and serve with lime wedges. A drizzle of really good olive oil is a nice touch, too.

Keys to Success

- Note that you can use really any cheap cut that likes long, slow cooking. Stewing hens, wild turkeys, pork hocks and shoulder, old pheasants, shanks of really any animal, oxtail, mutton, you name it.
- Don't like cilantro? Another very common garnish is mint. Parsley is common, too.
- Some versions of this stew add sausages, ranging from blood sausage to chorizo to butifarra. If you use sausages, add them in the last 20 minutes, then fish them out and slice into serving pieces before returning them to the pot.

SALPICÓN

PREP TIME: 20 MINUTES | COOK TIME: 3 HOURS | SERVES 6

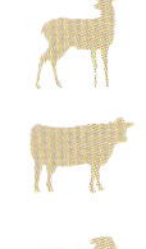

Salpicón de venado, a shredded venison salad with lots of fresh vegetables, is a specialty of Tamaulipas. It's easy to make, works with other meats, and is a cooling and perfect dish for hot weather. Pronounced something like "sahl-pee-CONE," salpicón basically means hodgepodge or a random mix of things. There are a number of dishes called salpicón in Latin America, including a salsa in Yucatan.

The most common version is salpicón de res, with beef, but you can see this done with shredded chicken as well as fish and seafood. I used the brisket from a nilgai I hunted in the RGV because that cut has a very defined grain to it, and it's lean—unlike beef brisket. That said, if you get a beef brisket trimmed of most of the fat, you're good to go. Other excellent cuts would be the eye of round from the hind leg, skirt or flank steak.

You don't brown the venison or beef. It just goes into a pot with some aromatics—onion, garlic, bay leaves, etc.—and simmers until it wants to fall apart. Remove the meat, let it cool a bit, then shred it finely. This can be done up to a day or two in advance.

Once you have your meat ready, chop vegetables, add lime juice and olive oil, and it's ready. What vegetables? In the traditional Tamaulipas salpicón it's romaine lettuce, serrano chiles, minced white onions, cilantro, and diced radishes. Always lime juice and sometimes olive oil. Avocado is a good addition, as are ripe tomatoes. I like to add a hit of Mexican oregano, too. I've seen mint instead of cilantro, habaneros instead of serranos, and cabbage instead of romaine lettuce.

Salpicón doesn't age well, so I like to shred tons of meat beforehand, then make batches of salad as I go. The meat will keep a week.

Meat

- 2 pounds venison or beef (see headnote)
- Salt
- 4 bay leaves
- 2 cloves garlic, smashed
- 1 tablespoon allspice berries, cracked
- ½ onion, sliced

Salad

- 6 romaine lettuce leaves, chopped
- 3 radishes, diced
- 1 to 4 serrano chiles, diced
- ½ cup chopped cilantro
- 1 teaspoon Mexican oregano (optional)
- 1 cucumber, peeled and diced
- 4 limes, juiced
- ¼ cup olive oil

Put all the meat ingredients in a large pot and cover with water by about 2 inches. Bring to a simmer. Add salt to taste. Simmer, covered, until the meat can be easily shredded, about 2 to 4 hours.

Pull the meat out of the pot and let it cool a bit. Shred finely with two forks or your fingers. This can be done up to 3 days before you make the salad.

To make the salad, toss all the vegetables with the shredded meat, and then dress with salt, olive oil and lime juice. Serve cool.

RED CHILE RABBIT

PREP TIME: 30 MINUTES | COOK TIME: 2 TO 3 HOURS | SERVES 4

This is one of the few recipes in this book that I've not had in its native state. I first learned about conejo en adobo in the rare-but-cool book *Cocina Familiar en el Estado de Tamaulipas*, and I've made it many times, notably at a hunting camp along the Mexican border in Arivaca, Arizona. I've tinkered with it over the years, based on experience and from an amalgam of recipes I've read in other Spanish-language cookbooks.

Basically, you make rabbit broth to cook the animal, then use some of that broth for the adobo. The adobo is a lot like a simplified mole sauce, with chiles, onion, garlic, and tomato, plus a little Mexican chocolate and some spices. It reminds me of a simpler mole coloradito or chirmol sauce, both of which are from southern Mexico. The adobo is useful on way more than just rabbit, so keep some in a jar in the fridge, where it will keep about 10 days or so; it can be frozen.

A couple things will take this to the next level: real Mexican oregano and real Mexican chocolate. Abuelita brand chocolate will work, but there are all sorts of better Mexican chocolates out there that are less sweet and processed. If you can't find the exact dried chiles I call for here, mix and match among the following: guajillo, pasilla, New Mexican, California, and cascabel. Note that the rabbit here is a farmed one. If you are using wild rabbits, you'll need two cottontails or a jackrabbit. They'll need more cooking time, too.

- 1 rabbit, cut into serving pieces
- 2 white onions, quartered
- 1 head garlic, cloves separated, unpeeled
- 1 sprig epazote (optional)
- 2 hoja santa or avocado leaves (optional)
- 2 tablespoons dried Mexican oregano, divided
- Salt
- 4 ancho chiles, stemmed and seeded
- 4 guajillo chiles, stemmed and seeded
- 2 plum tomatoes, sliced in half
- ½ teaspoon ground allspice
- 1 tablet Mexican chocolate, finely grated
- 2 tablespoons lard or vegetable oil
- 2 tablespoons chopped cilantro or green onions, for garnish

Pour 2 quarts of water into a large pot and bring it to a boil. Salt the water well, add the rabbit and return to a boil. Skim off any foam that forms, then drop the heat to a simmer. Add one of the quartered onions, the epazote, hoja santa, and half the oregano. Peel half the garlic cloves and smash them with the flat of a knife. Add them to the pot and let this simmer.

Get a comal or cast iron frying pan or similar pan warm. Toast the dried chiles over medium-low heat until they begin to blister a little, turning often. Don't let them burn. Move them to a blender with the allspice and grated chocolate.

When you are done toasting the chiles, put the other quartered onion on the comal or flattop to char, along with the remaining unpeeled garlic cloves and the tomatoes, cut side down. When you get some good blackening, peel the garlic and move all the vegetables to the blender, coarsely chopping them if need be. Add some of the broth you're cooking the rabbit in to the blender and purée. You want it to be the constancy of cream. I strain the purée through a fine-meshed strainer to remove any stray bits of chile skin and seeds, which are undigestible, but this is optional.

To finish the sauce, heat the lard in a pot over medium-high heat and pour in the purée. Stir vigorously to incorporate the fat and bring to a gentle simmer. Let this cook slowly while the rabbit cooks, about 15 to 20 minutes. Then turn the heat off until the rabbit is tender.

When you are ready to go, drop the rabbit pieces into the sauce, then move them to a plate. Garnish with the rest of the oregano and maybe some cilantro or chopped green onions.

NOTE: You will have sauce left over, which will keep a week or more in the fridge and is great with pretty much any meat, as well as oily fish or beans.

CUCUMBER AGUA FRESCA

PREP TIME: 10 MINUTES | SERVES 4

This is a simple, refreshing summertime drink common all over the borderlands. You can vary the amounts of salt, sugar, and lime juice to suit your tastes. You can also use honey instead of sugar. Agave syrup is a good choice, too.

Taste the peel of the cucumber: If it's not bitter, leave it, because you'll get a prettier color with the peel. Remove if it's bitter, though. I recommend those hothouse English cucumbers.

2 cucumbers, coarsely chopped

Pinch of salt

½ cup sugar

Juice of 3 limes

Put the cucumbers, salt, sugar, and lime juice in the blender. Cover with 6 cups of water.

Blend until totally smooth. Set a fine-meshed strainer over a bowl and push the liquid through it. Taste the liquid and add more salt, sugar, or lime juice to taste. Serve over ice.

Variations

- You can add an herb like mint, cilantro, lemon verbena, hoja santa, or some other sweet herb.
- Agave syrup is a good alternative sweetener.
- Adding grated lime zest adds a lot of flavor.
- You can make this an adult beverage by adding a shot of silver tequila, mezcal, bacanora, or sotol when serving.

"Salió más caro el caldo que las albóndigas."

"The broth is more expensive than the meatballs," meaning the solution is costlier than the problem

SOUTH & WEST TEXAS

If you've ever driven to El Paso, you can feel the weird. Hours and hours from the next nearest city of any size, the twin cities of El Paso and Ciudad Juarez really do look like the spaceport Mos Eisley on Tatooine in Star Wars. The sprawl emerges from the desert like an alien moon base, ten thousand lights twinkling in the dusty gloom. With only a few lights visible at first, you crest a rise on Interstate 10 and boom, the desert night dissolves and there it is: two adjoining cities, home to nearly 3 million humans.

Interstate 10 is the electric spine of El Paso, the main thoroughfare for a city that sprawls 30-plus miles east to west, its tidy, walled exurbs looking exactly like their cousins in Scottsdale and Glendale, Arizona: the Phoenix-ification of El Paso.

The air can take on that crystalline character only a desert wears without being gauche. But when the winds roar out of the northwest, they kick up dust storms so thick that everyone's cellphone blinks a warning to stay inside.

Few do. Because life goes on in El Chuco, er, Mos Eisley, er, El Paso, and ya gotta drive to wherever it is you're going. Traffic and the Janus-like double nature of the people of these cities leave strong impressions. Oh, and the burritos.

It is said that Juarez invented the burrito. And those bundles of goodness, held closely in a flour tortilla hug, are truly the best thing you can eat there. Far smaller and lighter than their California mission-style cousins—think of those Chipotle burritos as big as your head—a Juarez/El Paso style burrito feels only slightly heavier than a single taco.

Flour tortillas are thicker and doughier than the delicate and translucent Sonora-style flour tortillas. Corn tortillas, as a rule, are cheap, mass-produced things here, although there are a few exceptions, such as Taconeta.

Much as in the Rio Grande Valley, look to humbler, hole-in-the-wall places for more satisfying food than restaurants that strike a pose. Queen of them all is Lucy's Coffee Shop, the original of the Lucy's mini empire in El Paso. You can't get any more old school than Lucy's. The vibe is exactly like the White Diamond and the other chrome-walled diners I grew up with in Westfield, New Jersey—only Lucy's serves borderlands food.

Prickly pear cactus growing in Big Bend National Park.

Their signature is a machaca burrito with queso con chile: a poofy flour tortilla, a smear of refried pintos, tender machaca, and a healthy pour of the green chile-studded queso, which was probably Velveeta. I wanted to hate it but didn't, and it weirdly paired well with black coffee.

More notable were the conversations at Lucy's, which were emblematic of speech everywhere along the border: Everyone, and I mean everyone, even old, fat, pale, white dudes wearing pressed chinos and a severe blond-gray buzz cut, shifted effortlessly between English and Spanish—often in midsentence.

JRZ
ELP

Lucy's Café in El Paso is a national treasure.

This being Texas, the steaks are top notch. Places like the West Texas Chophouse can rival the menus of the best steakhouses in Sonora. At most of them, you'll find a borderlands greatest hits: All kinds of mesquite-grilled steaks; chicharron de ribeye (deep-fried chunks of ribeye served with tortillas and guacamole), a Mexican cousin to South Dakota chislic; queso fundido; and at the West Texas Chophouse, a real rarity, crab-stuffed chiles güeros called Toritos (page 278).

And everywhere cream of poblano soup, popular from Tijuana to Matamoros. Done right it is smooth, with a perfect mellow heat, smoky, and richly creamy.

Like many border towns, El Paso is both not quite Mexican, and not quite what you'd expect in the USA: all the sameness of Everywhere, USA, side by side with places like Lucy's and the Flores Meat Market, where I ate the signature dish of Juarez, colitas de pavo.

These are turkey tails, braised tender, chopped, seared and served either in a stew, in a burrito, or in tacos or tortas, which are to Mexico what a banh mi is to Vietnam. The story of colitas de pavo is emblematic of the border's cultural duality.

◀ The mural scene in El Paso is second to none.

Forty years ago, the US turkey industry needed a home for the tails; few people in the states eat them. So some enterprising cook from Juarez decided to buy a bunch, then performed that Mexican magic of turning trash into gold. Now they are the dish to eat if you want to get a unique flavor in Juarez or El Paso. Crispy, fatty, meaty. Chopped in a burrito, there is absolutely nothing off-putting about them. And I'll be honest: I was nervous at first, but they're so amazing I ate three on that first trip. And they would never be a thing without the synergistic relationship between the US and Mexico, which as of this writing is the United States' top trading partner.

—

If Brownsville marks the beginning of the border journey from east to west, El Paso marks the end of that beginning. At its shortest, the journey is 830 highway miles. But a true reckoning of the Texas border will only take you on Interstate 10 here and there. The good stuff is all off the highway.

Laredo is the only substantial city between Brownsville and El Paso, if you're hugging the border. San Antonio, at least to me, counts as South Texas, but it's sort of its gateway, not its heart. Laredo is a busy, gritty working town at the terminus of Interstate 35 (which you can drive 1500 miles north to Duluth if you care to). It is the only place where a breakfast taco is called, oddly, a mariachi.

Your next stop on the way to El Paso would be the twin towns of Piedras Negras and Eagle Pass. Piedras Negras is the purported birthplace of the nacho. As the story goes, some ladies who lunch crossed the border in 1943, but the restaurant they went to wasn't ready for service. The chef, Nacho Anaya, whipped up some totopos (tortilla chips), and topped them with whatever he had around. The ladies loved it, and history was made.

Drive a few miles further down US 277 and you'll come to Del Rio, which is home to Julio's tortilla chip factory, and, at least to me, is the Promised Land of the Taquito, that rolled, fried,

HOW TO MAKE A JUAREZ BURRITO

An El Paso or Juarez burrito is an exercise in restraint. Widely believed to be the birthplace of burritos, these rolled-up packets of awesome are simple, and open to your own sense of adventure. Often just refried beans, meat, and some cheese, they are sold folded over, not tucked in like a California—or a Chipotle—burrito. The reason is because it's expected that you will add to that minimalist base things that please you: pico de gallo, queso con chile, other salsas, shredded lettuce or cabbage, maybe pickled jalapeños. Then you tuck the ends yourself and carry on your merry way; everyone there knows how to fold a burrito. Even still, these burritos are smaller and slimmer than what you may be used to. It's not crazy to eat two.

chicken-stuffed corn tortilla cigar of goodness. Taquitos is a general Texas term, but around Del Rio you'll hear them called tapatios. A flauta is another word for them, although to some the difference between a taquito and a flauta is you use two tortillas for a flauta, making them longer and more, well, flute-like. In the West, a flauta is a rolled flour tortilla. I've also seen them called tacos dorados, but in most places that's a taco folded over and fried, not rolled. Go all the way to San Diego and you'll see taquitos called rolled tacos. All the same thing, all great.

From Del Rio, you shift to US 90, which takes you over the Big Bend National Park. Big Bend is one of the most beautiful places in Texas, and arguably the United States. The Rio Grande has cut towering gorges through the landscape, and the remoteness of Big Bend takes you back in time. The nights are dark and cool, the wind constant, and the people thin on the ground.

Nestled inside Big Bend is Terlingua, the alleged birthplace of Texas chili. Some will tell you that a Terlingua bowl of red is the godfather of all chilis to come after it, but *A Bowl of Red* is really just the title of a 1953 cookbook, and the Terlingua chili cook-off was organized to promote that book. Texas chili originated long before there was a Texas. It is itself a child of older dishes, like Caldillo de Carne Seca (page 146) or Guisado de Abigeo (page 186) or even Chile Colorado or Asado de Puerco (page 152). Big, powerful bowls of red chile-soaked meat, onions, garlic . . . and no beans.

In Texas, you eat charro beans *alongside* chili. The rest of the country simply dumped those charro beans into their bowl of red—unthinkable to any proper Texan. Charro beans really are essentially chili beans.

Along US 90, the three towns of Marathon, Alpine, and Marfa hold your attention. All sport excellent barbecue, excellent brisket tacos, fajitas, and top-notch Texas-style beef enchiladas. Marfa has become famous as an artist colony, and its Cactus Liquors boasts one of the best and biggest selections of agave spirits in the country.

From there, you can dip down US 67 to another set of twin towns, Presidio and Ojinaga, or continue on over the lonely final 200 miles through the Chihuahuan Desert until you see those lights of El Paso. And when you do, do yourself a favor and put on the Marty Robbins song "El Paso." I do, every time I see those lights in my windshield.

CHUCHOS FOR CHUCOS

There is a drink in Juarez, and to a lesser extent El Paso, that is unique to the world: chuchos, an infusion of a medicinal root in sotol that creates a slightly anise-like, golden drink. Chuchupastle is the local name for the root, which is known commonly as oshá in the United States, *Ligusticum porteri* in Latin. It's a native lovage. I first drank it in the city of Chihuahua, and Beto Petrosky, the owner of El Magico Bar there, explained how to make the drink.

Take the roots, which are gnarly and covered in a dark skin, and whittle off that skin, which is bitter. Chop the roots and infuse them into sotol or a silver tequila, and let it steep for a week or more. Strain and drink.

The drink was said to be invented at the bar Arbolito in Juarez in the 1940s, interestingly at the same time that Chucos became a thing. Chucos is a shortening of pachucos, which was the name for 1940s zoot suit–wearing young Mexican and Mexican American hipsters. They are credited with starting the Chicano low rider scene, which is still strong in El Paso today—so strong that the city is widely known as El Chuco.

LAREDO "Q" TACOS

PREP TIME: 20 MINUTES | COOK TIME: 20 MINUTES | SERVES 4

This is the legendary breakfast taco I mentioned in the Gulf chapter. I include it here because I actually first ate one at a Stripes in Laredo, where the company was founded. There isn't anything magical about this taco, only that it's really good and hits the spot early in the morning. You can wrap these up in foil and take them in the field or on the road with you—they keep for a few hours that way.

To make one, you do need a few things ready, notably refried beans. My refried beans recipe (page 35) is excellent, but any refried beans will do. You also need diced, parboiled potatoes. You can fully cook diced potatoes on the flattop, but it takes longer. I recommend cooking up a batch the day before so you can finish them at breakfast.

In Texas, melty cheese is yellow, and usually mild Cheddar or Colby Jack. But you can use whatever you want. For a salsa, the Fire-Roasted Salsa (page 38) is a great option. For store-bought hot sauces, Huichol is an excellent choice.

- 8 to 10 slices of bacon
- ½ pound potatoes
- 2 to 4 teaspoons chili powder
- 5 eggs, lightly beaten
- 1½ cups refried beans
- ½ pound shredded melty cheese
- 4 flour tortillas
- Salsa of your choice

If you are unsure about the potato prep, cut the potatoes into pieces the size of your thumbnail. You can leave the skin on if you want. I prefer to use russet potatoes, but waxy potatoes like Yukon gold are fine, too. Put them in a pot with water and a healthy pinch of salt. Boil until tender, about 5 minutes. Set them on a tray to steam off and lose more moisture before frying.

Fry the bacon until crispy. Eat a piece. Set the rest aside. Brown the potatoes in the bacon fat, which will take maybe 5 to 8 minutes. Sprinkle some chili powder over them as they cook. Turn the heat to medium and add the beaten eggs. Stir to combine.

Meanwhile, heat the refried beans and flour tortillas and keep them warm.

When the eggs have set, spread some refried beans on the tortillas, then divide the egg-potato mixture among them. Top with the shredded cheese, a slice (or 2) of bacon, and a splash of salsa. Wrap them up in foil to melt the cheese and have at it!

COLITAS DE PAVO

PREP TIME: 20 MINUTES | COOK TIME: 2 HOURS | SERVES 10 TO 12

If there's a more Juarez dish, I can't think of one. Turkey tails, slow-cooked in lard, deboned, and then crisped up and chopped for tortas, tacos, or burritos is a quintessential example of making something out of nothing. They are the platonic ideal of turkey: meaty, fatty, crispy skin.

Turkey tails can be tough to find when you're outside of the New Mexico–West Texas area, although they are becoming more common in large supermarkets, especially ones catering to a diverse customer base. They'll usually be in the freezer section.

You will often see these colored a lurid red after they've been braised. This is almost always done with red food coloring, but I suspect that someone decades ago made awesome colitas de pavo with lard colored with either achiote paste or red chile. You can color your lard the way I do, using achiote paste, or skip it, or yes, use a few drops of red food dye.

Restaurants that sell colitas de pavo usually buy them vacuum sealed, deboned and already slow-cooked, so they can pull some out and sear them crispy on the flattop. This means you can do the initial steps, then do what the restaurants do so you can make these easily later.

Bulk braising can be a double advantage because sometimes you have to buy many pounds of turkey tails on special order. Do the heavy lifting in one day, then you'll have chunks of the best turkey you've ever eaten for months afterwards.

- 2 quarts fresh rendered lard
- ¼ cup achiote paste or Red Enchilada Sauce (page 37)
- 3 pounds turkey tails
- Salt

Pick over the turkey tails and remove any stray feathers. Salt them well. Preheat the oven to 300°F.

Heat the lard and the achiote paste in a pot over medium-low heat until the paste starts to sizzle. Turn off the heat and strain the lard into a pot large enough to hold the turkey tails. Discard the paste.

Submerge the tails in the lard, cover the pot, and cook the tails in the oven until tender, usually about 2 hours. You don't want them falling apart, just tender. Always a good idea to start checking at about 90 minutes.

Remove the tails and let them cool. Strain the lard again; you can reuse it elsewhere. Slice off the meat and fat from the central bone on the tail in largish pieces. Discard the bones. This step can be done in advance, and you can let the meat cool and vac seal it in the freezer for months.

When you are ready to eat your colitas de pavo, take out the chunks and sear them hard on a flattop, comal, or in a frying pan. Once they're crispy, chop further and serve in a burrito, taco, or a sandwich.

NOTES: You can buy fresh lard and achiote paste in most Latin markets. Once you make the red lard, you can reuse it for other things, notably as the fat in the masa for the tamales on page 78.

PARISA

PREP TIME: 30 MINUTES | SERVES 4 TO 6 AS AN APPETIZER

I'll take a slight detour north of the border in this trip to Mendina, Texas, home of parisa. In case you're not familiar, Mendina is just west of San Antonio. Parisa is at its core a Texas steak ceviche. It has a Mexican cousin called carne apache, which hails from Michoacan, and that is finely chopped or ground meat mixed with a standard pico de gallo; I have never seen it in the north of Mexico. Parisa has its origins with the steak tartares of Europe, but with a decidedly Texas touch. It has several variations but is almost always served as an appetizer alongside Saltines or Ritz crackers.

I prefer using lean, fatless venison for this recipe, but any sinew-free, largely fat-free cut of red meat will do. Beef is customary.

There are two ways to serve parisa: immediately, like a more classic tartare, or marinated. I don't care for the marinated version because the lime juice turns the meat gray and unappetizing, but that's more common in Mendina.

1 cup white or yellow onion

¼ cup lime juice

1 pound finely chopped lean red meat

2 to 4 serrano or jalapeño chiles, deseeded and minced

2 small cloves garlic, minced

¼ pound finely shredded cheese (Monterey Jack or Cheddar)

1 teaspoon salt

Black pepper

1 tablespoon olive oil

Saltines or Ritz crackers, for serving

Soak the minced onion in the lime juice and set this in the fridge while you mince the meat and the other ingredients.

Mix the meat, chiles, garlic, cheese, salt and pepper and olive oil. If you are not serving the parisa right away, wait to add the lime-soaked onion until you are ready to serve. Keep everything cold.

To serve, you can either dump the juice and onions into the rest and mix, or drain off the lime juice and mix the onions in. I prefer the latter because it will keep the meat pretty and pink longer, but you'll still have that bright acidity from the lime juice on the onions.

Eat with Saltines or Ritz crackers.

TIP: Partially freeze the meat before slicing or partially thaw frozen meat. It makes it much easier to dice the meat very finely. You could also use very lean ground meat.

Variations

Some people like to add a pinch of ground cumin to their parisa. Some prefer to mince pickled jalapeños instead of using fresh ones. One of the testers for this recipe added pomegranate seeds, which is a nice touch.

TAQUITOS

PREP TIME: 20 MINUTES | COOK TIME: 20 MINUTES | SERVES 4 TO 6

I didn't grow up in the Taquito Belt, which, in America, runs from about Houston along Interstate 10 along into Southern California. You'll also see them called tacos dorados, rolled tacos, or, if you put two tortillas together you have a flauta. You can serve them as a snack, an appetizer, or as a main meal. When in Texas, I eat them for breakfast, usually from the fast-food chain Whataburger.

What are they? A corn tortilla filled with something spare, rolled tightly and fried in oil until crispy. You normally serve them with a salsa on top, sometimes sour cream, guacamole, cheese, or other good stuff.

The key to a taquito is to keep the filling limited, but tasty. Simple shredded chicken is nice, but it's better if you mix the meat in a sauce first. And it has to be dry enough so the filling doesn't blow out the tortilla when you roll it. Picadillo (page 238) or some other ground meat is another popular choice, and the filling of the enchiladas in this chapter is, too.

Most recipes will tell you to secure the rolled-up taquitos with a toothpick, but this isn't really necessary. You do need to roll them fairly tightly, then set them seam side down as you make more. Then, carefully pick them up with a spatula, seam side down, and place them in hot oil, again, seam side down. The taquito will then set firmly that way and won't unroll when you turn it over in the hot oil. Keep them hot on a rack set over a cookie sheet in a warm oven as you fry them.

Two last pieces of advice: Cook more than you think, because people will eat more than they think they can, and because leftovers are great the next morning.

3 cups cooked, shredded chicken, pheasant, turkey, etc.

½ cup Salsa Negra (page 71), hot sauce, or another smooth salsa

16 6-inch corn tortillas

1½ cups corn oil or other neutral vegetable oil

Salsa, for garnish

Sour cream, for garnish (optional)

Shredded lettuce, for garnish (optional)

Cotija or shredded cheese, for garnish (optional)

Mix the shredded meat with the salsa or hot sauce, breaking up any large pieces. You going to be rolling a delicate tortilla around this, so you want no big lumpy bits.

Heat the oil in a large frying pan over medium-low heat for about 4 minutes. Using tongs, dip the tortillas in the hot oil for a few seconds to soften them. Set them on a tray or plate.

Put a tablespoon or two of the shredded meat in a thin rectangle on the first third of a tortilla. Wrap it up tightly, but gently, as the tortillas are tender at this point. Slide the taquito, seam side down, aside. Repeat with the remaining taquitos.

Heat the oil to at least 325°F, and ideally 350°F. Using a thin spatula, slip the end of the spatula under the seam of a taquito—lengthwise, with the edge of the seam facing away from the spatula—and carefully place it in the hot oil, seam side down. Press on the top of the taquito for 10 seconds to hold it. Repeat with a few more taquitos. You will need to do this in batches so you can flip them.

Set a cooling rack on a baking sheet and put that in the oven, setting the oven to "warm." After 1 to 2 minutes, turn your taquitos over and fry them on the other side for another 1 to 2 minutes. Move them to the rack in the oven and repeat with the remaining taquitos.

Serve with salsa, lettuce, cheese, sour cream, or whatever makes you happy.

TEXAS-STYLE ENCHILADAS

PREP TIME: 90 MINUTES | COOK TIME: 30 MINUTES | SERVES 6 TO 8

Classic Texas-style enchiladas are easy to make, delicious, and are fantastic as leftovers. These are the sort of enchiladas you're probably thinking of when you think about enchiladas: shredded or ground meat, rolled corn tortillas, and lots of cheese.

Plus, these are baked, and not all enchiladas are. The net effect is more-or-less a Mexican casserole. You can fill this basic enchilada recipe in a variety of ways. This recipe uses a very simple, picadillo-like mixture with ground venison, but enchiladas have always been a great option for leftover meats, so get creative! A few especially good fillings would be:

- The Sonoran Picadillo (page 238), which is basically really good "taco meat".
- Leftover Barbacoa (page 87). Using the shredded meat is a great use for it.
- If you've made Carne Asada Tacos (page 248), dice any leftovers small and use that as a filling.

One thing I like to add to the filling is queso fresco. It's not a melty cheese, so it plays well with whatever filling you choose.

You can use canned enchilada sauce—if you have one you really like. If you live in Texas or the desert Southwest, there are lots of good ones. I make a simple sauce from a purée of chiles, a touch of tomato paste, onion, and garlic, all thinned out with broth. This sauce keeps for weeks in the fridge, so you can use it as a salsa later, for more enchiladas or, for the filling in the tamales on page 78.

The best way to build standard, rolled enchiladas is to briefly fry the corn tortillas in oil or reheat them on a comal or flattop, then paint or dip in the sauce, fill, roll, arrange in a dish, top with cheese, and bake. Briefly frying the tortillas in oil helps them hold up a little better than if you reheat them to make them supple.

Building enchiladas is messy, so do it near the sink. I find just going for it with my hands is the best option. Having sauce-spattered hands also keeps me focused.

As for the cheese topping, ideally, you'd top enchiladas with hand-shredded queso asadero, queso Oaxaca, or queso Chihuahua. They're all real-deal Mexican melty cheeses. But you can certainly use shredded Mexican blend, or if you want to lean Tex-Mex, go for that yellow longhorn cheese.

I will often serve venison enchiladas solo, maybe with a crunchy salad alongside. The Cactus Salad (page 88) is a great choice here. Leftover venison enchiladas keep for a week in the fridge, and they freeze well.

Sauce

3 ounces ancho peppers, stemmed and seeded

4 ounces guajillo, New Mexican, or colorado peppers, stemmed and seeded

½ white onion, quartered

3 unpeeled cloves garlic

2 chipotles in adobo

1 teaspoon ground cumin

1 teaspoon dried Mexican oregano

4 tablespoons tomato paste

Salt, smoked salt if possible

3 cups chicken broth

Sauce

To make the sauce, boil the ancho and guajillo chiles for a few minutes, then turn off the heat and let them soak. Heat a cast iron pan or comal on medium-high heat and lay down the pieces of onion and garlic. You want to blacken the onion on both cut sides, and get some char on the garlic peel. This process takes about 8 to 10 minutes. Remove the onion and garlic to a cutting board. Peel the garlic.

Put the garlic and soaked, drained chiles into a blender. Coarsely chop the onion and add that, too. Add all the remaining sauce ingredients, including about 1 teaspoon of the salt. Purée, adding chicken broth as needed, to make a pourable sauce. In some cases, you'll need to add some water, too. Taste and add salt if needed.

OPTIONAL STEP: I always do this, because it results in a smoother sauce that removes bits of seed and skin, which are undigestible. Push the sauce through a fine strainer with a rubber spatula into a bowl. Set aside.

Filling

2 tablespoons lard or olive oil

1 white onion, chopped

2 pounds ground venison

2 cloves garlic, minced

1 teaspoon Mexican oregano

½ pound queso fresco, crumbled (optional)

To Finish

Neutral oil, for frying

18 to 20 corn tortillas

½ pound shredded cheese (see headnote for options)

Filling

To make the filling, heat the lard or oil in a large pan over high heat. Add the chopped onion and the venison and brown well. This takes about 8 minutes or so. Stir the meat occasionally. When everything has mostly browned, add the garlic and oregano and cook a minute or two more. Turn off the heat.

Mix in a ladle or two of the sauce, using it and a wooden spoon to scrape off any browned bits stuck to the pan. Once this cools, add the queso fresco and mix well.

To Finish

Preheat oven to 350°F. Pour some oil in a frying pan, enough to float tortillas, and heat the pan over medium-high heat. Get paper towels or a kitchen towel ready. When the oil is shimmering, fry one tortilla at a time in the oil, flipping once or twice, for only a few seconds—you want to see them puff up. They should be very flexible. Do this for all the tortillas, setting them on the towel.

Spread a little sauce on the bottom of a casserole dish.

Set up a station where you can dip a tortilla into the sauce (or paint sauce on both sides of each tortilla with your fingers or a brush), then grab a bit of the filling (maybe 2 to 3 tablespoons), and roll up the enchiladas. Set each one, seam side down, into the casserole. Fill the dish snugly.

Sprinkle the shredded cheese on top and bake for 30 minutes.

BRISKET TACOS

PREP TIME: 30 MINUTES | COOK TIME: 30 MINUTES | SERVES 8

Brisket tacos are huge in Texas, and something like them appears in the neighboring Mexican states of Coahuila and Nuevo Leon. They are, in my opinion, the apotheosis of what brisket should be: fatty, smoky, but not overwhelming. These flavors are balanced with bracing heat from chiles and acidity from limes. A solid backbone to your taco will perfect it. What I mean by that is there should be something underneath the meat. You generally have three main options: Guacamole (page 272), Refried Beans (page 35), and/or grilled cheese or the Costra (page 75).

I feel strongly that a brisket taco should be on a flour tortilla, but if you must, you can eat them on corn tortillas. All this said, consider this a model for brisket tacos, not gospel. But you do need to have a fully smoked and ready brisket to make them. Not a smoker? Find a barbecue joint in town and buy a few pounds of their brisket, then use that.

- 2 pounds smoked brisket
- 3 tablespoons beef fat, lard, or oil
- ½ pound shredded cheese (Oaxaca, Jack, asadero, Chihuahua, "Mexican blend")
- 16 flour tortillas
- 1 batch Guacamole (page 272) or Hank's Refried Beans (page 35)
- ⅓ cup minced cilantro
- Salsa of your choice (I love the Monterrey Salsa on page 75 for this)

Slice the brisket to about ½ inch thick. Heat the beef fat or other cooking fat in a large pan, like a cast iron pan, and get it hot. Sear the slices of brisket on one side to crisp. Chop it small enough to be nice in a tortilla and keep it warm.

Heat a comal or griddle over medium-high heat. When it's hot, lay down some shredded cheese in a pile, somewhere around 2 tablespoons, depending on the size of your tortillas. When it starts to melt, set a tortilla over it and press down. Keep pressing down until you see the cheese reach the edges of the tortilla, or when cheese grease seeps out the sides. Let this cook for a minute or two, then, either using your hands or a metal spatula, remove the tortilla with the grilled cheese attached. This takes a little practice to perfect.

Now spread some guacamole or refried beans over the cheese, then top with the brisket. Add the salsa of your choice and some cilantro and you're ready to rock!

"That's as common as cornbread."

Old Texas saying

FAJITAS

PREP TIME: 15 MINUTES | COOK TIME: 15 MINUTES | MARINATING TIME: 2 HOURS | SERVES 4 TO 6

You can't talk about real Texas cooking without fajitas, which appear in Coahuila and Nuevo Leon, too. The word means little strips, for the way the meat is cut. It's vital to use tender meat and to cut it across the grain, otherwise, it will pull out of the tortilla when you bite into it. It's almost always made with skirt or flank steak, and while I have used these cuts off large deer, elk, and nilgai, beef in this case is far superior. Bison is almost as good.

The main key to cooking great fajitas is super high heat, so kick the spurs to the grill, or use your most powerful burner with your fan on high.

Marinated Meat

1 teaspoon garlic powder

1 teaspoon cayenne

1 teaspoon ground cumin

1 teaspoon dried oregano, crumbled

1 teaspoon salt

1 pound flank steak

Juice of a lime

To Finish

3 tablespoons canola oil or other high smoke point oil, divided

1 green bell pepper, cut into strips

1 red bell pepper, cut into strips

1 orange or yellow bell pepper, cut into strips

1 onion, sliced

¼ cup chopped cilantro or parsley

Juice of a lime

Salt and freshly ground black pepper

8 to 12 flour tortillas

1 avocado, sliced

Salsa of your choice (optional)

Mix all the dry ingredients for the marinade together, then rub them into the flank steak. Put this in a bag or plastic container in the fridge for no less than 2 hours, and up to a day. If you are only going to let it marinate 2 hours, add the lime juice right away. If not, add the lime juice with 2 hours to go.

You will need a grill, or a large frying pan, ideally cast iron. Start getting it hot. Take the meat out of the fridge, and wipe it dry with paper towels. Coat it in 1 tablespoon of the oil. When the pan is hot, I mean hot as in starting to smoke, about 500°F to 600°F, lay the meat in the pan or on the grill. If you happen to have a bacon press, put it on the meat. If not, no big deal. Let it sit there for 3 minutes. Turn the meat and let it cook another 2 to 4 minutes, depending on how you like your meat. I only give it the 2 minutes because flank or skirt steak will cook a bit more via carryover heat when it's on the cutting board. Move it to the board.

Coat the vegetables in the remaining oil and add them to the hot pan. Stir-fry a minute, then let them sit a bit to get some char. Move them once a minute for 3 minutes. You want them soft, but not mushy, and with some browned or even blackened bits. Turn off the heat and mix in the lime juice and cilantro, as well as salt and lots of black pepper.

Slice the flank steak against the grain, and serve with the vegetables in tortillas and topped with avocado and salsa.

NOTE: I make my flour tortillas before I even start making the fajitas, keeping them in a tortilla warmer. If you are reheating premade tortillas, you can do that either before you start or while the meat is searing.

Keys to Success

- You will want a variety of colors for your fajita vegetables. It's prettier, and the ripe ones add sweetness. You can skip bell peppers if you want and use poblanos, Italian frying peppers, Anaheims, or any pepper that isn't super hot.
- The meat must be cold when it hits the pan, otherwise you run a risk of it overcooking by the time you get some good char—and char is key for fajitas.
- Flour tortillas are traditional, as this is Tex-Mex, but corn are fine, too.
- Guacamole is a good choice for a salsa here (page 272). So is my Avocado Tomatillo Salsa (page 43).

DISCADA

PREP TIME: 20 MINUTES | COOK TIME: 35 MINUTES | SERVES 8 TO 12

Discada is more of a vibe than it is a recipe, though there are some similarities to every discada you'll encounter. At its core, discada is a sort of borderlands stir-fry usually cooked on a disco—originally an old plow disk, now more commonly a dedicated steel or aluminum vessel. A disco is essentially a shallow wok, and the best discada is served on a steel one heated by mesquite fire.

Discada is a meat lover's dream. I've never seen one with fewer than three meats, and there are often a half-dozen. Usually it's a combo of pork and beef, but sometimes chicken gets thrown in there, too. I've also never seen a discada without either bacon or chorizo (usually both), and sliced hot dogs are super common, although they're not in my recipe; add some if you like.

Beyond that, there are always onions, garlic, and peppers of some sort. My recipe uses roasted green chiles, but regular bell peppers of all colors are equally common. Canned chipotles in adobo are frequent visitors, and some sort of tomato product is vital, whether it's fresh chopped tomatoes, canned, tomato sauce, or hell, some even use a little V8.

A beer poured into the mix to deglaze it is also standard. Use a Mexican beer or some other light lager.

Serve discada with refried beans, rice, and lots of tortillas, corn or flour. It makes a great burrito filling, too. Use my recipe as a guide, not dogma.

Leftover discada is excellent. Add it to eggs, potatoes, breakfast burritos, you name it.

- 4 to 6 slices of bacon
- 1 pound chorizo
- 1 pound pork loin or country ribs
- 1 pound lean beef or venison
- 1 large white onion, chopped
- 4 cloves garlic, minced
- 1 pound roasted green chiles, or chopped bell peppers
- 2 to 6 serranos, chopped
- 2 cups crushed tomatoes
- 2 canned chipotles in adobo, with some of the adobo
- 1 can or bottle of lager beer
- Cilantro, limes and tortillas
- 1 recipe Hank's Taco Onions (page 46)

Heat the disco over medium heat and fry the bacon until crispy. Remove the bacon and chop it. Add the chorizo to the pan and brown that in the bacon fat.

While these two things are happening, chop the pork and beef into small pieces—remember you're serving discada in tortillas as tacos, so the meat needs to be fairly small.

Add the chopped meats to the pan and mix well. If your pan is getting full, scoop out the chorizo or do the meats in batches. You want things to brown at this stage.

Once all the meats are browned, if you're using a large enough pan, add the onions, then the peppers, then the garlic. If your pan is small, remove the meats to cook the vegetables.

When the onions are browned and the peppers mostly cooked, add back the bacon and meats, and the beer, tomatoes, and chipotles. Use a wooden spoon to scrape up any browned bits on the bottom of the pan. Let this all bubble away until the liquid thickens. Discada should not be watery.

Serve with tortillas, beans, and rice. When you make tacos, the lime-soaked raw onions cut through an otherwise heavy filling.

OPTION: If you plan on serving this at a party, where everyone can grab what they want off the disco with a hot tortilla, I'd suggest sprinkling grated cheese on top of everything. Then, when it melts, simply use a tortilla to grab a portion, cheese, meat, and vegetables. This is a classic Chihuahua move.

CREAMY GREEN CHILE SOUP

PREP TIME: 1 HOUR, IF YOU ARE STARTING WITH FRESH CHILES | COOK TIME: 20 MINUTES | SERVES 6 TO 8

This soup exists in some form all over the borderlands, and I've made it at Nixtaco in California. Think of it as a green chile bisque: smooth, lush, vegetal, and only mildly spicy. Depending on where you are, you'd use either poblanos or medium-hot green Anaheim chiles.

8 poblano or large Anaheim chiles

1 serrano chile (optional; see Notes)

3 tablespoons butter

1 white onion, minced

2 cloves garlic, minced

Salt

1 russet potato, peeled and diced

½ teaspoon dried Mexican oregano

Stems from 1 bunch of cilantro, chopped (optional)

1 teaspoon powdered chicken bouillon (optional)

1 cup heavy cream

½ cup Mexican crema

Cilantro for garnish (optional)

Roast the chiles according to the directions on page 32. Peel, stem, seed, and dice them.

In a soup pot, heat the butter over medium heat and cook the onions until soft but not browned. Add the diced, roasted chiles after a minute or three, then add the garlic. Salt everything well.

Let all this cook for a few minutes, then add the oregano and the diced potato, the cilantro stems, and bouillon, and water to cover. Simmer this until the potatoes are tender, about 15 minutes. Move all this into a blender and purée until smooth.

If you want to be fancy, push it all through a food mill or strainer. Return it to the pot, and add the crema and heavy cream. Bring this to a bare simmer, add more salt to taste, and serve.

NOTES: If your chiles aren't spicy, add the serrano. Every once in a while, poblanos get zippy. Taste each one as you dice them to be sure. Anaheims are rarely spicy unless they're marked as such.

You can also use chicken broth instead of water or vegetable broth. Other optional garnishes would be a few pieces of roasted chile, and some sweet corn kernels.

CHARRO BEANS

PREP TIME: 20 MINUTES | COOK TIME: 1 HOUR | SERVES 6 TO 10 AS A SIDE

A standard side dish all over Texas, Tamaulipas, Nuevo Leon, Coahuila, and even Chihuahua, these soupy, flavorful beans are the reason why the rest of the chili-eating universe puts beans in its chili: In Texas, chili with no beans is eaten alongside charro beans, which contain many of the ingredients non-Texans put in chili. Clearly someone dumped their charro beans in the chili one day and called it good. Fascinatingly, it could have been a Chihuahuan: Their Guisado de Abigeo (page 186) is often served mixed into or alongside charro beans.

Keep in mind this is a stripped down charro beans recipe. I've seen some with five meats in them. If you want to bulk things up, add some chorizo, hot dogs (yes, really), salt pork, or chunks of pork shoulder.

For best results, cook your beans separately or used canned beans. You have three choices: pinto, bayo, or flor de mayo beans. I've never seen anyone in the borderlands use beans other than these, but hey, you do you.

- 1 pound beans
- Sprig of fresh epazote (optional)
- ¼ pound bacon
- ½ white or yellow onion, chopped
- 1 to 3 jalapeños or serranos, seeded and chopped
- 3 cloves garlic, minced
- ½ cup roasted green chiles, chopped (canned is fine)
- 1 or 2 tomatoes, seeded and diced
- 1 teaspoon Mexican oregano
- 1 bottle of beer (Mexican lager)
- Salt, pepper, and chopped cilantro
- Cotija or queso fresco, for garnish

Simmer the beans in lots of water until tender. Let them cook for 30 minutes, then add the epazote, if using. Do not add salt until the beans are getting tender. The test for this is to eat 5 beans: If all 5 are nice, you're good.

Meanwhile, in another pan, fry the bacon in a medium pot until crispy. Remove the bacon and chop. If you are adding other meats, brown them in the pot, too. Add the onion and jalapeños and sauté until the onion is soft, then add the garlic and cook for a minute more.

Add the green chiles, tomatoes, oregano, and beer. Bring to a simmer, then, if the beans aren't yet ready, turn off the heat. Once the beans are ready, bring the pan back to a simmer and add the beans with some of their cooking liquid: How soupy you want your charro beans is up to you, but they should be wetter than the Border Beans (page 265). Let this cook at least 20 minutes to let the ingredients get to know each other.

When you are ready to eat, add the bacon, salt, pepper, and cilantro to taste, and garnish with the cheese.

If you are using canned beans, you'll want 2 pounds, which is about 2 cans. Add them when you add the green chiles, tomatoes, etc. Simmer 20 minutes and you're done.

NUEVO LEON & COAHUILA

Monterrey, Nuevo Leon is the Chicago of Mexico. Big, sprawling, vibrant, industrial, a city of business and strong shoulders. But with the heat and aridity, you'll have to toss in a bit of Phoenix to get the full vibe. It is also wealthy, home to the Beverly Hills of Mexico, San Pedro Garza Garcia.

It is a mountain city, a place where peaks and ranges separate neighborhoods, with a village of rascacielos, literally skyscrapers, in its center. Spanish and Middle Eastern influences are strong there, most visibly with the trompo, which most Americans know in its role as a vertical spit for Greek gyros and Turkish shawarma. Everywhere else in Mexico, see a trompo and you'll be eating tacos al pastor, a signature taco of Mexico City. Here, who knows what'll be on it. My favorite? The original: lamb thinly sliced off the trompo and served on micro pitas, which in Mexico feel like fat flour tortillas . . . because they are.

Meat is king in Monterrey. And the cooking method of choice is fire. It is the start of what I call the Fire Belt along the border, a belt that begins in Texas, dips down into Nuevo Leon, then stretches almost to the Pacific. This is the region of real carne asadas, real discadas—parties where the eponymous dish is the star. It's exactly like barbecue: You serve barbecue at a barbecue, and the meat in question was barbecued.

Grilled meat of all kinds is popular, but cabrito reigns supreme: Suckling kid goat is the prince of Nuevo Leon cuisine, and it is tragic that it's nearly impossible to find in the US outside of South Texas. Milk-fed goat is surpassingly good, and there are dozens of traditional dishes featuring it. The shepherding culture of both Nuevo Leon and neighboring Coahuila is strong.

A very Spanish tradition of cooking societies—until recently all male—thrives in Monterrey, and Patricio and I cooked at the one he belongs to. Nicknamed La Soci, pronounced "so-see," short for Sociedad Gastronomía Regiomontana, members take turns putting on a spread for the rest of the membership. This is where I first ate machito, the region's version of Greek *kokoretsi*, and first tasted the bliss of a buttered, rolled flour tortilla with grated, melted piloncillo mixed with pecans inside. Heaven. I cooked grilled octopus tacos with a chicatana ant salsa, grilled totoaba (a seabass), and made toritos. The salsa is very Oaxacan, and so won't be in this book, but you can find the toritos on page 278.

Nuevo Leon's countryside feels like Spain, only with a significant difference: Cartel activity remains an issue in some parts of the state, and it's considered dangerous to drive at night there. We toured the towns around Monterrey, and when an accident blocked our main road, a detour got sketchy when we had to roll through a place where it looked like the road was intentionally knocked out.

That said, there is amazing food to be had outside Monterrey. Las Comadres on the Rio Ramos just outside of Allende has become so famous it can take 90 minutes to be served the ladies' simple menu of beans, queso fresco, cortadillo stew, and homemade tortillas. The stew's recipe is a closely guarded secret, but it tastes almost exactly like my recipe for Sonoran Carne con Chile (page 240), only stewier with the meat cut into chunks.

At nearby El Principal del Blanquillo in Montemorelos, you'll also find grilled agujas (needles), which is a cut of the chuck roast above a cow's shoulder that includes a sliver of vertebra that acts as a handle—and as something to gnaw on. It's an outstanding cut I've seen in Latin markets in the US, and it'll be in any supermarket in South Texas. If you can find this cut, add it to your next carne asada. More on carne asada in the Sonora chapter.

CUAJITOS

PREP TIME: 35 MINUTES | COOK TIME: 3 TO 5 HOURS | SERVES 6 TO 8

I first had this dish at La Enramada in Cadareyta, Nuevo Leon. My friend Patricio was over the moon that they had it—although I was pretty sure it was off-menu, but Pato knows the owner. Cuajitos is a thick, meaty stew typically served alongside charro beans, chiles toreados—serranos blistered on a hot comal—and flour or corn tortillas.

Its origin is with the shepherds of the region, who would use the bladder of sheep (cleaned, of course) to cook the stew in. You can still get cuajitos this way in a few places, but it has become rare. The original meat was lamb or mutton, but veal and its bladder have also been used for generations. Venison is a good wild option, and aoudad sheep would be ideal.

Pay attention to the cooking technique here because it's what makes cuajitos special.

Once made, the stew will keep a week in the fridge, and it can be frozen or pressure-canned.

- 2 to 3 pounds meat, such as lamb shoulder
- 1 or 2 large yellow or white onions, chopped
- 2 or 3 bell peppers or poblanos, seeded and chopped
- 1 to 4 serranos, seeded and chopped
- 1 head of garlic, peeled and coarsely chopped
- 1 tablespoon black peppercorns
- 2 teaspoons cumin seeds
- ¼ to ⅓ cup fresh oregano, Mexican if possible (see Notes)
- Salt
- 2 cups crushed tomatoes
- 1 12-ounce bottle dark lager beer

Cut the meat into 2-inch chunks. Put it in a soup pot with the onions and peppers.

In a molcajete or mortar and pestle, grind the garlic, peppercorns, and cumin seeds to a paste, then grind in the oregano, adding a little water to ease this process. You want an intense salsa.

Add this, the crushed tomatoes, and about 1 tablespoon salt to the soup pot, and, using your hands, work everything together so it's well coated. Let this sit for at least 30 minutes and up to 1 hour at room temperature, or up to 4 or 5 hours in the fridge.

When you're ready to start cooking, pour in the bottle of beer—you're looking for something darker like a Negra Modelo or Bohemia—then enough water to cover the mixture by 1 inch. Mix well, bring to a simmer, and add more salt if it needs it. Drop the heat to low, cover the pot, and let this simmer very gently for . . . well, as long as you can stand it, but definitely 3 hours. You want this to be something of a hammered, cooked-down stew, with everything melded.

NOTES: Many old recipes for cuajitos use blood, but this method gets you very close because all of the liquid that bubbles up from the raw meat, undesirable in most stews, is vital here. You want it thick and rich and cloudy with all those proteins.

If you can't find fresh oregano, use 2 tablespoons dried. It is supposed to be a strong flavor in this stew.

◀ An ancient pecan tree grows next to a natural cistern in rural Coahuila, Mexico.

MONTERREY ENCHILADAS

PREP TIME: 45 MINUTES | COOK TIME: 20 MINUTES | SERVES 4

I include these as a hat tip to Cinthia Martinez, co-owner of Nixtaco, native of Monterrey, and a lover of this sort of enchilada. They're simple, humble, vegetarian, and pretty to look at. You'll want to use red corn tortillas if you can get them. Some Latin markets will carry them, but they are easily mail-ordered. If you can't find them or don't want to bother, make a batch of my Red Enchilada Sauce (page 37) and dip regular corn tortillas in that.

Have everything ready to go before you start because these enchiladas come together quickly.

- ½ white onion, minced
- ¼ cup freshly squeezed lime juice
- Salt
- 2 cups shredded iceberg lettuce
- 1 tomato, seeded and cut into chunks
- 4 serrano chiles
- 1 cup vegetable oil
- 16 to 20 red corn tortillas
- 1½ pounds queso fresco or panela, crumbled
- Mexican crema for drizzling
- Olive oil (optional)

Soak the minced onion in the lime juice. Add a pinch of salt to the mix.

Heat the vegetable oil in a pan large enough to hold 1 or 2 tortillas, and fry the serranos in that oil, turning them constantly until blistered. Remove and set aside. Lower the heat.

Drain the onion, reserving the juice, and taste the onion. It should not be bitter. If it is, you can either keep soaking it, or use it as a topping. Once the onions are tart and nice, mix them with ¾ of the crumbled cheese.

Pass the tortillas through the hot oil for a few seconds, just to heat and loosen them up. You can do them all at once, but they will stick to each other if you stack them after frying. I prefer to make an assembly line and heat a tortilla, fill it, roll it, then move it to a plate before I do a second tortilla. Once you get the knack of it, this goes quickly.

After the tortilla is nice and soft, set it on a work surface and fill it with some of the onion and cheese mix. Roll it fairly tightly and set, seam side down, on a plate. Repeat this with the remaining tortillas.

To finish, sprinkle some more cheese over the enchiladas and drizzle some crema over them. Toss the shredded lettuce and tomato with the lime juice and a little olive oil, or some of the vegetable oil from the tortillas. Serve that alongside the enchiladas, with a toreado—the blistered serrano—as a spicy side. You can peel the skin off the serranos if you want, and the idea is to take a bite of one as you eat the otherwise mild enchiladas.

When You Don't Have Red Tortillas

This is what you do with regular white or yellow corn tortillas to turn them red. In some ways, this is even better than the classic method. Heat red enchilada sauce to the steaming point. Get the oil ready as above.

Fry the tortillas—only this time fry a touch more, so they are thinking about getting crispy. Use tongs to remove them from the oil and immediately dip the tortilla into the warm enchilada sauce. Then fill and wrap.

This is a messier operation, but I think it's tastier.

EMPALMES

PREP TIME: 45 MINUTES | COOK TIME: 20 MINUTES | SERVES 8 TO 10

Empalmes are a very Nuevo Leon appetizer, usually at parties where carne asada or discada are the star. They are a sort of handheld enchilada: two corn tortillas, slathered with refried beans and cheese, sometimes some meat, brushed with chile-infused lard and seared. They are addictive.

Like a lot of Mexican appetizers, you'll want everything ready to go when you start making them. So have refried beans, shredded cheese, any meat you want—I recommend some cooked chorizo—and the chile-lard all set. You can use any red chile sauce. I use the Red Enchilada Sauce (page 37). Or you can rehydrate a few guajillo chiles and purée them with a bit of water and salt.

Use standard 6-inch corn tortillas for this.

Once you make empalmes, they are best right off the heat, but you can stack them and wrap them in foil to keep them warm for an hour or so.

- ¼ cup red chile sauce
- 1 cup lard
- 1 recipe Hank's Refried Beans (page 35)
- 12 ounces shredded melty cheese (mozzarella, Jack, asadero, Chihuahua, etc.)
- ½ pound Mexican chorizo, cooked and crumbled
- 20 corn tortillas

Preheat the oven to 200°F. Stir together the lard and chile sauce until they have combined. You want the lard to be soft, but still semisolid. Brush a healthy bit of this lard onto two tortillas, then set them together fat side to fat side, so they stick.

Holding the tortillas with one hand, spread some refried beans on the top tortilla, then some chorizo, then top with a healthy amount of shredded cheese. You can repeat this process with the rest of the ingredients. Get your comal or griddle hot. You can do this on a grill if the grates are narrow.

Now, very carefully slide the top tortilla, the one with all the good stuff, off the bottom one, and set it on the comal. Set the other tortilla—*lard side up!*—on top of the good stuff. Press down with a metal spatula. Let this sear for a few minutes, until the cheese starts to melt, then carefully flip them to sear the larded side. Press down again and cook until the tortilla is crispy and a little blackened, and the cheese has fully melted.

Slide the empalme off the comal and set in the oven. You can do this on a baking sheet or directly on the rack. Repeat with the other empalmes.

SOPES or CAZUELITAS

PREP TIME: 15 MINUTES | COOK TIME: 20 MINUTES | SERVES 8 TO 10

Mexican sopes, called cazuelitas in Nuevo Leon and parts of South Texas, are probably the best way to begin cooking with masa. These little tartlets can be made without a tortilla press, are easy to make—kids love making them—and can be filled with pretty much anything. Pronounced "so-pays" or "so-pez," they are traditional botanas, or appetizers, and can be found all over the borderlands. They come in as many colors as there are colors of corn.

Sopes can be made with either fresh nixtamal or with masa harina, although they are better when made with fresh masa. Sopes are made in one of two ways, and each has its advantage.

The first, and probably oldest method, is to pat out a gordita, a fat tortilla, by hand and then cook it over medium heat on the comal, to start setting the dough. Then you pull the gordita off the heat and immediately use your thumbs and forefingers to pinch out a raised rim around the disk. The rim is what makes a Mexican sope a sope and not some other masa shape. It's easy enough, but it takes a little getting used to—that masa is hot!

The other method is to form the sope from raw masa, then fry them to set. The advantage of this method is that you end up with a sope that has a taller, fuller rim. The disadvantage is that this frying is a violent process, and you will lose a few sopes to it; they can rupture or form big air bubbles.

The more traditional comal method is more foolproof, but you will not get as nice a raised rim.

Once made, they're best eaten within a few hours. In a pinch, you can let them sit a day in the fridge and then fry, or refry them right before you serve.

The only constant sope filling is the presence of beans, almost always refried beans. The reason for this is because refried beans serve as glue to keep whatever you put over them on the sope. After that, anything goes. That said, you will mostly see guisados. These thick stews are more successfully eaten on a sope than in a taco, because the sturdy shell of a sope contains the juicy guisado better. Some good choices in this book would be:

- Venison Carne Guisada (page 97)
- Carne con Chile (page 240)
- Asado de Puerco or Chilorio (page 152 and page 283)
- Pork Chicharron en Salsa Verde (page 68)
- Barbacoa (page 87)
- Tarahumara Mushrooms (page 188)

The pretty yellow masa sopes you see in the picture opposite are vegetarian, filled with a combination of fresh fava bean purée and my Avocado Tomatillo Salsa (page 43), plus the Quelites filling (page 53). Cilantro flowers make them fancy.

Your general rule for filling sopes is this: refried beans + protein + salsa + queso fresco or other cheese + sour cream, if you want it.

Most sopes are meant to be eaten in no more than three bites. This is both because they are meant to be appetizers, and because the corn masa dough can only be made so big without it collapsing. Roughly 45 to 50 grams is what you are shooting for, or about the size of a golf ball.

▶

SOPES or CAZUELITAS, continued

Sopes

2 cups masa harina

1¾ cups hot water

Vegetable oil for frying

Fillings

Refried beans

Filling of your choice (see headnote)

Salsa of your choice (see headnote)

Queso fresco or cotija cheese, crumbled

Mix the hot water with the masa harina: Add the water about ½ cup at a time, kneading and mixing at first with a fork, then your hands. You will likely need all 1¾ cups of water, but this will depend on how dry your climate is and how old your masa harina is. You want a very pliable, almost wet dough that doesn't stick to your hands when you roll it into balls. Do a tester: Roll a ball of masa and then flatten it. If it cracks all over along the sides, you will need a bit more water; start with a tablespoon at a time. If it sticks horribly, add a tablespoon at a time of masa harina, mixing well after each spoonful.

Preheat a comal or griddle or cast iron skillet over medium heat. You want it less than 400°F, and about 350°F is best.

Form the masa into balls of about 45 grams, or the size of a golf ball. Pat them into fat tortillas, gorditas, between your palms. You want them about ¼ inch thick or a little fatter. Nothing too thin yet.

Heat the gorditas on the comal. First side gets 1 minute. This will be the base of your sope. Flip and heat the other side for about 30 seconds.

Move the sope off the comal and use your thumbs and forefingers to form a lip around the edges of your sope on the side you just cooked, which will be more supple. Yes, it will be very hot. Push down the center of the sope a little so you have essentially a little tartlet. Repeat all this with the rest of the dough, setting aside the sopes for now.

When you are ready to serve them, heat up a decent amount of lard or vegetable oil in a pan, enough to cover the bottom by about ½ inch. When it's hot, about 325°F to about 350°F, fry the sopes until crispy, which should take a couple of minutes per side. You'll want to fill and serve them shortly after this.

Alternative Method

Mix the dough as above and pat out those gorditas. Only this time, heat lots of oil or lard in a pan to about 325°F. You need enough for the sopes to float in the oil, so about ½ to 1 inch deep.

After you've formed the gorditas, use your thumbs and forefingers to form the rims on the uncooked sopes, rotating the sope as you go so it doesn't stick to the cutting board or table. Form all of them before you start frying.

Fry a few sopes at a time, starting cup side down, so flat side up. Fry like this for about 2 minutes, then flip them. You will want to spoon hot oil into the cups immediately. You will see the inside of the cup bubble furiously, then calm down. When it calms down, remove the sopes to a cooling rack set over a baking sheet in the oven set to "warm."

These can hold for up to 1 hour before serving. Any more than that and you will need to fry them for about 1 minute per side to re-crisp them.

Keys to Success

- Have all the fillings made before you start the sopes. Most people make sopes a day or so after they've made the toppings so all that's needed is to reheat and fill.
- If you want these as party appetizers, don't overfill or people won't be able to pick them up and eat them. If you plan on having people use a knife and fork, stack toppings as high as you want.
- Don't stack the sopes themselves, or they will steam and get soft . . . and you will be sad.
- Broken or leftover sopes can be broken up and tossed in a stew. They're pretty great that way.
- If you are using fresh masa, I prefer the traditional method because fresh dough is wetter than dough made from masa harina. I've had more sopes explode and break when I use the frying method.

LODGE
12

PERICOS

PREP TIME: 15 MINUTES | COOK TIME: 15 MINUTES | SERVES 4 TO 6

Pericos, pan de pastor, corn fritters, these are Coahuila's answer to hush puppies. I'd heard about them for years before I got a chance to make these fritters with Norberto Arizpe, the manager of the Guadalupe Ranch outside of Muzquiz, Coahuila. They are easy to make, and the variable additions of minced onions, cracklins, and/or chopped bacon, plus sometimes chopped jalapeños, pickled or fresh, elevate the humble hush puppy.

Norberto upped the ante by frying the pericos in beef tallow. We were on a cattle ranch, after all. You can use any frying oil you want.

We ate our pericos with barbecued cabrito, rice, a goat offal stew called fritada, a version of the Fire-Roasted Salsa (page 38), and lots and lots of beer. They don't keep well, so eat them right out of the fryer.

- 1 cup cornmeal
- ⅓ cup flour
- ½ teaspoon salt
- 1 heaping teaspoon baking powder
- ¼ to ⅓ cup minced green onion
- ¼ cup cracklins or minced cooked bacon (optional)
- 1 egg
- ½ to 1 cup whole milk
- Oil for frying

Mix the cornmeal, flour, salt, baking powder, minced green onion, and cracklins, if you're using them. Add the egg and ½ cup of milk and stir well. You want a thick, semi-liquid batter that is just barely scoopable with a big spoon or ice cream scoop. Start with the ½ cup of milk, let the mixture rest for a few minutes —the cornmeal soaks up a lot, and add more milk if you need to while the oil is heating.

Pour enough oil into a large, heavy pot to reach a depth of about 3 to 4 inches; you can later strain and reuse this oil several more times. Heat it to 360°F.

Using a small ice cream scoop or a large spoon, scoop 2 tablespoons of the batter and carefully drop it into the hot oil. Fry until puffy and golden brown, turning the fritters with a slotted spoon to make sure they fry evenly.

Drain on paper towels and serve immediately.

CHICKEN RIO RAMOS

PREP TIME: 20 MINUTES | COOK TIME: 60 MINUTES | SERVES 6

This is a classic dish in Nuevo Leon, mostly associated with the town of Allende, a few miles outside of Monterrey. I'm including it because it's one of the rare chicken dishes along the borderlands. Mostly you'll see whole grilled chickens in adobo, or chicken wings, an imported treat from the United States. This is an older dish, one that makes a lovely sauce perfect for potatoes, simple white rice, or corn tortillas.

While you could pull this off with pheasant or grouse breasts and thighs, it is really better as a chicken dish. Whole quail would work, as would rabbit. It's definitely a white meat dish.

Once made, it keeps in the fridge a few days, and reheats well.

- ¼ cup lard or vegetable oil
- 1 chicken, cut into serving pieces
- Salt
- 3 to 6 chicken livers
- 2 bay leaves
- 1 white onion
- 2 green bell peppers, seeded and sliced
- 3 jalapeños, seeded and chopped
- 3 cloves garlic, minced
- 1 teaspoon dried Mexican oregano
- 2 teaspoons ground cumin
- 1 bunch fresh mint, chopped
- 1 pound tomatoes, seeded and chopped
- 1 pound tomatillos, husked and chopped

Salt the chicken well. Heat the lard in a large frying pan and brown the chicken pieces, paying special attention to the skin. Remove as each piece gets crispy and brown.

As the chicken is cooking, put the bay leaves in a small pot of water and bring it to a boil. Add one quarter of the onion. Do this by slicing the onion in half, and then slicing one of those halves in half. Save the rest of the onion. Drop the chicken livers into the pot and simmer for 5 minutes. Turn off the heat.

Slice the rest of the onion into strips, root to tail. Sauté the onion and the sliced green peppers in the pan. If you need to add more lard, do so. Cook the onions and peppers until barely soft, 3 minutes. Turn the heat to low.

Meanwhile, in a blender, purée the chicken livers, the piece of onion they cooked with, the jalapeños, garlic, oregano, cumin, half of the mint, tomatoes and tomatillos with a little salt. Add a little of the liver cooking water to the blender to make a sauce.

Return the chicken to the pan, pour over the sauce, and simmer, partially covered, until the chicken is tender, about 40 minutes to 1 hour. Taste, and add salt and more mint if you want. Serve with beans, rice, corn tortillas, and chile pequins.

MEXICAN LENTIL SOUP

PREP TIME: 20 MINUTES | COOK TIME: 30 MINUTES | SERVES 6

Sopa de lentejas exists in various forms all over the border, but it's most popular in Nuevo Leon. It's hearty, warming, and easy to make on a cold day.

The lentils I've seen in this soup are small and brown, so try to get those if possible. Green lentils will work for this recipe. You cook the lentils separately because there's lots of tomato in the recipe, and the acidity of it will slow the cooking of any sort of legume to a crawl. So I cook them in a separate pot. You can do this as a one-pot lentil soup by making it as normal, skipping the tomato until after the lentils are tender, then adding it and letting things get to know each other for a while.

You can easily make this soup vegetarian by skipping the chorizo and using vegetable broth to cook the lentils. This is done a lot around Lent. One alternative that will give you some of the chew and flavor that meat brings is to mince up a half pound of mushrooms and cook them as if they were the chorizo in the recipe.

Chorizo and bacon are very common additions, but I've also seen diced ham—ham and lentils is a classic combo—machaca, as well as link sausage cut into disks.

This recipe uses both mild-to-medium roasted green chiles as well as mega hot chile pequins. The green chiles act as a vegetable, the pequins as spice. You can use frozen or canned chiles, but they're not nearly as good. I prefer to roast Anaheims or poblanos specifically for this soup.

Lentils

- 1½ cups lentils (brown or green)
- ½ onion
- 1 sprig fresh epazote (optional)
- 1 quart chicken or vegetable broth
- Salt

Soup Base

- 8 ounces Mexican chorizo (see above for alternates)
- 1 cup minced white or yellow onion
- 1 large carrot, peeled and diced
- 2 stalks celery, thinly sliced
- 4 cloves garlic, minced
- ½ teaspoon cumin
- 2 roasted green chiles, seeded, peeled, and diced
- 1 cup crushed tomatoes
- Salt
- Chopped cilantro and chile pequin for serving

Put the onion and epazote in a pot and add the broth, plus another quart of water. Add the lentils and bring to a simmer. Simmer until the lentils are tender, but not mushy. You want them cooked, but still a little al dente. Add salt to taste and turn off the heat.

Meanwhile, in another pot, cook the chorizo—it should be fatty enough that you don't need to add more fat or oil—until well rendered, then add the onion, carrot, and celery. Cook these until soft, then add the garlic and cook for another couple minutes.

Stir in the cumin, green chiles, and tomatoes. If the lentils are done, add them, plus as much of the lentil cooking liquid as you want; I prefer a soupy soup, but add less liquid for a thicker stew. If the lentils aren't done, turn the heat off the soup base until they are.

Once everything's all together, simmer another few minutes, adding salt to taste. Serve with chopped cilantro and as many chile pequins as you can stand.

CALDILLO DE CARNE SECA

PREP TIME: 30 MINUTES | COOK TIME: 45 MINUTES | SERVES 6

Caldillo de carne seca, which translates to little stew of dried meat, is widespread in its various incarnations all over the border, notably Arizona and southern New Mexico. I've had many great versions in Monterrey.

I love how this recipe can be made with almost entirely dried ingredients while out on the range or off the grid. Caldillo de carne seca—or machaca, depending on where you are—hinges on jerky, usually beef, sometimes venison. And while normally you'd use freshly roasted green chiles, you can absolutely use their dried form, chiles pasados (page 181). Onions, garlic, some herbs if you want, potatoes to bulk it up, and some sort of tomato: fresh, puréed, or even dried ones.

The resulting brew is outstanding, and different enough from what you think of as chili to make it stand on its own.

It'll keep a week or so in the fridge, too, so you can make it on a weekend and bring it for lunches.

- 3 tablespoons lard or oil
- 1 large onion, coarsely chopped
- 8 ounces beef or venison carne seca, chopped into chunks
- 3 cloves garlic, minced
- 1 teaspoon dried Mexican oregano
- 1 teaspoon groundcumin
- 2 cups tomato purée
- 1 quart beef or venison broth
- 1 quart water
- 1 pound roasted green chiles, chopped
- Salt
- 1 pound potatoes, cut into chunks
- 2 Roma tomatoes, seeded and chopped (optional)
- Cilantro, for serving

Heat the lard in a soup pot over medium-high heat. Brown the onions. This takes time, so I have that started before I begin with the carne seca.

Cut the carne seca into pieces you'd eat with a spoon, then pull it apart with the grain a little more. If you're using the preshredded machaca, you're good to go. Oh, and if you're using the sort of machaca that looks like meat cotton candy, use only 6 ounces of it.

Stir the onions a couple times as you do this. Add the jerky to the pot with the minced garlic and cook until the garlic begins to brown. Add the green chiles, oregano, cumin and tomato purée, then the broth and water. Stir well and bring to a simmer.

Taste for salt. It may not need any. Cook this for about 15 minutes, then add the potatoes and cook until they are tender, maybe another 20 minutes. Add the chopped fresh tomatoes and some cilantro, and serve.

NOTE: You can use canned roasted green chiles here, or frozen ones. Fresh are great, but they add quite a bit of time to making this recipe. Use poblanos or Anaheim (Hatch) chiles if you do roast your own.

Tacos de Atropellado

Basically "roadkill" tacos—because they look terrible—this is a signature dish of Nuevo Leon, and it's closely related to caldillo de carne seca. To make it, follow the directions above, with these changes:

- Skip the tomato purée and the water.
- Reduce the stock to 1 pint.
- Use 6 tomatoes instead of 2.

Be sure to chop every ingredient small enough to go into a tortilla. Cook everything down until it's a thick stew that won't soak a tortilla. Serve on either corn or flour tortillas, with some chopped cilantro or guacamole on top.

NOPALES NAVEGANTES

PREP TIME: 45 MINUTES | COOK TIME: 20 MINUTES | SERVES 6 TO 8

I've eaten this dish in Coahuila, but it appears all over Mexico, and I've seen it on menus in both Tijuana and Hermosillo. I'm not entirely certain why it's called navigator's cactus, but it's a wonderful vegetarian stew that highlights the nopales in a mild chile-based sauce. It is usually served with a hard-boiled egg either tossed in with the stew or served alongside.

Making the stew is something of an odd, three-step process: You cook the raw nopales, make a roasted salsa, boil eggs—but put together, the sum is far tastier than the parts might suggest. You can use precooked nopales, even jarred ones, but they will be softer than freshly boiled cactus. You can also purée the Fire-Roasted Salsa on page 38 and use that, if you happen to have some lying around.

Once made, the stew will keep a couple days in the fridge, but the nopales will get sad after that.

Salsa

5 Roma tomatoes, sliced in half lengthwise

1 white onion, peeled and quartered

2 unpeeled cloves garlic

2 to 4 chipotles in adobo

4 ancho chiles, stemmed and seeded

Stew

4 cups diced nopales, about 4 paddles

Salt

½ teaspoon baking soda

3 tablespoons lard or oil

1 quart chicken or vegetable stock

¼ cup chopped fresh epazote, divided

Salt, smoked if possible

¼ cup chopped cilantro

6 eggs

To make the salsa, heat a comal, flattop, or heavy pan on medium-high. Char the tomatoes cut-side down. Let them cook until the cut faces of the tomatoes are black, then use a metal spatula to scrape it all up; you want that char. If you have room, blacken the cut sides of the onion, as well as the unpeeled garlic cloves. If not, do this after the tomatoes. When you have room on the hot surface, quickly toast the ancho chiles, maybe 15 to 30 seconds per side. Do not let these burn.

Peel the garlic, then put all of the salsa ingredients, plus the canned chipotles with some of their adobo in a blender and purée. Add water if you need to. The salsa should have the consistency of cream.

Meanwhile, boil the nopales in salted water. Make sure your pot has at least 2 inches of room above the level of the water. Boil for 8 minutes, then add the baking soda. The water will froth up, so stir constantly until this passes—this is why you need headspace in the pot. Boil another 2 to 4 minutes, then drain and rinse under cold water. Set aside.

You can also boil your eggs at this time. Set the eggs in a pot and cover with water by 1 inch. Bring to a boil, let this boil 1 minute, then turn off the heat. Let the eggs sit in the hot water for 10 minutes, then submerge in cold water and peel.

To finish the stew, heat the lard or oil in a soup pot over medium heat. Pour in the salsa and stir constantly until the fat emulsifies with the salsa. Pour in the stock and stir until it has combined with the salsa. Add the nopales, half the epazote and add salt to taste; smoked salt is excellent here. Simmer 15 minutes.

Add the rest of the epazote and the cilantro. Put a peeled, boiled egg in each person's bowl and serve the stew over it.

Tips and Variations

- You can use the salsa verde in the Chicharron en Salsa Verde (page 68) instead of the red salsa.
- You can add chopped-up carne seca if you want meat in your stew.
- Use older eggs if you can, because they peel easier.
- A little cheese, queso fresco or cotija, is a nice touch.
- You can grill all the vegetables for the salsa instead of using a comal.
- You can cook the nopales, eggs, and salsa up to a day before if you want to save time when you serve.

GAONERAS

PREP TIME: 20 MINUTES | COOK TIME: 5 MINUTES | SERVES 4 TO 6

While not quite my Deathbed Tacos (page 74), these are close. Believed to have been invented at Taqueria El Califa de León in Mexico City in the 1960s, the taco is an homage to Mexican bullfighter Rodolfo Gaona's signature move, where the torero runs at the bull with his red cape draped across his back. They are essentially a thin sheet of meat on top of a tortilla, corn in Mexico City, often flour in Monterrey.

At its most minimalist, this taco is simply a corn tortilla with a very thin piece of ribeye on top. You can then dress it as you will. In Monterrey, I ate them with a costra, that fantastic grilled cheese coating on the tortilla.

Eat enough gaoneras and you will encounter those that are too thick, or chewy, and this makes the taco tricky to eat. So I pound the meat ultra thin, then sear it in lard that has almost hit its smoking point for only a few seconds per side. It's so tender your teeth have no trouble biting through, and a topping of Hank's Taco Onions (page 46), cilantro, and a blazing hot salsa are all it needs. Want to gild the lily? Of course you do. Roast some bone marrow as in the Deathbed Tacos (page 74) and spread that on the meat before the final garnish.

Ribeye is most common, but I find venison backstrap even better because it's leaner and I can pound it thinner. A tip is to slice the meat partially frozen. Another tip is to use a bacon press to hold the meat flat in the pan. Definitely crank your stove fan on high for this one.

- 1 pound sirloin, ribeye, venison loin, etc
- Salt
- ¼ cup lard, beef tallow, or vegetable oil
- 12 to 16 corn or flour tortillas
- ½ pound shredded melty cheese, like asadero, chihuahua, mozzarella, or "Mexican blend"

For Garnish

- Hank's Taco Onions (page 46)
- Hank's Pico de Gallo (page 46)
- Chopped cilantro
- Salsa of your choice for garnish
- Marrow bones (optional)

When the meat is partially frozen, slice it thinly, about ⅛ inch. If it's a little thicker, that's OK. Put the slices between two pieces of plastic wrap and pound them very thin with a meat mallet or rubber mallet, or the side of a wine bottle. Pull off one side of the plastic and salt the meat. Repeat with the remaining slices, stacking the finished slices.

When ready to make gaoneras, I like to get a system going. Heat the oven to "warm" and put in a baking sheet with a cooling rack set in it. Make as many costras as you think you're going to eat; procedure is on page 75. Set each cheese-coated tortilla in the oven.

Heat the lard in a large pan or comal over high heat. Turn your fan on high. Sear each side of the meat for about 30 to 60 seconds. If you have a bacon press, use it to press the meat down. Add a little more salt to the meat as it comes off the pan. Ideally, you'd then set it on the costra-topped tortilla and give it to someone to dress with the various garnishes, but you can sear all the meat and put the cutlets in a pan, then build all the tacos and serve. Do not let the meat sit on the tortillas too long, or things will get soggy.

If you're adding the roasted bone marrow, make that first, then turn the oven off and use its remaining heat to keep everything warm. Scoop marrow onto the meat as you build tacos. The other garnishes go on top.

ASADO DE PUERCO

PREP TIME: 30 MINUTES | COOK TIME: 1 HOUR 30 MINUTES | SERVES 8 TO 10

Asado de puerco, or asado de boda, is a classic of northern Mexico. Rich chiles that aren't too hot, lots of pork, and spices make up this dish. The recipe is slightly different in Nuevo Leon from Sonora, and it changes in Durango and Chihuahua, too. You'll also see it called asado de boda because it's a traditional wedding dish. Head to New Mexico and you'll notice that asado de puerco bears a strong resemblance to New Mexican carne adovada (see page 154).

I've seen asado de puerco made with all sorts of cuts of pork, from shoulder—the most common—to hams to even loin. For me, this dish should be all about the shoulder. Wild hog is a great choice here as well because asado de boda is a long-simmering dish, so tougher cuts work fine. Javelina is another option.

The chiles are usually a mix of ancho and guajillo chiles, sometimes with pasilla chiles tossed in. Those are common no matter where you go. Two other flavors show up in asado de puerco that vary from place to place: orange rind and avocado pit.

I can hear you: *Who eats avocado pits?!* It is an ingredient I rarely see in recipes anywhere. But adding a little bit of the pit—about ¼ pit—adds a singular flavor that sets those versions apart. The flavor of an avocado pit is bitter, fatty, and floral all at once. I've never tasted anything like it. Start by adding no more than ⅛ pit to see how you like it. Too much will ruin the dish. They slice easily, but are slippery, so take care.

Some recipes toss in another part of the avocado, too: the leaves. Mexican avocado leaves impart a subtle anise flavor to whatever they are in, and if you can find them, use them. But they must be Mexican, because the leaves from the sorts of avocados that live in the US are not edible. Bay leaves are your obvious substitute.

I have eaten asado de puerco on corn tortillas as tacos, but mostly I see it as part of the standard platter with rice and beans. A little cotija cheese crumbled on it is a nice touch.

Leftovers will keep in the fridge for a week, and it freezes well.

- 3 pounds pork shoulder (see headnote for alternatives)
- Salt
- 3 avocado leaves or bay leaves
- 3½ ounces dried guajillo chiles (100 grams)
- 3½ ounces dried ancho or pasilla chiles (100 grams)
- 10 grams árbol or cascabel chiles (about 5 to 7)
- 4 cloves garlic, minced
- 1 teaspoon ground cumin
- 1 teaspoon dried thyme
- 5 whole cloves, crushed, or ¼ teaspoon ground
- ⅛ to ¼ avocado pit (optional)
- Stock (optional)
- ¼ cup lard, bacon fat, or oil
- Zest and juice of an orange

Cut the pork into chunks between 1 and 2 inches across and set them in a soup pot. Barely cover with water and bring this to a simmer. Skim any froth. Add salt to taste and the avocado leaves and simmer uncovered until the water has almost cooked away.

Meanwhile, set the guajillo, ancho, and árbol chiles in a bowl, pour boiling water over them, then let them steep to rehydrate. When they're soft, drain the chiles and add them, the garlic, cumin, thyme, cloves, and avocado pit to a blender. Add some water or stock and purée. You want the mixture to be about as thick as melted ice cream or housepaint.

When the water has mostly evaporated from the pot, remove the avocado leaves and add the lard. Don't toss the leaves. Turn the heat to medium-high and brown the pork, stirring often.

Once the pork has browned, pour in a little water or stock and use a wooden spoon to remove any browned bits off the bottom of the pot. Now pour in the contents of the blender and stir. Add a little water to the blender to get any good stuff out of it and add that to the pot, too. Return the avocado leaves to the pot, add the orange zest and juice, and salt everything to taste. Let this simmer until the sauce thickens a bit, about 15 to 20 minutes. Serve alongside rice and beans, or in a corn tortilla.

Variations

- Some cooks add a bottle of Mexican Coke to the mix; this is most common in Coahuila.
- You can skip the orange juice and use ¼ cup of cider vinegar.
- Sometimes you will see a little Mexican chocolate added. If you want to do this, grate half of a Mexican chocolate tablet and add it to the blender.

CARNE ADOVADA

This recipe for Asado de Puerco is so similar to New Mexican carne adovada that you can basically follow it with a few minor changes. First, skip the cloves and avocado pit. Double the cumin to 2 teaspoons. Add ¼ to ½ cup cider or white vinegar, tasting as you go. It should be sour. And if you want, swap out the cascabel or árbol chiles with one or two peppers from a can of chipotles in adobo.

Old pans hanging in the kitchen of a century-old ranch in rural Coahuila, Mexico.

CABRITO AND MACHITO

CABRITO

Suckling goat is religion in Nuevo Leon, and Monterrey has any number of palaces of cabrito dotted around the city. To be cabrito, the kid goat must have only suckled its mother's milk. Once it eats grass, it's no longer cabrito. The flavor is, as you would imagine, mild. The meat is white, and so very tender. Cabrito appears most traditionally barbecued, cut into largish pieces and served with an array of side dishes, like the Cactus Salad (page 88), and beans con veneno, charro beans with a little of the fiery red sauce from asado de puerco added.

You'll see cabrito in stews and occasionally in tacos, but normally you make your own tacos with the tortillas they give you as the roasted cabrito arrives on your table.

I did not include recipes for cabrito here because it is very difficult to get cabrito in the US outside of South Texas, where it appears in supermarkets. In an exhaustive search both in Sacramento and in the Twin Cities, I could not find proper cabrito anywhere. A larger survey proved that my experience was common all over the US. You can mail order cabrito, but it is frighteningly expensive. And even kid goat a month older than a true cabrito just isn't the same.

My advice is to mark this dish on your "to eat" list the next time you're in South Texas, or better yet, Nuevo Leon or Coahuila. You will not be disappointed.

MACHITO

A quasi sausage of a suckling goat's organs wrapped in its cleaned intestines that is then slow-grilled until crispy on the outside, machito is, seemingly, not for the faint of heart. Except that once you eat some, you'll find nothing objectionable or "barnyardy" about it—this is because the kid goats slaughtered for cabrito are so young they haven't yet begun eating grass. The flavor is fatty and crispy and smoky and the innards are tender, creamy even, and very mild. The preparation is very similar to Spanish zarajos or Greek *kokoretsi*, and I suspect that every shepherding culture has a dish like this. I do not have a recipe for it here because it's simply impossible to get suckling kid goat offal with any regularity in the United States—except in South Texas, where you can buy it in HEB supermarkets, of all places.

Should you get a chance to eat some, do it. You'll thank me later.

Patricio Wise and Cinthia Martinez prepare cabrito.

Machito, a barbecued "sausage" of suckling goat innards, is way better than it sounds.

NEW MEXICO

New Mexico is the Louisiana of the West. Like the Bayou State, New Mexico has an older, more defined culture and cuisine set apart from its neighbors Arizona, Colorado, or Utah. Chile is king, thus the Official State Question—yes, that's real—"red, green, or Christmas?" in which a server asks customers whether they want a red sauce, a green sauce, or a bit of both.

Interstate 40 is the unofficial dividing line between north and south New Mexico. South of I-40, in places like Las Cruces and Hatch, with the exception of green chile cheeseburgers and green chile grits, the fare leans more pure Mexican, while north of that highway Indigenous and Anglo influences strengthen. Both regions take pride in a great many set-piece recipes like enchiladas, posole, and carne adovada.

Those of you who speak Spanish, or know Mexican food, will note that in NewMex, it's posole not pozole, and carne adovada not carne adobada. These are emblematic of the quirks in New Mexican cuisine. It's Mexican . . . ish.

By far the biggest difference between New Mexico and neighboring Chihuahua is that in the Mexican state I've seen a far greater flexibility, idiosyncrasy, and whimsy than I have anywhere in NewMex. New Mexican cuisine feels like a rich, spicy France, where set dishes like cassoulet show up on every regional menu, and the question is who makes the dish the best. You see this with adovada, posole, green chile stew, even the iconic green chile cheeseburgers.

To be clear, I love New Mexican food. It is by far the richest and spiciest of American regional cuisines, with only Louisiana as a contender for that title. Its pillars are two: sauces and the green chile-fication of standard American Anglo favorites.

Wheat plays a huge role, as does blue corn. Lamb—even mutton—is a thing here, and there's way more pork than I would have expected for a desert state.

But then again, New Mexico is more than the desert. Much of it is above 5000 feet, and the cooler climate there is better for wool sheep and pigs than the scorching desert near the border. In the mountains, when the monsoon rains come in summer, as in Chihuahua and Arizona, you can find atop these sky islands an array of edible mushrooms both wondrous and tasty.

A petroglyph of corn in Caja del Rio, near Santa Fe, New Mexico.

New Mexico does not have a taco culture the way Mexico does. Yes, you can get tacos in many places. But they tend to either be straight-up Mexican, or, when New Mexican, are larger and filled with the beloved standards like carne adovada—very similar to asado de puerco—or shredded chicken or ground beef, then topped with a Tex-Mex-like trio of shredded yellow cheese, lettuce, and pico de gallo. Great, but nothing like, say, street tacos in Sonora or Tijuana.

Where New Mexican food shines is in cool, even cold, weather. New Mexico gets snow. It can even snow in Hatch, just an hour away from El Paso and the border. The hearty guisados of New Mexico, like green chile stew and their version of Mexico's red pozole, not to mention most of the thick, meaty Indigenous dishes, are all perfect for a place that feels very borderlands, but with ski resorts.

Their flour tortillas reflect that. New Mexican flour tortillas are markedly thicker than a Sonora-style flour tortilla, and the reason for that is those guisados—you need a thicker tortilla to sop up that stew. The translucent Sonoran tortillas are way better for a taco, but would flop with a bowl of stew.

Most of all, I love the "green chile in everything" thread in New Mexican cuisine. Green chile in New Mexico means an Anaheim-type pepper that has been roasted, skin peeled off, stemmed, and seeded. It is the chile verde of Sonora and the chilaca of Chihuahua. It can be as mild as a poblano (some are even heatless like a bell pepper), all the way to scalding. Thankfully, they are, for the most part, labeled so you don't accidentally hurt yourself. You need to know what you're working with because many green chile dishes require at least some heat, therefore many add chopped serranos or jalapeños to spice up "weak" green chile dishes.

The standards are a green chile sauce and green chile cheeseburgers, but you'll see green chile in basically everything, from cornbread and mac and cheese to queso to casseroles—even apple pie. Your imagination is your only limit.

Red chiles, normally the ripe versions of green chiles, have thinner skins and softer flesh so you don't see them in the same forms as the green ones. These are the legendary ristras of New Mexico, which many bring home as souvenirs that get dusty from disuse. The red chile, equally variable in heat as its unripe green form, is the base of the red sauce that's everywhere in the state.

A word on the sauces. Only New Mexico, which has more of an Anglo and Spanish influence than most of Mexico proper, uses a flour-and-fat roux as a base for either a red or green sauce. I've never seen this done anywhere else along the borderlands, although I bet someone somewhere does it, because it tastes great. It tames fierce chiles and makes more of a gravy than a Mexican-style sauce.

Along with Arizona and arguably El Paso, New Mexico is the citadel of American Southwestern cuisine. And to me, that means a fusion of indigenous and Mexican ingredients with more mainstream, Eurocentric cooking styles and techniques. This is not at all a bad thing.

At its most basic, Southwestern cooking can be as simple as "add green chile to everything." But the cuisine has evolved into dishes far more delicate—and durable, having been preserved over centuries in some cases—that use touches of this or that indigenous ingredient to create something unique. There is no shortage of fine dining restaurants in New Mexico, and the food at places like the Coyote Cafe in Santa Fe and the Level 5 restaurant in Albuquerque does this well.

It must be said that whole books—hefty ones, at that—are devoted to the cuisines of New Mexico and the Desert Southwest. What you see in this chapter and the Arizona chapter are simply some of my favorites.

Looking for Carne Adovada? You'll find it over in the Nuevo Leon chapter as a variant to Asado de Puerco *(page 152).*

◂ Ristras of chiles hanging at The Hatch Chile Store in Hatch, New Mexico.

GREEN CHILE GRITS

PREP TIME: 15 MINUTES | COOK TIME: 30 MINUTES | SERVES 4 TO 6

Green chile grits are common between Arizona and El Paso. Once you remember that the Anglo settlement of this region was initially dominated by people from the American South, seeing grits on a menu in, say, Bisbee, Arizona, or Deming, New Mexico makes a lot more sense.

Many recipes simply used canned roasted green chiles, and that's fine, but freshly roasted will taste better: You'll get a firmer chile, more of those blackened charred bits, and the juice that the peppers exude adds flavor to the grits.

You want real grits, not quick grits, which are an abomination. I highly recommend War Eagle grits, or Palmetto Farms, Anson Mills, or even Bob's Red Mill. If you are in a place where grits are not a thing, like North Dakota or New Hampshire, you'll have to buy online. Other than that, easy-peasy.

These grits make a great vegetarian lunch or dinner, especially if you feel like frying an egg and putting that on top. Leftovers? Pack into a container and cover while still a little warm, then set in the fridge. This will let the grits set up without creating that hardened edge on the side exposed to air. Then, when you want to serve your leftover grits, they'll still be sticky enough so you can dust them in cornmeal or flour and fry crispy.

- 4 tablespoons butter, divided
- ½ cup minced white or yellow onion
- 2 cloves garlic, minced
- 4½ cups water
- Salt
- 1 cup grits
- 2 to 5 roasted green chiles, chopped, about 1 cup
- 1 teaspoon dried Mexican oregano or marjoram
- 1 cup shredded longhorn, Jack, or Chihuahua cheese
- 1 serrano pepper, seeded and minced
- ¼ cup minced cilantro
- Black pepper

Heat 2 tablespoons of the butter in a medium pot over medium heat. Cook the onions and garlic until soft and translucent, but not browned, about 4 minutes. Stir occasionally, and salt them a bit as they cook.

Add the water and a pinch of salt and bring this to a boil over high heat. Turn the heat to medium and pour in the grits in a stream, stirring constantly in one direction; this helps prevent lumps. Stir well and lower the heat so the mixture is simmering, not roiling. Cook this for about 15 minutes, stirring often to prevent the bottom from sticking and scorching.

When the grits are close—they need to be soft and creamy, not, well, gritty—stir in the Mexican oregano and the chopped green chiles, with any juices that have collected. Let this cook another 5 minutes. Note that you want the grits to be loose, so you might need to stir in a little more water.

Stir in the minced serrano, the cheese, and the remaining 2 tablespoons butter. When this has fully melted in, taste the grits and add salt if needed. Add some black pepper and a little of the chopped cilantro.

Options

- You can mince cilantro stems from your bunch and add them to the grits when you add the green chiles. You can also thinly slice another serrano for a spicy garnish, or fry an egg to your liking and top your grits with it.
- If you want to, you can add chicken or vegetable stock up to 50 percent of the water needed. More than that and you'll discolor the grits, and get too strong a broth flavor, which detracts from the green chile flavor.

STEAK DUNIGAN

PREP TIME: 15 MINUTES, IF YOU ALREADY HAVE ROASTED CHILES | COOK TIME: 30 MINUTES | SERVES 4

After a great mushroom hunt in the high country of New Mexico, laden with red-capped porcini, I was at a party and said that I wanted to make a dish with both wild mushrooms *and* green chile, in honor of New Mexico. Several people said, almost in unison, "Steak Dunigan." *Never heard of it.* They said it has been a standard at the venerable Santa Fe restaurant the Pink Adobe for generations, named for a patron—Pat Dunigan, best I can tell—who wanted green chiles with his steak. Good man.

A few recipes for Steak Dunigan pop up online, even one from the famous singer Dan Fogelberg, who apparently loved the dish. It's steak, mushrooms, onions, green chiles, and maybe garlic. Butter is the typical cooking fat. What's not to love?

There's nothing difficult about this dish. It's easy enough to make on a weeknight. You can use any sort of mushroom you like, and any cut of steak you like.

I used those New Mexico porcini and venison steak, along with roasted green chiles given to me by my friend Jesse Deubel of the New Mexico Wildlife Federation. They were spicy, so I didn't need extra heat in the dish, but if your green chiles are mild—all Anaheims will be in the supermarket—I suggest adding a minced serrano or a few jalapeños.

Steak Dunigan is great with crusty bread or rice, and it's damn good if you chop everything up and put it in a tortilla as a taco or a burrito. I ate leftovers right out of the fridge the next day.

1½ pounds to 2½ pounds steak, any kind

Salt and black pepper

2 to 3 tablespoons lard, butter, or oil

1 cup minced onion

1 cup minced mushrooms (see Options)

1 large clove garlic, minced

1 cup chopped roasted green chiles

1 minced serrano chile, if the green chile is mild

½ teaspoon dried Mexican oregano (regular oregano is OK)

1 to 2 tablespoons minced fresh cilantro

Porcini powder (optional)

Take the steaks out of the fridge and salt them well. Chop and mince everything else while the meat comes to room temp.

Heat the lard or oil in a large pan over medium-high heat. Cook the onions until they start to brown, maybe 6 minutes, stirring occasionally, and then add the minced mushrooms. Cook these until they brown, too, which will take another 4 to 6 minutes. Keep stirring once in a while, but not too often because you want some nice browning. This is important for flavor.

When the onions and mushrooms are pretty and brown, stir in the garlic and cook 1 more minute, then add the chopped green chiles and the serrano. Add the oregano and salt and mix well. Cook this another minute or three. You want it just a little wet, but not soupy, so you might want to add a splash of stock, water or beer to the pan. If you have any stuck-on bits in the pan definitely do this—the chiles often wet the pan enough to release the browned bits.

Turn off the heat, mix in the cilantro and add more salt and black pepper to taste. Set this aside.

Get another pan hot over medium-high heat, then add a high-smoke-point oil like grapeseed, canola, safflower or avocado. Get this hot. Pat the steaks dry with paper towels, then set them in the hot pan. Sear untouched a minute or three, then flip to sear the other side. Turn the heat to medium or even medium-low if the steaks are thick, and keep cooking, flipping occasionally, until they are done to your liking. I prefer medium-rare.

Remove the steaks to a cutting board, grind black pepper over them, and sprinkle porcini powder on both sides, if you're using it. Let the steaks rest 5 to 10 minutes.

To serve, put some of the sauce on a plate and top with a steak, or vice versa. Up to you.

BONUS STEP: If you want to be fancy, you can leave out some mushroom caps, slice, and crisp them up in a pan for garnish. Definitely do this if you are lucky enough to have some little porcini buttons! And if you have pretty little chanterelles? Sauté some whole and add to the mix—the contrast of green chile and yellow chanterelles is gorgeous!

Options

- I prefer to roast, peel, and seed my green chiles. Frozen roasted chiles work fine, and if you are pressed for time, canned ones are OK. Not great, but better than nothing.
- Literally any mushroom you can cook in butter or lard works here.
- I used venison backstrap steaks. You can use any red meat, and pork chops would be great with this sauce. So would a tuna steak.

GREEN CHILE CHEESEBURGER

PREP TIME: 20 MINUTES | COOK TIME: 10 MINUTES | SERVES 4

Chances are, if you've been anywhere from Texas to Colorado to Southern California, you've at least heard of a green chile burger. It's an icon in the Southwest. What makes them so special? The green chiles, of course. I use Hatch. Freshly roasted is best, but you can use thawed ones or even canned. And there's no reason other than authenticity not to use some other green chile, or even a red one if you wanted to made red chile burgers or somesuch. Poblanos are an excellent supermarket substitute.

And, as you can see in the picture, green chile burgers are almost always actually green chile cheeseburgers, because you use cheese to glue the chiles onto the burger patties. What cheese you use is up to you, but American, Cheddar, and Monterey Jack, specifically pepper Jack, are most common.

Making Burger Patties

If you've read any of my other books, you know that I am particular about hamburgers. I've worked at restaurants that specialized in serious burgers, so I got my personal rules from there. Short version: A perfect burger is just meat, fat (pork or beef), and salt. And the salt is added after you make the patties. You choose whether you like them thick or thin.

Your grind matters. The finer the grind, the thinner the patty can be. If you want to make thin, diner-style patties for something like a smash burger, you will need a fine grind. Grilled burgers are better with a coarser grind.

Either way, when you form your burger patties, make sure you press an indentation in the centers. This keeps your burger from balling up when it cooks. This happens because when raw meat hits the hot pan, it contracts. The indentation in the center offsets this.

Salting the outside of the patties, not the mix, helps keep the burger slightly loose and tender. Think crab cake, not meatball.

Cooking

Like all hamburgers, you have your choice of cooking methods. When it's warm out, I grill my burgers, and when it's cool, I use either a cast iron skillet or some other pan that can handle high heat. Nonstick is out.

Depending on how hot your heat is, it will take about 3 to 5 minutes per side for a burger cooked medium, which is how I like my mine. Add or subtract time if you like your burgers rare or well-done.

After you flip, grind some black pepper on the burgers, lay down the chiles and top with cheese. Now bring the lid down on the grill or cover the pan with a lid to melt the cheese. It should be nicely melted by the time the other side is ready.

Toppings

Other than the green chile and cheese, it's up to you. I do like the classic lettuce and tomato, and if your green chiles are mild, a good splash of hot sauce. Ketchup is common, as is mayo. Try the Serrano Crema (page 72). You can play around as much as you like.

Keep it simple. Use great ingredients. You won't be sorry.

▶

4 to 8 green chiles, such as Hatch, poblano, or Anaheim

1¼ pounds ground elk or other meat

Salt

Canola, grapeseed, or safflower oil

4 large slices tomato

4 to 8 lettuce leaves

4 burger buns

2 tablespoons butter or vegetable oil

4 slices Cheddar or Monterey Jack cheese

If you are starting with fresh chiles, roast them, remove the skins and seeds, salt them, and set aside. You can either keep them in fairly large pieces if they are well-roasted, or chop them coarsely. This can be done a few days ahead of time, and of course you can use canned or frozen chiles.

Make four burger patties. I prefer ⅓-pound burgers, but you can make them any size you want. Pro tips: Press the weighed-out, ground meat into a large circle mold for more evenly shaped patties. Press a dimple about the diameter of a walnut in the center of each patty. Salt your patties.

Cooking Options

Grilling: Get your grill hot. Scrape down the grates well, and grill your burgers with the grill cover open. Leave them on the grates for at least 3 or 4 minutes so you get grill marks and a good crust. Flip and cook to order. Typically a medium burger will need another 3 minutes.

Stovetop: Preheat oven to 200°F and set a rack over a baking sheet. Heat a cast iron pan or pan that can handle high heat over medium-high heat. When it's hot, slick the pan with some canola or other high-smoke-point oil, like grapeseed or safflower. Set the patties down and press gently with a spatula to get good contact with the pan. Cook as above.

No matter how you cook your burgers, when you flip them, lay the chiles over them, then cover with a slice of cheese. Close the grill cover or put a lid over the pan to melt the cheese.

On the stovetop, you usually have to cook in batches, so you will put each finished burger in the warm oven as you do the rest.

When you are ready, paint your burger buns with the butter or oil and set them on the grill or pan to brown. Keep an eye on the buns so they don't burn. Set aside once browned to your liking.

Build your burgers. I like to go bun, lettuce, tomato slice, patty, bun. But do whatever you like best. Enjoy!

Keys to Success

- If you are grinding your own meat, make sure to have some fat in your burger patties, otherwise they will be dry and will fall apart. Absolute minimum would be 5%, but most people prefer 15%. Any meat works here, not only beef or venison.
- Don't skip the indentation step in making the patties, unless you are going to make smashburgers.
- If you are worried about undercooked burgers, leave the patties out on a cutting board for 30 minutes or so before you cook them. Salt them at this time.

GREEN CHILE STEW

PREP TIME: 20 MINUTES | COOK TIME: 2 TO 3 HOURS | SERVES 8

When you make a recipe with only a few ingredients, technique becomes more important. Such is the case with green chile stew. It's a New Mexico favorite, but you will see it all over the borderlands.

Green chile stew is almost always made with either beef or pork; I used venison. All of these meats are ideal, and javelina, bison, elk, moose, lamb or mutton, or goat would all be fine.

Variations exist with this recipe. Some use tomato; I do not. Some use either sweet or field corn; I do. Most use potatoes, lots of roasted, peeled, and seeded green chiles—Hatch (Anaheims) would be natural here—and all feature a touch of cumin, garlic, and onions.

Some versions use no thickener. Some use a flour-and-fat roux. I use the old European technique of flouring the meat first, then browning. Over time, the flour in the pot that comes off the meat will thicken the stew.

And thickness is your call, too. What I like to do is make the initial batch properly stewy, as you see in the picture here. You eat it with a spoon and there is broth. Later, however, I will cook it down, and smash the potatoes and meat with a potato masher, and then it becomes more of a Mexican guisado, and in fact it is similar to my recipe for venison carne guisada on page 97.

Pro tip: Use this thickened, cooked-down green chile stew as a filling for empanadas, burritos, or as a taco filling. Here you definitely want flour tortillas.

About technique. You want to take your time browning both the meat and the onions because this makes or breaks the stew. Be patient.

Also, you will want to determine how much you want to actually see the roasted green chiles. They will dissolve as they cook, so you will either have them as a ghostly presence in your stew, or, if you put them in during the final 30 minutes, you'll have them as a vegetable. Up to you. I do both. Mild chiles go in early, hot ones late.

Which chiles you use is also a judgment call. Ideally, you would use Hatch chiles from New Mexico. But Anaheims are the same basic variety. Poblanos are an excellent alternative, but any large, not overly hot green chile will work. And you can use canned or dried.

Finally, corn or no corn? I like using chicos, the dried corn common in the Southwest. It's firm, even after long cooking, and starchy, not sweet. Use chicos if you can get them, otherwise simple fresh or frozen sweet corn is fine. Or leave it out.

Once made, this will keep in the fridge a week. It can be pressure-canned or frozen, too.

- 1 cup dried field corn (chicos), (optional)
- ¼ cup vegetable oil or lard, divided
- 2 to 3 pounds venison stew meat, or beef or pork
- Salt
- ½ cup flour
- 2 cups chopped white or yellow onions
- 4 cloves garlic, chopped
- 1 tablespoon cumin
- 1 tablespoon Mexican oregano (optional)
- 1 quart venison or beef broth
- 1 pound roasted, seeded green chiles, chopped
- 1½ pounds Yukon gold potatoes, cut in chunks
- Black pepper and hot sauce to taste

If you are using the dried corn, put it in a pot of water and start boiling it before you start anything else, because it can take a long time to soften.

Salt the venison well, then dust it in the flour, pressing the flour into the meat. Heat 2 or 3 tablespoons of the lard or vegetable oil in a Dutch oven or similar pot set over medium-high heat.

When the oil is hot, brown the meat in batches. Make sure no piece is touching another, and take your time with this. You want each piece well browned. Move them to a bowl as you go. You will likely need to add another tablespoon of oil late in this process.

When the meat is all browned, add the final tablespoon of oil and the onions. Stir this well, as the moisture from the onions will deglaze the pot. You want that. Sauté the onions until they too are nicely browned. This whole process, meat and onions, can take 30 minutes or more.

Add the garlic to the pot, stir well, and cook a minute or two. Return the meat and all of the accumulated juices in the bowl to the Dutch oven. Add the cumin, oregano, and broth, then a quart or even two of water. Stir and bring to a simmer. Add salt to taste. If you are using the field corn, use a slotted spoon to move it from the plain water to the Dutch oven now to continue cooking. Save the corn water, and use it to top up the stew if you need to later.

If you want green chiles as an invisible presence in your stew, add them now. Or add some now and some later. Regardless, simmer the stew until the meat is mostly tender, anywhere from an hour for pork to 3 hours for an old deer or elk.

When the meat is getting close, add the potatoes and chiles, if you haven't already. You can add sweet corn here, too, if that's the choice you made. Simmer gently until the potatoes are ready, then add salt and pepper and serve with hot sauce.

> "Coyote is out there waiting. And Coyote is always hungry."
>
> Navajo saying

GREEN CHILE MAC AND CHEESE

PREP TIME: 30 MINUTES | COOK TIME: 45 MINUTES | SERVES 8

Sometimes you just want macaroni and cheese, right? I've seen recipes for green chile mac and cheese in several of those homey, spiral-bound cookbooks that the Junior League or somesuch puts out in places like El Paso and Santa Fe and Lordsburg.

Many times they will include shredded chicken, so really any white meat works, from turkey to rabbit, pheasant, quail, you name it. I actually think shrimp or crawfish tails would be good, too. Or skip the meat.

This is one of those cases where you really do want good roasted green chiles, either professionally roasted and frozen, or one you've roasted yourself. Canned chiles will make a weak mac and cheese.

Everyone makes mac and cheese differently. My mom made it the old-fashioned way, with buttery breadcrumbs on top, casserole style, with lots of cheese and not a ton of sauce. So that's how I make it, too. If you want a saucier mac and cheese, add up to 1 extra cup of whole milk. And it needs to be whole milk, or half-and-half. Lowfat milk can separate in this cooking process, which is gross.

You will be adding in the meat towards the end, so it needs to be precooked. If you are using pheasant, chicken, quail, turkey breast, etc., I recommend that you poach it in some broth, or even salted water if you don't have any broth handy. This method will keep the meat tender.

- 1 pound pasta, cooked and drained
- 5 tablespoons butter
- 1 large white or yellow onion, chopped
- 3 cloves garlic, minced
- 1 tablespoon dried Mexican oregano (optional)
- 1½ cups chopped roasted green chiles (see headnote)
- 5 tablespoons all-purpose flour
- 2 cups half-and-half
- ½ cup whole milk
- 1½ cups shredded Gruyère cheese (or similar)
- 1 cup shredded white Cheddar cheese
- ½ cup grated pecorino or Parmesan cheese
- 8 ounces shredded cooked pheasant or chicken (about 1 cup)
- ¼ cup chopped cilantro or parsley
- ½ cup breadcrumbs

Heat the butter in a large sauté pan over medium-high heat. Sauté the onion for about 5 minutes, stirring often, then add the garlic and cook another minute. Preheat the oven to 350°F.

Add the flour to the pan and stir it in well. Drop the heat to medium, and let the flour cook a few minutes, stirring often. You don't want the flour to brown, but you do want it to color a bit. Look for an ivory-beige color, which should take about 5 minutes.

Stir in the roasted green chiles and the oregano, if using. Now start stirring in the half-and-half and whole milk, little by little. Do this about ½ cup at a time, stirring each time. Wait until the mixture begins to simmer before adding the next ½ cup.

When the cream and milk are all in there, start doing the same thing with the shredded cheeses, adding them about ½ cup at a time, stirring until they are melted and incorporated before adding the next ½ cup. Mix in the cilantro and add salt and black pepper to taste.

Stir in the cooked pasta and the meat. Move all this to a casserole dish (a standard 9 by 13-inch pan is what I use), and pack it down evenly. Top with the breadcrumbs. If you want to add other seasoning—I'd suggest chile powder—do that now. You can also dot the top with more butter if you'd like.

Bake this uncovered for about 25 minutes, or until the breadcrumbs start to brown. Take the casserole out and let it sit for 5 minutes before serving.

BISCOCHITOS COOKIES

PREP TIME: 20 MINUTES | COOK TIME: 15 MINUTES PER BATCH | MAKES 6 DOZEN SMALL COOKIES

Biscochitos are an easy-to-make little sugar cookie very popular in New Mexico; most are flavored with either anise extract or anise seeds. There are similar cookies throughout the borderlands. Hojarascas are almost identical, and are common in South Texas, Tamaulipas, Coahuila, and Nuevo Leon.

Biscochitos are great as a snack or simple dessert, especially alongside ice cream. Pine nut ice cream would be my recommendation. They're fantastic road trip snacks, or good with your morning coffee. They're sweet enough so that unsweetened coffee really balances it all out. If you prefer a less sweet cookie, you can reduce the sugar by ¼ cup.

I got my recipe from Viola Vigil, a friend of my friend Jesse Deubel in Albuquerque. Hilariously, the original recipe makes "approximately 20 dozen." Um, great if you are serving an army. I tinkered with the recipe to make it closer to something a smaller group would love.

They'll keep a week, covered, at room temperature.

- 1 cup sugar
- 2 teaspoons ground cinnamon
- ⅓ pound of lard or room temperature butter
- 1 egg
- 1 teaspoon anise seeds (optional)
- 1 teaspoon anise or vanilla extract
- 2 cups cake or all-purpose flour
- 1 teaspoon baking powder
- Pinch of salt
- 1 tablespoon water

Preheat the oven to 350°F. Either grease 2 baking sheets with butter, or line them with parchment paper.

In a small bowl, combine ¼ cup sugar with the cinnamon.

In a large bowl, beat the lard or butter with the remaining sugar until it's fluffy. Beat in the anise extract and the egg.

Mix the flour, baking powder, and salt in another bowl, then mix this in with the wet ingredients. Sprinkle over the anise seeds, if using. Add the water and mix it all well.

Roll this dough on a floured surface to a thickness of about ¼ inch or a little thinner. Use a cookie cutter to cut out small cookies. I use a 1½-inch round cutter, but you can vary the cookies as you wish. Move the cookies to the baking sheet—spacing them at least 1 inch apart—and sprinkle with the cinnamon sugar.

Bake for 12 to 15 minutes, until the cookies' edges start to brown. Let them cool on the baking sheet for 10 minutes or more, then you can move them to a cooling rack. They are best eaten at room temperature.

SOPAPILLAS

PREP TIME: 25 MINUTES | COOK TIME: 10 MINUTES | MAKES 24 SOPAPILLAS

Beloved in New Mexico, common in Chihuahua, and rare everywhere else, sopapillas are a staple for both sweet and savory meals. They are, more or less, fried bits of flour tortilla—squares, rectangles, and triangles are most common—that can either be served sweet or savory.

I love them alongside green chile stew (page 167), carne adovada or any of the myriad, comforting stews of that state. Add a bit of sugar to the dough, and drizzle the sopapillas with honey, and you have the snack of snacks, or a dreamy dessert next to pine nut ice cream.

My sopapilla recipe is an amalgam of several I've received from friends.

2 cups flour

1½ teaspoons baking powder

1 teaspoon salt

3 tablespoons lard or butter (room temperature)

¾ cup water or milk

Oil for frying

Mix together the flour, baking powder and salt. Work the lard or butter into the dry ingredients until the mixture looks like a coarse meal. Add the water, then mix and knead the dough until it is smooth. Divide the dough into 8 balls. Put the balls in a plastic bag and let this rest for 20 minutes to 1 hour.

Heat a few inches' worth of oil in a pot over medium-high heat until temperature reaches 360°F. Turn your oven to "warm" and set a baking sheet with a cooling rack inside.

Using a rolling pin or a tortilla press, roll out the dough into what are essentially flour tortillas. Slice each tortilla into quarters. Add those pieces, one at a time, and fry until puffy and golden brown, about 15 to 30 seconds per side. You'll likely need to do this in batches.

As they finish, move the sopapillas to the cooling rack in the oven.

TIP: For a more interesting texture, before frying use a knife to slice shallow little slashes in each triangle from cut side to cut side. When they fry, it will alter the shape of the sopapilla. I learned this trick from Pati Jinich.

FRY BREAD

Fry bread is very close to sopapillas. A product of colonialism—and a controversial food item in the Indigenous community—fry bread is reviled by some, and embraced by others who view it as an example of Native ingenuity; making something delicious from very little. Well-made fry bread is absolutely delicious, and is not overly greasy (despite the popular song of that name). It's mostly used as a sort of hybrid flatbread/tostada, topped with meat and traditional New Mexican taco toppings: shredded lettuce, pico de gallo, yellow shredded cheese. It can also be served sprinkled with sugar, like a giant Italian zeppole.

I've seen fry bread recipes exactly like the sopapilla recipe above, notably Juanita Tiger Kavena's in her book *Hopi Cookery.* Most Navajo fry bread recipes substitute the lard with full-fat powdered milk.

The biggest difference in execution is that once you make the dough, you make only 4 balls, and you need not press them in a tortilla press. Simply roll or even flatten with your hands into a disk that you then fry in hot oil. I suggest you double the sopapilla recipe if you're making fry bread.

PINE NUT ICE CREAM

PREP TIME: 15 MINUTES | COOK TIME: 30 MINUTES | SERVES 8 TO 10

Pine nuts and honey are a great combination, and you don't need to get an esoteric honey for this recipe. And while I use Mexican or American pine nuts, you can use any pine nuts. Italian stone pine nuts are an excellent, if expensive, alternative.

You will need an ice cream maker to make this.

- 1 cup shelled pine nuts
- 2 cups whole milk
- 2 cups heavy cream
- ¾ cup honey, plus more for drizzling
- ½ vanilla bean, scraped, or 1 teaspoon vanilla extract
- Pinch of salt
- 5 egg yolks

Toast the pine nuts in a dry pan on medium-high heat until they begin to brown. Keep an eye on them, as pine nuts can burn very easily. As soon as they start to brown, move the nuts to a bowl and set aside.

Put the pine nuts and the remaining ingredients (except the egg yolks) into a heavy pot and heat to steaming over medium heat. If you have a thermometer, you want the cream to get to 160°F or so. Turn off the heat, cover and let steep for 1 hour. Refrigerate until cold, up to a day.

Strain the mixture and discard the vanilla bean. Save the pine nuts and reserve.

Reheat the cream mixture over medium heat to 160°F. Beat the egg yolks slightly in a bowl. Now, using two hands—one with a small ladle, the other with a whisk—slowly pour in some of the hot cream into the egg yolks, using your whisk hand to whisk in the hot cream. Do this a little at a time so you don't scramble your eggs.

After you have 2 to 3 ladles in the egg yolk bowl, start whisking the hot cream mixture in the pot. Slowly pour in the hot egg yolk–cream mix and whisk well. Allow this to cook below a simmer, stirring often, for 5 minutes. It will thicken.

Strain the mixture once again and chill. Once chilled, pour it into your ice cream maker. Allow the ice cream to churn until it's a soft-serve consistency. Move the ice cream to a large, chilled bowl and fold in the pine nuts. Chill hard, then serve with some honey drizzled over the top. Note that prep time does not include the chill time for the custard.

PINE NUTS IN THE BORDERLANDS

Two nuts dominate the cuisine of the borderlands: pecans and pine nuts. Most of the pecans are farmed, most of the pine nuts are wild. Universally known as piñons, or more properly piñones in Spanish, there are two main kinds: *Pinus edulis* and *P. cembroides*.

P. edulis is by far the most common. I've seen them for sale all over Arizona, Sonora, Baja, and New Mexico, and the trees range up into Utah; incidentally, there is a third piñon, *P. monophylla*, which I picked for years in California, that lives mostly in Nevada, but is does occur in Utah and Arizona, too. *Edulis* and *monophylla* both yield ivory-colored nuts that are one of the most delicious foods I have ever eaten: so rich in fat, vitamins and carbohydrates, even a handful will sustain you all day in the woods.

The pink nuts of *Pinus cenoides* are prized in Mexico.

(Another edible pine nut comes from California's *P. sabiniana*, the gray pine. These nuts are excellent, but their shells are so tough they need to be cracked with vise grip pliers.)

Mexico prizes *P. cembroides*. This is the pink pine nut, little known outside Mexico—although I have seen them for sale online. This pine nut is noticeably sweeter than its cousins, and commands a price several times higher than the others. It's almost exclusively used in sweet preparations, while the other two are perfectly at home in either sweet or savory dishes.

Cembroides lives mainly in both Sierra Madre mountain ranges, but interestingly, you can find them in the Chisos and Davis mountains of southwest Texas, near Big Bend and Marfa.

Look to buy in-shell pine nuts from early autumn through spring. I've seen American pine nuts for sale online, too. Alas, it is very difficult to find them shelled.

The best way I've found to shell pine nuts for recipes—as opposed to eating them like a vastly superior sunflower seed—is to lay nuts on a terrycloth towel in one layer, then cover with another terrycloth towel, then roll over it all with a rolling pin. This will crack the shells, many of which will stick in the terrycloth. It's still tedious, but is still faster than trying to crack them one at a time.

If you buy online, check that they are American or Mexican pine nuts, not piñons from China. The vast majority of all pine nuts sold in the United States are from China. It is believed that nuts from the Asian tree *Pinus armandii* are the cause of the dreaded "pine mouth," which causes everything you eat to taste metallic for days or even weeks. But recent research suggests that it could be caused by a person's genetics, no matter what species of pine nut they eat. This is similar to why some people think cilantro tastes soapy. The science remains unclear.

Store pine nuts in the fridge or freezer, as their fats go rancid relatively quickly. Frozen and in the shell, they will keep for a couple years.

CHIHUAHUA

If you wanted to sum up the cuisine of the Mexican state of Chihuahua, you could do worse than the dish I ate for lunch one day at Los Mezquites in the capital city: seared skirt steak with roasted green chiles and lots of melty cheese, served with flour tortillas. These three ingredients—beef, green chiles, and cheese—dominate, but the cuisine is much, much more diverse than that.

Climate and culture dictate any cuisine, and that of Chihuahua is no different. The majority of the Chihuahan Desert lies within the state, and this desert is higher and starker than the neighboring Sonoran Desert. It snows on the regular in the city of Chihuahua. And where Sonora's native influences are primarily Tohono O'Odham, Yaqui, Mayo, and Seri, the Apache, Pima. and Tarahumara dominate in Chihuahua.

Desert living means drying things, and no one does it better than Chihuahua. Chiles pasados—roasted, peeled, dried green chiles—are everywhere. As is carne seca and the machaca made from it.

Chihuahua's take on what most Americans know as chili is called guisado de abigeo, cattle rustler's stew, made with beef jerky, beans, chiles, onions, garlic, and often potatoes. While mostly a home-cooked dish, you can find it in some restaurants specializing in classic Chihuahuan dishes.

In every market you'll find chacales, called chicos in New Mexico, a variety of dried corn: Unhusked ears are roasted, then dried, kernels taken off the cob and cracked for eating later. They're then stewed in things like green chile stew. You actually want them beat up and crushed a bit, so the starch gets into the broth.

Pinole is a big deal, too. Normally pinole is corn flour, but the Tarahumara made this stuff famous because they add seeds of the superfood chia to it, and their legendary long-distance running abilities eating mostly pinole diet have helped make chia a worldwide commodity.

Chihuahua, like Sonora, is in love with the globular wild chiltepin chiles; the bullet-shaped chiles pequins start to dominate one state to the east, in Coahuila.

Lunch at Los Mezquites is about as Chihuahua as you get.

Unlike Baja, fish and seafood play only a minor role here—although Chihuahua is the main place to find actual, real wild trout in Mexico, and there's a catfish stew confusingly called caldo de oso that's big here, too. (Oso means bear but there's no bear in it.) Higher-end places, like my friend Chris Duthoy's Sulawe, will fly in fish, but if you are going to a mom-and-pop place for seafood, maybe only go to restaurants with big lines.

Nowhere else in Mexico does cheese play a more important role. So many varieties, many named for the towns they come from, most melty and semisoft. A big reason for this has been Mennonite immigrants, who first began coming to Chihuahua a century ago.

Queso fundido, which is to Texas queso what the sun is to a match, is everywhere, usually with roasted "chilaca" chiles in it; the quotes around chilaca are because the long, skinny, dark green

chile chilaca in the rest of Mexico is not the chilaca of Chihuahua. Here, a chilaca is a synonym for a Hatch/Anaheim/chile verde chile.

The signature snack of the city of Chihuahua, the montado, requires a healthy bit of melty cheese, too. A montado is a giant flour tortilla with cheese and beef (usually) inside, that you then open and add whatever toppings you want inside before closing and rolling like an impromptu burrito. The montado alambre, which adds grilled onions and peppers to the beef, is especially good at El Tren near the city's center.

Beef in general is excellent here, although I'd say Sonoran beef is a bit better. There's more pork in Chihuahua than Sonora and Baja, but other than the ubiquitous al pastor tacos, it isn't as prevalent as in, say, New Mexico. Chicken is nonexistent other than whole roasted pollos asados or, oddly, wing restaurants. There's even a Buffalo Wild Wings in Chihuahua. Don't go there.

Underpinning everything in the city are the Tarahumara, the region's most numerous Indigenous group. Statues of famous Tarahumara dot the city. Tarahumara women wear their bright dresses everywhere, a happy, gaudy change from the dusty city. Chihuahua does a lot to advance their visibility, and you can easily buy crafts either directly from them on the street, or in one of several nonprofits set up to aggregate Tarahumara artists' works and funnel the profits back to them.

Foodwise, the most interesting ingredient the Tarahumara (also known as the Rarámuri) bring to the table is arí, a resin made by ants on a shrub that only lives in the region. The resin is crushed with citrus and salt and chiltepin chiles for a simple, umami-rich salsa.

The strong influence of native groups in Chihuahua also brings corn to the fore far more than in neighboring Sonora. Corn tortillas are generally factory-made, wretched things in Sonora and Baja. Not so in Chihuahua.

You can definitely thank the Indigenous groups for that, and one of the best bites you'll find is a knockout quesadilla with melty cheese, squash blossoms or fresh huitlacoche (a corn mushroom), on a blue or green corn tortilla made right on the spot at the city center's farmers market.

Where tequila is Jalisco, mezcal is Oaxaca, and bacanora is Sonora, sotol is Chihuahua. Sotol is as idiosyncratic a drink as any other Mexican spirit, and each distillers' personality lurks within each bottle. A great place to sample a ton of sotol is El Magico, a bar near the city center. If you're nice, they may pour you a swig of chuchos, an infusion of sotol with the herb *Ligusticum porteri*, known as oshá in the United States. (see page 111)

Beerwise, Chihuahua is a pivot point between Carta Blanca and Tecate. Both are good. And there are a growing number of excellent Mexican craft beers, too. I recommend a night at the brewpub El Gardenia.

When it comes to sweets, get ready for an onslaught of pecans and apples. Chihuahua is Mexico's main producer of both. You'll see literally anything you can do with pecans, apples, and the local pine nuts—there's even a pink one. Cookies, pies, cakes, candies, you name it. And, thanks to the Mennonites, you can literally say something's "as Chihuahuan as apple pie." Pretty cool, no?

The murals of the City of Chihuahua range from whimsical to political.

CHILES PASADOS

PREP TIME: 30 MINUTES | COOK TIME: 35 MINUTES | DRYING TIME: 2 DAYS OR UP TO A WEEK

The quintessential ingredient of Chihuahua and Durango, these are, to my knowledge, the only instance of dried roasted and skinned green chiles in all of Mexico. Literally meaning stale or worn chiles, you can make them with a dehydrator or you can do it the old-fashioned way, by hanging the skinned chiles from their stems in the hot, breezy shade.

Why bother doing this? First, because it's really interesting. Second, the dried chiles are light and portable and need no refrigeration. Third, they taste great and pop up in so many Chihuahuan recipes. The rehydrated fire-roasted green chiles, when added to tacos or included in tamales or in a guisado, are similar but different from their fresh cousins. Their texture is meatier, and the flavor more concentrated.

Traditionally you would use a Hatch-style chile, like an Anaheim. They can be either hot or mild. Poblanos work, too, but are not traditional.

10 green Hatch-style chiles like Anaheim or poblanos

Roast the chiles. I do this over an open gas flame on my stovetop, but it's better done over a ragingly hot, smoky wood fire. You don't want to really cook the chiles, which is why I don't use my broiler or oven, but if this is all you have, go for it—broil the chiles, turning often.

I char the skins of the chiles over the open flame until they are almost universally black.

When you've blackened each chile, put it in a covered bowl to steam. When they're all done, let them steam until cool enough to work with. Remove the skins. I do this by scraping the skins off with a butter knife, from stem towards the point. Do not rinse the chiles, as this removes a lot of flavor.

To dry your chiles, hang them by the stem with the string in a hot, airy, dry place, like a garage in summer, or under a porch. Do not sun-dry them, as this will bleach the chiles. Shade is key.

Alternatively, you can dry your chiles pasados in a dehydrator set at about 115°F, more or less.

There's a trick to this: The section of the chile closest to the stem will take a long time to fully dry. When you hang the chiles, it dries them more evenly. If you are dehydrating, you will need to turn the chiles over a few times. It can take a full day in a dehydrator, up to a week in open air.

To speed things up, you can remove the stems, open the peppers up, and remove the seeds, then lay them flat in a dehydrator.

CHILE CON QUESO

PREP TIME: 15 MINUTES, IF YOU ALREADY HAVE ROASTED GREEN CHILES | COOK TIME: 15 MINUTES | SERVES 4

It's tough to contemplate borderlands food without thinking about queso. If, in your head, you're saying that word with a Texas accent, this is not *that* queso. Banish me from the Lone Star State if you must, but I am not a fan of typical Texas queso . . . until you get to El Paso, where it's like this. Queso fundido is popular in neighboring Coahuila and Nuevo Leon, but my all-time favorite is the Chihuahuan version, loaded with roasted green chiles. It's easy to make, especially if you have the roasted green chiles handy. Canned are OK, but fresh or thawed ones are better.

Obviously, since this is a molten cheese dish it should be eaten straight away, either with tortillas or as a filling for a burrito or even on toasty bread. It's just barely too thick and gooey for tortilla chips—unless you add more half-and-half or crema. If this is what you want, keep adding until you get something less molten and thick, and more flowy and dippy.

2 tablespoons butter

½ white onion, chopped

2 cloves garlic, minced

½ teaspoon dried Mexican oregano

5 green chiles, roasted, skinned, seeded, and chopped (roughly 1 cup)

1 cup full-fat milk, Mexican crema, or half-and-half

4 cups shredded melty cheese, ideally queso Chihuahua or asadero (about 12 to 14 ounces)

Black pepper

Heat the butter in a large pan and sauté the onions over medium-high heat until translucent, but not browned. Add the garlic, oregano, and green chiles—along with any juices or charred flecks on the cutting board—into the pan and cook, stirring occasionally, for 10 minutes.

Stir in the milk or crema and turn the heat to low. See the headnotes for exactly how much to use for different styles of queso. After everything gets hot, stir the cheese in, a little at a time, adding more when the previous bit has melted.

Taste and add salt if needed; it depends on the cheese. Grind some black pepper over it all and serve.

To keep the cheese melted, serve it from the pan on a trivet on the table, or warm a bowl in the oven while you make the queso.

Variations

- If you use poblano peppers, you'll get closer to the queso served in Nuevo Leon.
- You can add 1 or 2 seeded, chopped plum tomatoes if you want.
- Queso asadero, a rich, melty Chihuahuan cheese that is far tastier than mozzarella, is the ideal cheese here. You can find it in Mexican markets. But any white melty cheese works. If you want to get all Texas, use a yellow cheese. Please don't use Velveeta. Or if you do, don't tell me . . .

PASTEL DE POLLO

PREP TIME: 1 HOUR | COOK TIME: 30 MINUTES | SERVES 8

Pastel de pollo is one of the many names for pastel azteca, which is basically Mexican lasagna. There are as many variations as there are cooks. This rendition is from Chihuahua, and I am indebted to Aída Garcia de Orduño's recipe in the book *Cocina Familiar en el Estado de Chihuahua* for the inspiration for this recipe. The flavor of this casserole feels a bit more like Greek moussaka than Italian lasagna because it's so creamy.

If you can find them, use hot green chiles for this recipe, ideally hot green Hatch peppers. The reason is because everything else in this dish is mild, bordering on bland, so the heat really perks things up.

Once made, this will keep in the fridge for a few days, and it can be frozen. I reheat it by covering in foil and setting it in a 325°F oven for a half hour or so. A microwave would work, too.

- 4 Roma tomatoes, sliced in half lengthwise
- 18 corn tortillas
- Oil for frying
- Butter or oil for greasing the pan
- 1 pound shredded, cooked chicken
- 1 cup Mexican crema or sour cream
- Salt
- 2 teaspoons dried Mexican oregano
- 6 poblanos or Anaheim peppers, roasted, peeled, seeded, and cut into strips
- 4 ounces cotija or feta cheese, crumbled
- 1 pound Chihuahua, Oaxaca or mozzarella cheese, grated

Get a comal, griddle, flat top or cast iron pan very hot, and char the cut side of the tomatoes. You want them nicely blackened. When they are, put them in a bowl and cover it to steam them. Remove the skins and seeds, then chop the tomatoes coarsely.

While the tomatoes are steaming, heat about 1/4 inch of oil in a pan until it hits about 350°F. Fry the tortillas for about 30 seconds or so -- enough to stiffen them up a bit, but not enough so they are actually stiff like tostadas. I start checking them at about 15 seconds. You want semi-limp. Set the tortillas on a cooling rack.

Preheat the oven to 425°F.

Mix the shredded chicken with the crema and the oregano. Add salt to taste.

Butter or oil a standard casserole pan, 9 by 13 inches or thereabouts. lay down a layer of 6 tortillas, slightly overlapping; some people cut the tortillas to fit the pan. Spread half the chicken mix evenly over the top. Then add half of the tomato pieces and half of the strips of roasted green pepper.

Sprinkle over half the cotija cheese, then one-third of the shredded Chihuahua or Oaxaca cheese. Top another layer of tortillas, then repeat the process. The top should be tortillas covered with the rest of the melty cheese. Bake for 30 minutes, until the cheese starts to brown. Let the dish sit for 10 minutes before serving.

NOTE: if you can't find Mexican crema, thin regular sour cream with a little buttermilk, milk, or cream to get you closer to the real thing. It should be very thick but pourable.

GUISADO DE ABIGEO

PREP TIME: 30 MINUTES | COOK TIME: 1 HOUR | SERVES 6

Another of the chili-like, red chile meat stews of the borderlands, this one is a Chihuahuan classic. It translates to cattle rustler's stew, and is a dish that can easily be made from staples carried in a saddlebag. According to the book *Los Sabores de Mi Tierra*, the modern dish became popular in the 1940s at a restaurant owned by Sadot Venegas in Meoqui, a town a little southeast of Chihuahua City. Carne seca, jerky, got the nickname "cattle rustlers' meat" because during the Revolution of 1910–1917, the revolutionaries who raided the haciendas of the well-to-do would steal cattle and dry the meat to sustain themselves on their adventures.

This guisado is a stripped-down version of the caldillo de carne seca on page 146, plus charro or border beans. The beans and stew are usually mixed in the same bowl, making this the most chili-like dish in the book.

- 2 guajillo or colorado chiles, seeded and stemmed
- 2 to 4 dried morita chiles, seeded and stemmed
- 2 pasilla chiles, seeded and stemmed
- 3 cloves garlic, minced
- 3 tablespoons lard or oil
- 1 large, onion, coarsely chopped
- 8 ounces beef or venison jerky, chopped into chunks
- 2 ounces machaca (optional)
- 1 teaspoon dried Mexican oregano
- 1 teaspoon ground cumin
- 1 quart beer
- Salt
- Cilantro, for garnish
- 1 recipe Charro Beans (page 127)
- Hot sauce, for serving

OPTIONAL: Heat a comal or griddle or large pan over medium heat and toast the dried chiles by letting them blister a little on each side, turning them a couple times. Do not let them char. Each chile should only need maybe 20 to 40 seconds to get a little toasty. Toasting adds another level of flavor.

Rehydrate the chiles by putting them in a bowl and pouring boiling water over them. Cover the bowl and let steep while you chop other ingredients. Drain and purée the chiles with the garlic in a blender. If you want, push this purée through a strainer to remove any bits of seed or skin.

Heat the lard in a soup pot over medium-high heat. Brown the onions. This takes time, so I have that started before I begin with the jerky.

Cut the jerky—it must be real jerky, not the ground kind—into pieces you'd eat with a spoon, then pull it apart with the grain a little more. If you're using the preshredded machaca, you're good to go.

Stir the onions a couple times as you do this. Pour in the chile purée. It will spatter, so keep stirring until everything combines.

Add the jerky to the pot with the oregano and cumin, then the beer. Stir well and bring to a simmer.

Taste for salt. It may not need any. Cook this for about 20 minutes, or until the jerky is tender enough to eat. Serve garnished with the cilantro alongside the charro beans. Some people mix the beans and stew into the same bowl. Serve with hot sauce at the table.

MONTADOS

A montado is not a recipe, but a structure. It is essentially a burrito crossed with a quesadilla. The only rules are that the tortilla must be large and flour, and that it has melty cheese, usually queso asadero. They usually also have a base of refried bayo or pinto beans, and then the item you order as the type of montado, for example, carne asada or barbacoa or shredded chicken.

You get them minimalist, like a Juarez burrito, and then you can dress your montado up as you wish with salsas, cilantro, raw onions, pickled jalapeños and the like.

My all-time favorite way to eat montados is with Discada (page 125).

- Slather half of your big, warm flour tortilla with refried beans.
- Add as much discada (or whatever) as you dare.
- Top with a hot salsa or hot sauce, cilantro, and white onions.
- Sprinkle shredded asadero cheese over the top and fold the montado in half to make a great big quesadilla.
- Heat the montado up on a comal or flattop or even a grill, pressing down with a spatula to melt the cheese and let it stick everything together. Flip once or twice, then eat.

TARAHUMARA GREEN CHILES AND MUSHROOMS

PREP TIME: 45 MINUTES | COOK TIME: 30 MINUTES | SERVES 6 TO 8

Mushrooms play a significant role in Mexican cuisine, especially wild mushrooms, called hongos. The country is a haven for all sorts of species that range from the jungles of Chiapas and Yucatan to arid Chihuahua. But don't look for mushrooms in the desert. They're up high in the sky islands above the desert floor, often at elevations higher than 9000 feet. It's the same basic mushroom array as in Arizona and New Mexico, which get excellent flushes after summertime monsoon rains.

The Tarahumara are excellent cooks who make wide use of wild mushrooms. This guisado is one of those dishes. I found it in a rare cookbook called *La Milpa Rarámuri en las Gorditas Chihuahuenses*.

The soul of this recipe is the combination of roasted green chiles and mushrooms. Ideally, you'd use chiles pasados (page 171). But you can also use freshly roasted chiles. Interestingly, the mushroom in the book is the sohachi, which is the Caesar's mushroom of the desert Southwest, *Amanita cochiseana*. It's a wonderful mushroom I've picked in Arizona. But it belongs to a family that includes deadly mushrooms like the death cap, so you need to know your stuff if you're going to pick that one.

I used chanterelles. Any mushroom will do. The original recipe is meatless, but I added shredded grouse. I think it adds a lot to the dish; shredded chicken, quail, or pheasant would be good. Shrimp would be nice, too.

Serve this alongside rice and beans, or as a taco or in a burrito. Corn or flour tortillas are just as good here. Once made, this will keep in the fridge a week, and you can freeze it.

- 8 to 10 chiles pasados, or Anaheim or poblano chiles
- 4 Roma tomatoes
- 3 tablespoons lard or vegetable oil
- 1 white onion, chopped
- 2 cloves garlic, minced
- Salt
- 1 pound mushrooms, any kind, cut into bite-sized pieces
- ½ pound shredded chicken or other white meat (about 1 cup; optional)
- 1 teaspoon dried Mexican oregano

If you're using chiles pasados, rehydrate them in hot water. If using fresh chiles, char the skins all over and put the chiles in a bowl and cover it to let them steam for 20 minutes. Scrape off the skins, and remove the seeds and stems. Once the chiles are ready (rehydrated or prepped), chop coarsely. Save the rehydration water if you used the dried peppers.

Meanwhile, heat a skillet or comal over high heat. When it's hot, slice the Roma tomatoes in half lengthwise and sear the cut sides until they're black. Use a metal spatula to scrape them off the skillet. Put them in the bowl you used for the chiles and cover to steam them, too. Remove the skins and seeds of the tomatoes and chop coarsely

Heat the lard or oil in a large pan over medium-high heat. Cook the onions, stirring often, until they start to brown, then add the garlic and cook another minute. Salt everything.

Add the mushrooms and toss to coat with lard. You might need a bit more. Cook the mushrooms until they give up their water, and when most of that water boils away, add another pinch of salt.

Add the tomatoes and chiles, along with any juices that have collected with them—if you're using the rehydrated chiles pasados, add maybe ½ cup of the soaking water—along with the oregano. If you're using the shredded chicken, add it, too. Let all this cook down until it's thick.

Serve with beans and rice, or on tortillas as tacos.

SQUASH BLOSSOM QUESADILLAS

PREP TIME: 15 MINUTES | COOK TIME: 15 MINUTES | SERVES 4

Squash blossom quesadillas, called quesadillas de flor de calabaza in Spanish, are tasty, easy, and can be made in less than 30 minutes. I ate both these and huitlacoche quesadillas at the Chihuahua farmer's market, and I loved them both. The Tarahumara vendors used blue corn tortillas, but flour are fine—and way easier to make large; forming a corn tortilla larger than about six inches requires serious skill.

You will want to use any melty cheese here. I use queso Chihuahua, which melts nicely. Queso Oaxaca works well too, as does mozzarella . . . or, let's face it, so does that "Mexican blend" you see in the supermarket. Monterey Jack is another good choice.

These are really very simple, with only cheese, the blossoms, and an herb of your choice. I prefer epazote, which is traditional, but cilantro works, too. If you have them, little green or ripe chiles pequins are a nice surprise in there as well.

Once made, your quesadillas are best eaten right away, but I've eaten them cold and they were still good.

- 8 flour or corn tortillas
- 1 pound queso Chihuahua, or other melty cheese, shredded
- 1 sprig epazote, or cilantro
- ½ pound squash blossoms, coarsely chopped
- Chopped chiles pequin (optional)

Heat a comal, griddle, flat top or large cast iron pan over a large burner. If you are doing flour tortillas, you want medium-high. If you are doing corn, you want high heat. Corn tortillas are best around 500°F, where flour is better around 400°F.

Lay down a little shredded cheese on one side of a tortilla, then some chopped squash blossoms, a few epazote leaves, and a little chopped chile. Top with a little more cheese. Fold over carefully and press the quesadilla down on the hot comal with a spatula until the cheese melts and holds it together. Let this sear a few minutes, then flip and repeat. You want the cheese a little browned on the edges. Repeat with the remaining tortillas.

NOTES: When buying or making tortillas, you want them around 8 inches in diameter, larger than those for street tacos. When I make the flour ones, I measure out about 40 grams per tortilla.

Keys to Success

- Fresh epazote really adds a lot to this, so use it if you can find it. It'll be in many Latin markets. No huge deal if you need to skip it, though.
- Chop the stem ends off the squash blossoms and they will lay flatter in the tortillas. If I have lots and lots of them, I only use the yellow part.
- Serve your quesadillas with a nice salsa on the side. I am partial to my Fire-Roasted Salsa (page 38), or my Tomatillo Salsa Verde (page 70).

CHACALES SOUP

PREP TIME: 15 MINUTES | COOK TIME: 2 HOURS | SERVES 6 TO 8

Chacales are roasted, dried, and cracked corn kernels typically cooked in soups or as a sort of porridge. There is an uncracked version in New Mexico called chicos, and variations of this sort of corn appear all the way up to North Dakota, where the Lakota and Mandan use them. Chances are you'll need to mail order chacales, but I'll give you some easier options below.

Also called chichales or chuales, chacales make a great meatless soup for Lent. The stewed corn stays chewy and almost meaty—it definitely tricks your mouth into thinking you're eating meat—and the accompaniments are perfect for late winter or early spring.

Chacales soup is almost always a mix of the corn, onions and garlic, something red—chiles or tomatoes—cilantro, and cheese. I've seen both roasted, peeled, seeded and chopped green chiles as well as chiles pasados. The red thing is usually tomatoes of some sort, usually peeled and hand-crushed. Alternatively, I've seen what is essentially a red enchilada sauce poured into the chacales soup at the end, which gives it a vivid red color.

Either way, the main chore in cooking chacales is getting the corn tender enough to eat. You can soak it overnight or boil it for an hour or so before you start the rest of the soup. You want the kernels to be chewy, but pleasantly so.

The soup keeps a week in the fridge, and it freezes well. You could also pressure-can it.

In Mexico, you usually see chacales served with corn or flour tortillas. Oh, and you absolutely can add meat to your soup if you want.

8 ounces chacales or other cracked corn

Salt

3 tablespoons lard, bacon fat, or vegetable oil

1 white onion, chopped

2 cloves garlic, minced

1 teaspoon dried Mexican oregano

1 28-ounce can, whole, peeled tomatoes

½ cup chopped cilantro

½ pound melty cheese (asadero, Chihuahua, mozzarella, "Mexican blend"), grated

2 limes, cut in wedges

Soak the corn in water overnight if you can. Boil the corn in plenty of water until it's chewy, but pleasantly so, about 1 hour. Add salt late in the cooking process, about 45 minutes in.

When the corn is mostly ready, fry the onions in the lard or bacon fat over medium heat until transparent and a little brown on the edges. Add the garlic and cook another minute more.

Usually the water level in the boiling corn has reduced enough to be a nice soup consistency. You want it milky looking and covering the corn by about 1 inch. If there's too much water, drain some. If not enough, add some. Scrape the onions and garlic into this pot and continue to simmer.

Hand-crush the peeled tomatoes into the pot. Add the tomato juice from the can if you'd like. Stir in the oregano. Let all this cook for 10 minutes, and add salt if needed.

Stir in the cilantro, and bring the soup to a rolling boil. Ladle it out very hot into bowls and add the grated cheese on top, for everyone to stir in. Serve with lime wedges and hot sauce on the side.

Alternate Salsa

If you want to go the red salsa route for the soup instead of, or in addition to, the tomatoes, use the Red Enchilada Sauce (page 37).

MAKING CHACALES OR CHICOS

If you want to make your own chacales, it's not terribly difficult. In Mexico, it's always starchy corn, never sweet. But in New Mexico, I've seen sweet corn done this way.

You roast, steam or smoke ears of corn, in the husks, until they are nicely cooked. Strip the husks off and then dry the ears in the sun or a dehydrator. Once completely dry, which takes days or weeks depending on your climate, you strip the kernels off.

This process typically cracks a lot of the kernels, which is good, because that opens the starch up in them to thicken soups or stews. Once made, chacales keep for years if kept dry.

CALDO DE OSO

PREP TIME: 25 MINUTES | COOK TIME: 30 MINUTES | SERVES 8 TO 10

Bear stew? Nope, it's just a confusing name for a hearty catfish stew emblematic of Chihuahua. Like most of these stews, there are many variations. I've eaten it in the City of Chihuahua in some humble restaurants, although this is mostly a home-cooked dish.

The legend is that this stew was served to copper miners day after day after day, until it became known as caldo odioso, hated stew, and somehow the name got changed around. It really is wonderful . . . if you don't eat it for weeks on end.

You don't need catfish here, but catfish live in most of the rivers of Chihuahua, where they're called bagre. I've even seen this recipe made with the heads of huge blue catfish. If you happen to have fresh fish or seafood broth, use it in place of water, but water is far more common in Mexico.

¼ cup lard or cooking oil
1 large white onion, sliced root to tip
4 cloves garlic, minced
2 large carrots, cut into chunks
1 pound waxy potatoes, peeled and cut into pieces the size of the carrots
Salt
1 cup tomato purée
2 teaspoons dried marjoram or Mexican oregano
2 bay leaves
1 4-ounce can diced, pickled jalapeños, or 2 jalapeños, seeded and diced, plus ¼ cup vinegar
2 pounds skinless fish fillets
½ to 1 cup chopped cilantro
4 green onions, chopped
Black pepper
Hot sauce or chiles pequins
Saltines (optional)

Heat the lard or oil in a soup pot over medium-high heat. Cook the onions in the pot until they are slightly browned, then add the garlic, carrots, and potatoes. Salt them, too. Cook all this, stirring often for 4 minutes or so, then add the tomato purée, marjoram, bay leaves, and the chiles with the vinegar. Pour in a quart to a quart-and-a-half of water—you want a loose stew, and this won't cook down too much. Add salt to taste.

Let everything simmer until the carrots and potatoes are tender. Meanwhile, cut the fish into chunks. When the vegetables are ready, add the fish to the pot and cook 5 minutes. Add the cilantro, green onions, and black pepper to taste.

Serve with Saltines and let everyone add hot sauce or crushed dried chiles to taste.

CAGUAMANTA

This is a stew common in Baja, Sonora, and Sinaloa. Originally made with sea turtles, caguamas, this practice has been illegal for a generation. So cooks have substituted other sea creatures, most commonly skates and rays, mantarraya. Thus the portmanteau of caguamanta. But any fish or seafood you have will do. I ate a wondrous rendition of this stew in Ensenada made with opah fish. Structurally, caguamanta is close enough to caldo de oso to use the same recipe, with these modifications:

- Rehydrate and purée 2 or 3 stemmed and seeded ancho or pasilla chiles, adding them with the water.
- Add 1 teaspoon ground cumin.
- Chop 1 or 2 stalks celery.
- Substitute the pickled jalapeños for chopped fresh ones.

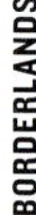

EMPANADAS DE SANTA RITA

PREP TIME: 90 MINUTES, INCLUDING RESTING TIME FOR THE DOUGH | COOK TIME: 30 MINUTES | SERVES 12

These empanadas are a relic of an earlier age, when sweet and savory went together more often. Think English mincemeat pies and you get an idea. They are little fried hand pies exclusive to Chihuahua, and only widely available for the festival of Santa Rita in late May. But the filling is easy to make, and the dough is the basis for all fried empanadas. For Santa Rita empanadas, you will want the anise and sugar in the dough.

Once you have the dough recipe down pat, you can fill them with anything. Just make sure whatever the filling is, it's cut into little pieces or is soft—otherwise it will pierce the dough when you fold the empanadas over. And you will need about 1 pound of whatever the filling is.

Other good choices would be the filling for the Shrimp Empanadas (page 93), the Chilorio (page 283), the filling for the Texas-Style Enchiladas (page 118), the Sonoran Picadillo (page 238), the shrimp meatball mix (page 260), the filling for the Marlin Tacos (page 275), or the Carne Guisada (page 97).

Once made, these empanadas will keep in the fridge a week, and once cooked, they freeze well.

Dough

- 2¼ cups flour
- 1 teaspoon salt
- ½ teaspoon baking powder
- ½ cup lard, butter, beef tallow, or vegetable shortening
- ⅓ cup ice water
- 2 teaspoons distilled or white wine vinegar

For Sweet Empanadas

- ½ teaspoon ground anise seeds
- 1 to 2 teaspoons sugar

Dough

Mix the flour, salt, and baking powder in a bowl, as well as the anise and sugar, if using. Add the lard and combine with your fingers until the mixture looks like sand. Add the ice water and vinegar and knead into a fairly soft and pliable dough. You can add a little more ice water if you need to.

Divide the dough into balls about 50 grams, or 1¾ ounces. You should be able to make 11 or 12. Put the balls into a plastic bag and set aside for 1 hour.

Filling

While the dough is resting, make the filling. Heat the lard in a pan and brown the ground meats. Add the onion and potatoes, then salt everything well as it cooks. Add the raisins and pecans and let this cook until the potatoes are soft.

Add the peas, sweet wine, and spices and mix well. Add salt and black pepper to taste.

Finishing

Heat 2 or 3 cups of lard or oil in a frying pan; you want it at least 1½ inches deep, and 2 inches is better. (Remember you can later strain the oil and reuse it several times) You're looking for 350°F. Set a cooling rack over a baking sheet in your oven and set the oven to 200°F.

Get a little bowl of water ready and grab a fork to seal the empanadas.

While the oil is heating up, line a tortilla press with two pieces of plastic cut from a plastic bag. Squash one of the balls into a round. Fill it with a couple tablespoons of the filling, dip a finger into the water, and wet the outside rim of the dough. Fold it over and seal. Pick the empanada off the plastic and set on a cutting board. Crimp the edges with the tines of the fork.

Santa Rita Filling

2 tablespoons lard or oil

½ pound ground pork

½ pound ground beef or venison

1 white onion, minced

½ pound waxy potatoes, peeled and diced small

Salt

⅓ cup raisins

¼ cup finely chopped pecans

½ cup peas

½ cup sweet wine, ideally a sweet sherry

1 teaspoon ground cinnamon

¼ teaspoon ground clove

Black pepper

Lard or oil for frying

If you are good, you can do this assembly line–style and just make and fry. If you are starting out, you probably want to make at least half of the empanadas before you start frying.

When you are ready, slip a few empanadas into the hot oil, bottom side down. Usually only a little of the top will bob above the surface of the oil. Fry until golden, 2 or 3 minutes, then flip. When both sides are golden brown, move the empanada to the cooling rack in the oven and continue with the rest of the empanadas.

NOTE: If you want to play around with flours, start by replacing the regular flour with ½ cup of your alternate. I like doing this with acorn or mesquite flour, or that amazing roasted wheat flour from the Tohono O'Odham in Tucson. Different flours will change the flavor and color of the empanadas.

Keys to Success

- Watch the oil temperature. Let it return to 350°F between batches, and tinker with the heat to keep it there. Never let it get below 325°F or higher than 365°F.
- Don't be tempted to overstuff your empanadas. I love the filling as much as you do, but overstuffed empanadas explode.
- If you would rather bake these, set the empanadas on a parchment-lined baking sheet. Paint with a mixture of 1 egg beaten with 1 tablespoon milk or cream. Bake 20 minutes at 400°F.
- Lard is the best fat for the dough, but those other fats I mention all work. I dislike vegetable shortening, however. I've done empanadas with oil, too, and it's a little trickier but it will work.
- I highly recommend using those little raisins called, oddly, currants (they're not actually currants): They integrate better with the rest of the filling. Or chop bigger raisins.

GREEN CHILE APPLE PIE

PREP TIME: 90 MINUTES, INCLUDING CHILL TIME | COOK TIME: 80 MINUTES | SERVES 8

I could easily have put this in the New Mexico chapter because this unusual pie is served in both places. Green chile apple pie *sounds* weird, but it's amazing—so long as you use mild or medium chiles. This is not a place for ultra hot Hatch chiles. In New Mexico, I ate a slice of this at the Las Cruces Farmer's Market that had pine nuts in it, then again in Chihuahua, where it had pecans.

As the son of the most Yankee New England mom who ever lived, I happen to like Cheddar cheese on my apple pie. And Cheddar on a green chile apple pie that has nuts in it may be the best dessert in the world, at least to me.

I am indebted to my friend Elise Bauer of Simply Recipes for the base apple pie recipe, and for her outstanding pie crust.

Crust

- 2 sticks room-temperature butter (225 g) diced
- 2 cups (280g) all-purpose flour
- 2 teaspoons sugar
- 1 teaspoon salt (skip if using salted butter)
- ½ cup (115ml) full fat sour cream

Filling

- 3 pounds cooking apples
- 2 tablespoons freshly squeezed lemon juice
- ½ cup roasted green chiles, coarsely chopped
- ½ cup pine nuts or chopped pecans
- ½ cup sugar
- 3 tablespoons all-purpose flour
- 1 teaspoon ground cinnamon
- ½ teaspoon ground allspice
- ¼ teaspoon ground nutmeg
- 1 teaspoon vanilla extract

To make the pie crust, whisk together the flour, sugar, and salt. Cut the butter into the mix with forks or a pastry cutter until it all looks like a coarse meal. It's OK if there are a few larger patches of flour-covered butter.

Stir the sour cream into the flour and butter mixture, then gather the dough together into a ball. It's OK to knead it slightly, but do not overwork the dough or it will get tough. Cut it in half, then form into two 6-inch disks with no cracks. Sprinkle with a little flour and wrap in plastic. Chill for 1 hour, or up to 1 day.

Meanwhile, peel, core, and chop the apples into ½-inch chunks or thin slices. Toss them in a bowl with the lemon juice as you go to keep them from browning too much.

Toast the pine nuts in a dry pan on medium-high heat. Toss them frequently, and keep an eye on them so they don't burn. Once most of them have at least a little browning, move them to a bowl.

Mix the apples, chiles, and pine nuts in a large bowl. Add the vanilla extract. Combine the sugar, flour, allspice, nutmeg, cinnamon, and add this mixture to the apple bowl.

After the dough has chilled for an hour, remove it and let it sit for 5 to 10 minutes so it's easier to roll out. Sprinkle your work surface with flour. Roll out each disk to a circle 12 to 13 inches wide and an even thickness, about ⅛ inch thick. As you roll the dough, make sure the bottom is not sticking. If it is, lift it and sprinkle a little flour underneath.

Preheat the oven to 375°F. Place an oven rack in the lowest position and put a baking sheet on it to catch drippings from the pie. Put the next rack right above it.

To Finish

1 large egg yolk

1 tablespoon cream or half-and-half

Gently place one piece of rolled out dough onto a 9-inch pie plate. Press down to line the pie dish with the dough. Add the filling, mounding it in the center. Place the top crust over the filling, trim the edges to about ½ to ¾ inch over the sides, then crimp the edges. Do this by folding the dough under itself so that the edge of the fold comes right to the edge of the pan. Press the top and bottom dough rounds together as you flute edges using thumb and forefinger, or press with a fork.

Mix the egg yolk with the cream and paint the top crust. Cut steam vents in the top.

Bake the pie at 375°F until the crust begins to lightly brown, about 20 minutes, then reduce heat to 350°F. Bake until the crust has nicely browned and the juices are bubbling all over, an additional hour or up to another hour and a half, depending on the type of apples you are using. If you are looking for an internal temperature, the filling should hit 200°F at its center.

If the crust is browning too much, tent the edges or even the whole pie with foil.

Let this pie cool for 1 hour before serving, ideally with pine nut ice cream or slices of very sharp Cheddar on top (not both).

NOTE: Good cooking apples include Granny Smith, Jonagold, Fuji, and Braeburn. You'll need 4 to 8, depending on size.

"Desayunar como rey, comer como príncipe y cenar como mendigo."

Eat breakfast like a king, eat at midday like a prince, and have supper like a beggar.

ARÍ SALSA

PREP TIME: 20 MINUTES | SERVES 4 TO 6

Arí is a burgundy resin made by ants on a particular shrub in the Sierra Madre Occidental, and is unique to Chihuahua. First used by the Tarahumara, it adds umami to whatever it is added to—usually salsas. Think of it as Tarahumara MSG, only without the side effects.

Alas, I know of no source for arí in the United States, and it is expensive even on the streets of Chihuahua: A typical sandwich bag full can cost 1000 pesos, close to $50. But it never goes bad and you only need a little, so if you ever find some, buy it.

Should you ever find arí, here is the traditional salsa.

- 1 or 2 pieces of arí, about 10 grams
- 2 cloves garlic
- Pinch of salt
- A few dried pequin or chiltepin chiles
- ¼ cup freshly squeezed lime juice
- ¼ cup water

Grind the ari with the salt into a powder. Add the garlic and chiles and grind to a fine paste. Slowly stir in the lime juice, then add the water to taste. This salsa is amazing on carne asada or other simple meat or fish preparations.

NOTE: This salsa is only made in a molcajete, the basalt mortar and pestle used everywhere in Mexico. You grind the arí to a powder first. This is important because it's a resin, and won't be fun to eat if it's still in chunks. A regular mortar and pestle is fine for this, as are some spice grinders—I've had mixed success with them.

My friend Christian Duthoy, chef of the award-winning restaurant Sulawe in Chihuahua, fancies up his version:

- 10 grams arí
- 10 grams dried chiltepin chiles
- 500 grams Clamato
- 125 grams freshly squeezed lime juice
- 125 grams freshly squeezed orange juice
- 5 grams dark soy sauce

Grind the arí with the chiles in the molcajete, then add the liquids. This creates a magic brew that is fantastic as a base for aguachile, a Clam Ceviche (page 268) or as a splash in your beer for a michelada.

CHRIS'S SALSA MACHA

PREP TIME: 20 MINUTES | COOK TIME: 15 MINUTES | MAKES 3 CUPS

Salsa macha has been having a moment these days, with a thousand versions from a thousand cooks available even in many supermarkets. It's a spicy oil-based sauce that plays well with a huge array of dishes; a little goes a long way and it keeps for months in the fridge. Think of it as Mexican chile crisp. Patricio's Salsa Negra is similar (page 71).

This is another recipe from my friend Chris Duthoy. According to the *Larousse Diccionario Enciclopédico de la Gastronomía Mexicana*, salsa macha originated in Veracruz, but it has since spread far and wide in both Mexico and the United States.

Chris is a chef, so he uses exact metric measurements. I'll provide volumetric equivalents, but for the real recipe, weigh everything out.

- 75 grams dried chipotle meco (the tan chipotles), 2½ ounces
- 20 grams chiles de árbol, ¾ ounce
- 25 grams New Mexican or colorado chiles, 1 ounce
- 25 grams guajillo chiles, 1 ounce
- 75 grams sesame seeds, 2½ ounces
- 12 grams pink peppercorns, ¼ teaspoon crushed
- 10 grams salt, 2 teaspoons
- 25 grams ground dried ginger, 1 ounce
- 10 bay leaves
- 7 star anise pods
- 3 grams ground cardamom, 1½ teaspoons
- 75 grams garlic, chopped coarsely (about ½ cup
- 15 grams sugar, 4 teaspoons
- 250 grams neutral oil, like canola or peanut, 9 ounces
- 250 grams extra-virgin olive oil, 9 ounces
- 50 grams vinegar, ¼ cup

Stem and seed all the chiles. Toast them for a few seconds on a comal or grill, or smoke them all for an hour if you happen to have a smoker running for another recipe. Tear the chiles into little pieces.

Toast the sesame seeds until fragrant, being careful not to burn them. Put all the ingredients except the olive oil and the vinegar into a pot and heat it all over low heat until the garlic sizzles a bit. Let the garlic sizzle for 1 minute, then remove the pot from the heat and let it cool down.

When it's cool enough to handle, put the chile mixture plus the olive oil and vinegar into a food processor and pulse it until the solids are small; if you've ever seen Chinese chile crisp, it's like that. Pour into jars, where it will keep for ages. Either use the oil, or stir the salsa before using.

NOTE: You can use a mild olive oil, too. Olive oil is very common in Veracruz.

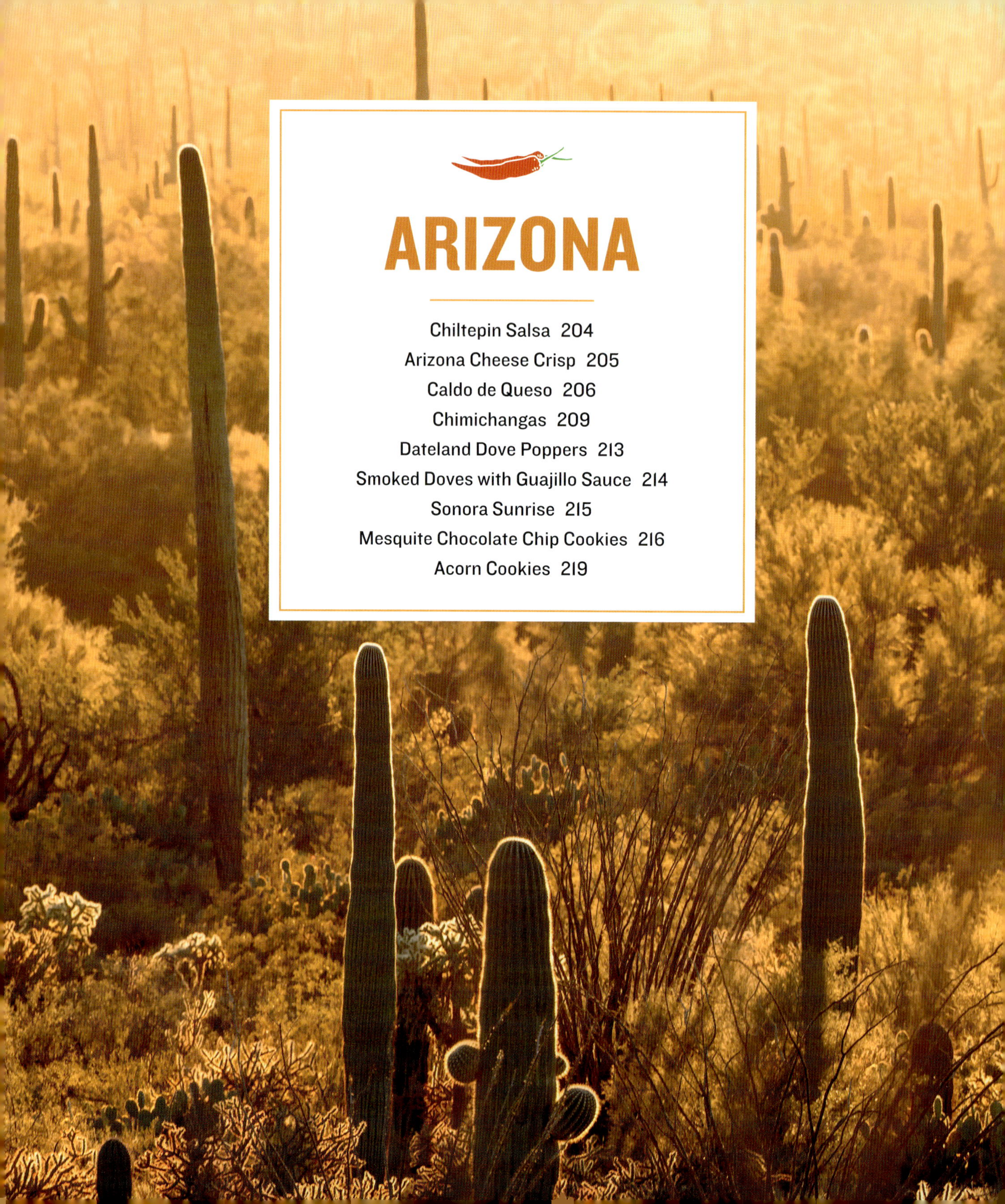

ARIZONA

The line between Arizona and Sonora is far blurrier than the line between New Mexico and Chihuahua. Where New Mexico has its own distinctive, fully formed cuisine, Arizona simply doesn't. Yes, there are unique dishes to that state, but much of the beauty of Arizona's food is directly derived from the Mexican state of Sonora to its south. All of southern Arizona, almost to Phoenix, *was* Sonora until the Gadsden Purchase of 1854.

Today, Arizona is a state where you can find a café serving food right out of the American South next to a Mexican restaurant that has been open for generations.

Unlike New Mexico, Spanish and Mexican influences are almost complete north of Interstate 40, and they begin to fade north of Phoenix. The 14,500-square-mile megalopolis of Phoenix is certainly a polyglot city, and there is some excellent Mexican food there. But it's largely Sonoran or dishes imported from whatever area of Mexico the restaurant owners came from.

Tucson is the great exception. Tucson embraces the desert, is fully bilingual, and has the closest thing to an amalgamated cuisine Arizona offers. Here you'll find the few great stars of Arizona's cuisine: cheese crisps, chimichangas, and a host of Sonora specialties so good you need not cross the border to enjoy la mera neta—the real deal.

The most original and wondrous foods of Arizona are to be found among Indigenous groups. The Hopi, Navajo, Tohono O'Odham and other tribes live there, and each adds unique and excellent foods to the state's tapestry: cholla buds, saguaro syrup, candied barrel cactus, mesquite.

Arizona's excellent hunting and gathering opportunities enrich the cuisine—dove hunting is as big a deal in places like Yuma as is it 1000 miles away in Brownsville, Texas. Organizations like Desert Harvesters spread the word about the bounty of the Sonoran Desert, where you can get fat on wild foods—if you know what to look for, and how to cook it.

Keep in mind as you read this chapter that almost everything in the following chapter on Sonora can be found in Arizona as well. The recipes that follow are those dishes I've either eaten more on the American side of the border, or, as in the case of the cheese crisps, are truly an Arizonan dish.

▲ View across the border of Arizona into Mexico.

CHILTEPIN SALSA

PREP TIME: 10 MINUTES | COOK TIME: 15 MINUTES | MAKES 1 CUP

This one'll get ya. It looks like a rather thin, mild, tomato-based salsa, but within lurk the fruity fires of the wild chiltepin chile. I include this recipe in the Arizona chapter instead of Sonora solely because I perfected my own version of this iconic sauce at a hunt camp in Arivaca, Arizona, which is just a healthy hike away from Mexico. You can use this salsa as your baseline "hot" salsa for any dish in this book. And if you cannot get chiltepin chiles, your next best would be the bullet-shaped chiles pequins, then after that chiles de árbol, which are widely available.

- ½ pound plum tomatoes, halved lengthwise
- 2 large unpeeled cloves garlic
- 1 to 3 heaping tablespoons chiltepin chiles
- 2 teaspoons dried Mexican oregano
- Salt, smoked if you have it
- ¼ cup white or cider vinegar

Heat a comal or flattop on high heat. When it's very hot, set the garlic and the tomatoes cut side down to blacken. Let them char for a solid 5 to 10 minutes. Use a spatula to flip them, scraping the bottom of the tomato up with the rest; you really need that char. Let them cook on the uncut side for a minute or two, then move the tomatoes to a bowl and cover to let them steam a bit. The garlic is ready when the skins are charred.

Peel the tomatoes and the garlic and put them in a blender. Add the remaining ingredients and purée well. You want this salsa to be smooth. Adjust the flavor with more vinegar, salt, and some water as needed.

Once made, it will keep in the fridge for a month or more.

ARIZONA CHEESE CRISP

PREP TIME: 15 MINUTES | COOK TIME: 10 MINUTES | SERVES 2 AS A STARTER

A specialty of Tucson, the cheese crisp is effectively grilled cheese on a giant flour tortilla, with some roasted green chile thrown in for good measure. They are spare, crispy, cheesy, and make a stellar starter for a Southwest meal. The best I've eaten were at a place called El Minuto in Tucson, but you can find them all over Arizona.

You need large, ideally thin, Sonoran-style flour tortillas for this. You'll want to match the size of the tortilla with the size of your largest frying pan, usually 12 inches or so. If you can only get the thicker tortillas, fry them a bit longer.

This recipe can be scaled up infinitely. I can eat a whole one easily.

- 1 large flour tortilla, ideally a thin Sonoran-style one
- 3 tablespoons lard or oil for frying
- 1 roasted, skinned, and seeded green chile, chopped coarsely
- ⅓ cup grated Cheddar cheese
- ⅓ cup grated Monterey Jack cheese

Heat the lard or oil in a large frying pan over medium-high heat. When it's hot, slip the tortilla into the oil and fry it until crispy, 30 to 60 seconds. Push the tortilla down with a spatula to keep it fairly flat, although it will puff up. Flip it to crisp the other side. Set the tortilla on a cooling rack set over a baking sheet. You can do this up to a day ahead.

When you are ready, turn your broiler on to "high."

Arrange the green chiles around the tortilla like a pizza, then mix the cheeses and sprinkle them evenly over the tortilla.

Set a baking sheet under where you are going to broil your cheese crisp to catch any drips, then slide the crisp on the highest rack under the broiler. Keep an eye on it, and rotate the tortilla if you have hot spots. It's done when the cheese has melted and browned in places.

Slice like a pizza and serve at once.

CALDO DE QUESO

PREP TIME: 30 MINUTES | COOK TIME: 30 MINUTES | SERVES 6

I'll never forget my first caldo de queso. My friend Jonathan O'Dell was helping me complete the "squirrel slam"—hunting and cooking every species of tree squirrel in America; yes, I know, I am weird. Several species only live in Arizona, and we were hunting the Arizona gray squirrel, *Sciurus arizonensis,* near Fort Huachuca. As we neared our spot, it started snowing. In Arizona. A scant 20 miles from the Mexican border.

We got our squirrels and headed east to Bisbee in a full snowstorm. It was wild, like nothing I ever expected. We skidded into the old mining town and hit up a little restaurant to warm ourselves. Jonathan ordered the caldo de queso, and I followed his lead. It was like nothing I'd eaten before.

Caldo de queso is unusual in that the cheese, in a way, takes the place of meat in the soup. You cut it in chunks that only melt a little, so you can savor them. Several different cheeses can be used, but queso fresco is the most common. Queso panela and sometimes Mexican-style queso Manchego is used, too.

There are two ways to serve the soup: all from one pot, or a two-step where you put the cheese, and maybe the chiles and tomatoes, in everyone's bowls, then ladle the soup over that and serve. Serving from one pot is easier, but unless you are going to eat up the whole pot right then and there, the cheese will begin to melt and you will be sad when you go to reheat your caldo.

Doing the fancier two-step is nicer. The cheese warms gently, and neither the roasted chiles nor the peeled tomatoes overcook.

- 4 Anaheim, Hatch or poblano peppers
- 1 white onion, chopped
- 2 tablespoons butter or oil
- 1 pound potatoes, peeled and diced
- 6 cups chicken broth
- ½ pound Roma tomatoes
- 1 pound queso fresco cheese, diced
- ½ cup whole milk
- Crushed chiltepin chiles or black pepper (optional)

Roast the chiles over a gas flame or broiler until the skin has blackened. Put them in a bowl and cover the bowl with a lid to steam for a few minutes, then peel and seed the peppers and cut into strips. Or use canned or frozen roasted green chiles. This is what I do.

In a large heavy, lidded pot, heat the butter or oil over medium-high heat and sauté the onions until wilted, but not browned. Add the potatoes and broth and bring to a simmer. Cook until the potatoes are tender, about 15 to 20 minutes.

Slice an X in the base of each Roma tomato and drop it in the soup. About a minute later, fish the tomatoes out and peel them; the X makes them easier to peel. Discard the skins and seeds, and dice the tomatoes.

When the potatoes are done, add the tomatoes and strips of green chile, and the milk. Let this simmer a minute or two. Put the diced cheese in everyone's bowls and ladle the soup over them. Serve with chiltepin chiles or black pepper over the top, and with flour tortillas or bread alongside.

Keys to Success

- Avoid cheese that melts easily, like Oaxaca or mozzarella. Queso fresco or a fresh farmer's cheese is best.
- Caldo de queso is very mild. So spice things up by crushing chiltepin chiles over the soup.
- This can be made in advance: Leave out the milk and cheese until you serve. The base broth, potatoes, onions, green chiles, and tomato can sit in the fridge for a week. When you reheat it, add milk to taste and then put cheese in everyone's bowls and pour the soup over it.

CHIMICHANGAS

PREP TIME: 20 MINUTES | COOK TIME: 10 MINUTES | SERVES 4

A chimichanga is basically a fried burrito. There are all sorts of origin stories for this dish, and lots of places claiming to have originated it. I ate one at El Charro, in Tucson, where, a century ago, then-owner Monica Flin allegedly accidentally dropped a burrito into the fryer and started to shout "chingada!" which is basically the f-word in Mexican Spanish, but caught herself and said the nonsense word "chimichanga" instead. The chimi there was good, but I question that this is the original.

Why? Because the same dish, called a chivichanga, has existed in Mexico prior to the Tucson origin story. You can't tell me that burrito makers took decades to try deep-frying one. It makes too much sense.

And yeah, chimichangas can be heavy fried things. This is why that shredded lettuce and pico de gallo around it are so vital. You eat a chimi with a knife and fork, enjoy a heavy bit of goodness, then balance it with some of the lettuce and pico. Back and forth, it's a great meal.

What's inside the burrito? Up to you. I've seen damn near everything inside one. But the meat or main item—a green chile relleno is a phenomenal vegetarian option—almost always has red rice and refried beans along with it, and sometimes cheese, too.

Make chimichangas a day after you've already made some other yummy thing, like carne asada, chilorio, discada, puerco asado, or whatever.

Chimichangas don't store well, so make them and eat them.

- 4 large flour tortillas
- 2 cups refried beans
- 2 cups red rice
- 2 to 3 cups meat filling (see headnote; your choice)
- 1 cup shredded cheese (queso Oaxaca, longhorn, queso Chihuahua, etc.)
- 2 cups vegetable oil, for frying
- 3 to 4 cups shredded lettuce
- 1 to 2 cups pico de gallo
- Crema or sour cream

Pour the oil into a pot or pan that will barely hold one or two chimichangas. Doing this means the oil will come higher up the sides of the chimi, getting you close to deep-frying without actually deep-frying. Heat the oil to 350°F.

Either right over a gas burner, or on a comal or flattop or large pan, warm the flour tortillas so they are pliable. You could also cover the tortillas in a damp paper towel and microwave them for 30 seconds.

As the oil heats, make 4 burritos with the refried beans, rice, meat filling, then some of the shredded cheese. Keep in mind these are suggested fillings. You do you. Err on underfilling the burrito because you really want it completely wrapped, with none of the filling poking out.

Set one or two chimis in the hot oil seam side down and fry for 2 to 3 minutes, then turn and fry the other side for 2 minutes. Then repeat with the rest of the meat and filling.

Serve on a bed of shredded lettuce, drizzled with crema and pico de gallo.

YUMA DOVE HUNTING

No hunt along the border is more anticipated than the annual Labor Day dove hunt. And nowhere is that anticipation greater than in Yuma, Arizona. Doves don't like cold weather, and even though states as far north as Minnesota have dove seasons, the cultural tradition of hunting these birds is really a Southern thing.

Sometimes you do something to enjoy it, other times to experience it. I'll be blunt: The Yuma dove hunt is a borderline circus, but like the Minnesota State Fair, you go anyway. Tens of thousands of hunters, almost all driving large white pickups, descend on the southwest Arizona town of about 100,000 on August 31. Every hotel room is booked. Sprague's, a gun shop that has sponsored a "big breast" contest since the 1980s—heaviest dove breast, to be clear—is mobbed with what looks like the bar scene from Star Wars, only instead of drinking (that comes later), they're all buying licenses, Sprague's swag, and ammo.

Lots of ammo. National statistics show that the average dove hunter uses five shotgun shells for each dove he or she kills. Yeah, they're that hard to hit, juking and diving around at 55 miles an hour—but also remember that every casual hunter in the region comes out for this, so you have a ton of terrible shotgunners out there, increasing the average.

The downside to all this is a whole lot of lead entering the environment, to the point where some states require hunters to use steel shot, which works fine. The upside is that since 1937 there has been an 11 percent tax on ammo: the Pittman-Robertson Act, which funds wildlife projects all over the country.

As my friend Jonathan O'Dell likes to say of the thunderous, PTSD-inducing roar of gunfire on opening morning, "Ah, the sweet sound of conservation . . ."

Nowhere are there more dove hunters in such a relatively small area as in Yuma. Texas has fantastic dove hunting—the best dove hunt I ever had was in Brownsville at the farm of my friend Mike Ortiz—but down there it's all private land. Yuma has both public land and private land opened up for dove hunters through a partnership, so there are trucks—and doves—everywhere.

We decided to hunt away from the infamous firing line, along a fallow field that backed up on the big levee, across from an irrigation canal. A small wash of saltbush and tamarisk and other scrubby plants was our backstop. The ultrafine Arizona dust covered everything. It was 93 degrees at 4 a.m., with no breeze. The air felt like an attic.

My friend Sharon and I got hemmed in. Another party had set up 100 feet to our right. Nice enough guys, but still. All morning, it was a case of stopping your shotgun's swing so you don't accidentally shoot another hunter. A dove isn't worth shooting a person. The locals weren't so considerate, and Sharon got peppered at least once.

But I was not there for the hunting. I was there more to soak in this weird experience. Yuma is not a pretty town. It feels like a gigantic, sprawling open-air mall. Chain stores and strip malls are everywhere. It wasn't always this way.

The town was originally a Yuman village before the Spanish arrived in 1540; they built a mission nearby in 1780. Later, the US built Fort Yuma in 1848 to guard the area, which is the best way to cross the Colorado River for many miles—believe it or not, the Colorado used to be a big river, but has since been crippled by dams and overuse of its water.

Eventually Yuma became a major farm town, and it's still the source of most of America's winter lettuce. It's the ag that brings the doves, who love eating little seeds. Millet, corn, wheat, sorghum, flax, you name it. Doves—mourning, white-winged, and now Eurasian collared doves—are the dominant bird on the landscape.

Watching the fiesta is worth all the hassle. The whole town gets up for this hunt. There are "welcome dove hunters" signs on the streetlamps, banners at all the gas stations, and many restaurants will cook your doves for you. Bacon-wrapped jalapeño poppers are the rule here. All the hotels have tables with a trash can outside so hunters can clean their birds. And there are at least a couple places where kids earn money for school trips by cleaning hunters' doves. It's a party.

Would I return? Maybe. The remarkable thing about the Yuma dove hunt is how a community comes together to celebrate a hunting event. But as a hunting experience? Endure Day One for its anthropological curiosity. Enjoy the rest of the 15-day season. It'll be quieter. There will still be lots of birds, and you can head over to Chretin's to have them cooked up for you. Get the relleno.

Clockwise: Sunrise on dove season in Yuma; the whole community comes out for the hunting opener; a good start to the day's hunt.

DATELAND DOVE POPPERS

PREP TIME: 30 MINUTES | MARINATING TIME: 8 HOURS | COOK TIME: 15 MINUTES | SERVES 4 TO 6

One day, after one of those Yuma dove hunts, Holly and I stopped at Dateland, a little roadside stop that features Date Shakes (page 288) as well as an array of various date products. I bought some dates because I had an idea forming inside my head: a new take on a bacon-wrapped jalapeño popper, this one a combination of dove and dates. Sweet and meaty.

In 1927, Dateland was designated as an "official" place to grow dates by the King of Morocco when his country was threatened by a date blight. So seed stock from the highest quality Moroccan dates was grown there, and since then a small but significant date industry has expanded in Arizona and into Southern California. Morocco led me to my marinade for the doves: chermoula. Chermoula is an herby, citrusy, spicy mixture often used to marinate fish or meats.

Small honey dates are best because they don't overwhelm the dove. Medjools are too big, so if that's all you can find, cut them in half. Another tip is to half-cook the bacon so the dove breasts won't overcook by the time the bacon crisps on the grill.

Fatty-smoky-crisp bacon, soft and sweet dates, and meaty dove laced with the bright, spicy marinade. Super good, fun to eat—but rich! I ate six and was full.

12 to 16 dove breasts (24 to 32 halves)

12 to 16 small dates

1 pound bacon (not thick cut)

12 to 16 toothpicks, soaked in water

Chermoula Marinade

2 tablespoons olive oil

Zest and juice of a lemon

1 bunch cilantro or parsley, chopped (about 2 cups)

4 teaspoons ground cumin

2 teaspoons paprika

1 teaspoon hot paprika, Aleppo pepper, or cayenne

1 teaspoon salt

½ teaspoon black pepper

1 preserved lemon quarter, chopped (optional)

4 cloves garlic, minced

Put all the ingredients for the chermoula in a food processor or blender and buzz until smooth. Mix with the dove breasts and set in the fridge, covered, for up to 8 hours.

Cook the bacon until it gives up some fat and is limp. You want it about half-cooked, but not crispy. Set it aside to cool.

Slice the dates open vertically to remove the pit. Unfold the date to flatten it out. Take a dove breast, shake off excess marinade, and wrap it around the date.

Wrap a piece of bacon around the dove-date tightly and secure with a toothpick. If you want, you can double up on the dove-dates if you want a bigger popper.

Get your grill hot, leaving one side with no coals or with no burners turned on. Set your poppers on the grill with the seam side of the bacon facing down. Grill with the cover up, turning the poppers frequently to crisp the bacon on all sides. If you are worried the dove might not be fully cooked, set the poppers on the cool side of the grill when the bacon crisps, then cover the grill and cook for an additional 2 to 4 minutes.

SMOKED DOVES WITH GUAJILLO SAUCE

PREP TIME: 30 MINUTES | BRINING TIME: 12 HOURS | COOK TIME: 2 HOURS | SERVES 4 TO 6 AS A STARTER

I don't generally like stewed doves. Overcooked dove tastes like liver to me, and not in a good way. But if you cure and smoke your doves first, then bathe them in your sauce, whatever that sauce may be, you have a fantastic compromise.

To start, brine the birds with salt and a touch of Instacure curing salt; you use it when smoking meats for food safety and to give meats that characteristic rosy color. You can get it in butcher shops and online. You can skip the curing salt, but I prefer the flavor and the color that comes with it. Brine, rinse, chill, then smoke the doves before bathing them in the sauce.

16 to 20 doves, quail, snipe or sora rails, or 8 pigeons or teal

½ cup kosher salt (I use Diamond Crystal)

2 quarts water

1 teaspoon Instacure No. 1 curing salt (optional)

Guajillo Sauce

8 dried guajillo peppers, stems and seeds removed

2 tablespoons tomato paste

1 small white onion, quartered

5 cloves garlic, unpeeled

1 teaspoon dried Mexican oregano

¼ teaspoon allspice

¼ teaspoon ground coriander

2 to 6 hot chiles, such as chiltepin or arbol

Salt and freshly squeezed lime juice

Dissolve the salt and curing salt into the water and submerge the doves in it. Set this in the fridge for no less than 4 hours; I prefer 12 hours. Remove, rinse briefly, and pat dry.

Get your smoker going to about 170°F to 200°F. Use whatever wood you like, but I prefer mesquite or oak. Smoke your doves for 2 hours, with smoke going the whole time.

Meanwhile, make the sauce. Pour boiling water over the dried chiles to rehydrate them. While this is happening, char the onion and garlic in a hot, dry skillet until you get some nice blackening. Peel the garlic and put it in a blender. Coarsely chop the onion and put that in there, too.

Put the guajillo chiles, tomato paste, oregano, allspice, coriander, and hot chiles to taste into the blender and purée. Thin the sauce with some of the chile soaking water, lager beer, or water. Adjust the seasoning with kosher salt and lime.

You can either paint the doves with this sauce in the last hour of cooking, or you can remove the birds from the smoker, cut them in half with kitchen shears or a knife, and then bathe them in the sauce. Serve with plenty of napkins and a bone bowl. Watch out for birdshot!

SONORA SUNRISE

SERVES 1

This is the one cocktail in this book, and it's a good one. I came up with it after harvesting a bunch of Christmas cholla fruit at the San Bernardino National Wildlife Refuge, which straddles the border and is about 30 miles east of the twin cities of Douglas and Agua Prieta. This cholla has tasty crimson fruit with no needle-like glochids, unlike other cholla fruit. They're teeny, though, so I made a syrup out of them. Add some spicy rim salt, and it all came together.

- 1 shot bacanora, sotol, or mezcal
- Juice of 1 Key lime
- A glug of Christmas cholla or prickly pear syrup, about 1½ tablespoons
- 1 or 2 chiltepin chiles, crushed, or 1 arbol or other small, hot, dried chile
- 3 tablespoons Tajin

Wet the rim of a glass with a little of the lime juice and apply the Tajín as a rim salt. Shake the lime juice, bacanora, syrup, and chiles together, and pour into the glass over ice.

NOTE: Tajín is a widely available chile-lime-salt mix often used to spice up fresh fruit.

MESQUITE CHOCOLATE CHIP COOKIES

PREP TIME: 20 MINUTES | COOK TIME: 20 MINUTES | SERVES 8 TO 12

These cookies are flat out fantastic. No, they're not traditional or even super common, but mesquite chocolate chip cookies do exist outside my imagination: You can find them occasionally in Tucson, where mesquite flour is so popular that Desert Harvesters hosts special days where everyone can bring their dried mesquite beans to have them turned into flour.

These cookies are a wonderful celebration of the Sonoran Desert's bounty—especially when you add pine nuts or black walnuts, both of which grow in the desert. And pecans are an important crop throughout the borderlands.

I prefer to use gram measurements here because I made a great many versions of these cookies before I got where I wanted. And yes, it was *so* horrible eating so many cookies . . . That said, you can use the standard volumetric measurements and get close enough.

You can find mesquite flour in many fancy supermarkets, and you can buy it online.

You'll need 2 baking sheets lined with parchment paper for this recipe.

- 330 grams cake flour or all-purpose flour, 3½ cups
- 150 grams mesquite flour, a scant cup
- 6 grams baking powder, 1 teaspoon
- 6 grams baking soda, 1 teaspoon
- 6 grams salt, 1 teaspoon
- 225 grams room temperature unsalted butter, 8 ounces
- 200 grams sugar, 1 cup
- 50 grams brown sugar, ⅓ cup
- 3 eggs, room temperature
- 2 teaspoons vanilla extract
- 160 grams rolled oats, 2 cups
- 100 grams toasted pine nuts or chopped pecans, 1 cup
- 200 grams chocolate chips, 10 ounces

Preheat your oven to 375°F.

Mix the two flours, baking powder, baking soda, and salt in a bowl.

Beat the butter until soft, then beat in both sugars until the mixture is fluffy. Beat in 1 egg at a time, then the vanilla extract. Mix in the flour in 3 or 4 batches, making sure it's all incorporated after each one. Stir in the nuts, oats and chocolate chips.

Scoop up heaping tablespoons of the dough, and with wet hands, roll into a ball. Set on a baking sheet lined with parchment paper and pat into a disk. Repeat with remaining dough.

Bake the cookies 11 to 12 minutes. If your oven has hot spots, rotate the pans halfway through. Remove the baking sheets from the oven, let the cookies set for about 3 minutes, then use a thin spatula to move them to a cooling rack.

The cookies will keep at room temperature, covered, for a few days.

ACORN COOKIES

PREP TIME: 20 MINUTES | COOK TIME: 20 MINUTES | SERVES 4

I was surprised to see acorn cookies along the border, but there they were: galletas de bellota. It does make some sense: The Sonoran Desert is the land of the Emory oak, *Quercus emoryi*, which has such low levels of bitter tannins that its acorns can be roasted whole and eaten without prior leaching—unlike most other species of acorns.

The first cookies I saw were classic egg white cookies, a mix of egg whites, sugar, and acorn flour. Light, nice and fun. I've since seen them as butter cookies, and that was the inspiration for these snowballs. Think of this as a mashup between a butter cookie and a Mexican wedding cookie. They're simple to make, and as a bonus are gluten-free.

Obviously, acorn flour is the pain point here. I make my own, and if you live where the Emory oak does—Arizona, New Mexico, West Texas, Sonora, Chihuahua, or Coahuila—you can gather your own acorns, shell, and grind them. Or you can use acorns from other oaks, but they need to be leached. I have full instructions for this on my website Hunter Angler Gardener Cook. (huntgathercook.com)

You can buy acorn flour online, but it is expensive. An excellent, easier-to-find substitute would be to use chestnut flour or some other nut meal.

- 150 grams acorn flour, 1¾ cups
- 100 grams room temperature butter, 7 tablespoons
- 50 grams sugar, ¼ cup
- 3 grams salt, ½ teaspoon
- 2 grams ground allspice or cinnamon (1 teaspoon)
- Powdered sugar for dusting

Preheat your oven to 325°F.

Mix the flour, sugar, salt, and allspice in a bowl. Cut the butter into small cubes, then work it in with your fingers or a pastry cutter. You want the mixture to look like sandy meal.

Use your hands to compress the mixture into balls about the size of a small walnut. Really compress the balls, or they may fall apart.

Set each one on the baking sheet lined with parchment paper. Bake for 20 minutes.

Remove from the oven and let the cookies rest 5 minutes before carefully dusting them with the powdered sugar. They are fragile, but should hold together while you eat them.

The cookies will keep at room temperature, covered, for a few days. You might need to freshen them up with more powdered sugar after a day or two. They do not freeze well.

BARREL CACTUS

Barrel cactus fruit are large, juicy, and shine with a canary yellow that always makes me smile. They are spine-free—unique among cactus fruit—and easy to pick, if you keep away from the nasty spines on the main cactus.

Two species inhabit the borderlands, *Ferocactus wislizeni*, and *F. cylindraceus*. The former is more common in the Sonoran Desert, the latter in the Mojave, Baja, and California. Interestingly, the spines on *F. cylindraceus* point downward, and the whole plant leans southward, giving it the name compass cactus. Useful if you're lost in the desert.

The fruits, which look like mini pineapples, ripen slowly and are available from November to April, but each cactus is idiosyncratic: One may be loaded with fruit, the next barren. And I've seen ripe fruit even in May in Arizona.

To prepare barrel cactus fruit, slice off the top where the old flower petals were, slice the fruit in half, then dig out the little black seeds with a small spoon. Save these. Eaten fresh, the fruit is an almost perfect mashup of lemon, green pepper, and okra. I like them raw, but they are a little mucilaginous, like all cactus.

If you then cook the fresh fruit, that slime will get bothersome. So unless you want to use barrel cactus fruit like a tart okra in a stew, I recommend drying it first. Much like with nopales or cholla buds, the act of drying these foods tames the slime.

I dry barrel cactus fruit in rings or slices, then add them to stews like the Pozole Blanco (page 236) or the Green Chile Stew (page 167). You can also cook the fruit a long time with sugar to make a chutney or jam. It will need pectin.

Another fun use for the dried fruit is to grind it into a powder. You can use it combined with salt and ground chile to make a phenomenal rim salt for cocktails; it's a perfect addition to the rim salt for the Sonora Sunrise (page 230). It's also good sprinkled on ice cream or dusted on other fruits.

As for the seeds, you can use them as you would poppy seeds. I prefer toasting the seeds in a hot, dry frying pan before using, because their flavor goes from vaguely gritty and neutral to crunchy and nutty. Just toast and toss the seeds until they start to pop, then move them to a cool bowl so they don't burn.

You can keep the seeds as-is and include them in muffins, breads, or crackers. Or you can grind the toasted seeds into a powder and add that, sparingly, to flour tortillas, cookies like the Bizcochitos (page 172), even the Mesquite Chocolate Chip Cookies (page 216). Start with a tablespoon or two in those recipes, increasing in subsequent batches if you want a stronger flavor.

Flower buds of barrel cactus are edible and are delicious as a pickle. You'll need to pry them off the plant with a screwdriver or tongs or pliers, plus a knife. You can then pickle them using any cucumber pickle method you like. I've seen these offered as escabeche alongside tacos in Sonora, much like the more common jalapeños, carrots, and onions you'll see served with tacos elsewhere.

I should note that a candy was once made from the flesh of the barrel cactus itself, using a method very similar to the Candied Squash (page 252). But doing so kills the cactus, which can take decades to grow to maturity. The cacti were so overharvested that in most places in Mexico, it is illegal to kill one now. That said, I've eaten the candy in Tijuana. It was . . . OK. Definitely not worth killing a 100-year-old cactus for!

Barrel cactus fruit look like little yellow pineapples and have no spines.

MESQUITE BEAN SYRUP

Mesquite trees can be found in Southern California, southern Nevada, Arizona, New Mexico, the southeast corner of Colorado, most of Texas, and in little scattered pockets of Oklahoma, Kansas, and Missouri. All told, there are about a dozen species, the best of which are honey mesquite (*Prosopis glandulosa*), velvet mesquite (*P. velutina*), and the screwbean mesquite, which is *P. pubescens*. Any variety works.

Simply gather your beans and make sure they are very dry, which normally isn't hard in the desert. You'll notice little holes in the beans. These are caused by bruchid beetles, whose larvae bore their way *out* of the dry pod. So they are exit holes, not entry, which means you are not likely to eat a ton of little larvae. Even if there are some in your beans, who cares? They're teeny and will be cooked to death with the bean pods as you make the syrup. So don't sweat it.

Very occasionally the fungus *Aspergillus flavus* can infect mesquite beans, and this will make you sick. Desert Harvesters in Tucson recommends that you pick your pods before the summer rains, and only pick from trees, not on the ground, unless you're picking above about 3500 feet.

One flavor caveat: *Different trees will produce pods that taste different.* This is from Mike Mayer, who runs La Madera Mesquite in Tucson:

"You have to taste the pods first. Every tree will produce pods with a different flavor—some are bitter, some sour, some tasteless, some sweet, maple, or a combination. When the pod is dry, break off a small piece and chew it up carefully to get the flavor. If it tastes good it will make good syrup. If it tastes bad it will make bad-tasting syrup."

So how to make mesquite bean syrup? It's very simple because the bean pods are naturally sugary; there is no sugar added. In a nutshell, you break up the pods, steep them in water, and that water eventually becomes your syrup.

I use a ratio of 1 gallon of water to 1 pound of beans. Smash them up as best you can. I put the beans in a heavy-duty plastic Ziploc and bash them with a rubber mallet. You'll never completely crush the seeds, but that's fine.

You don't want to boil or even simmer the water. This is very important. Beer brewers will know why: Higher temperatures extract tannins and other bitter compounds from the pods, which can wreck your syrup. Very slow and very low is the key. Patience.

You can do this in a low oven, or on the stovetop set on low, but the best method is in a slow cooker. Put all your crushed beans and water in the slow cooker, set it so it will never even simmer, put the lid on and walk away.

How long? At least overnight, and 20 to 24 hours is better. Strain the liquid through a fine-mesh strainer first, then again through a paper towel or cheesecloth to get the fine suspended particles out.

You now have an awesome liquid the color of dark chocolate, with a high enough sugar content to brew into alcohol if you wanted to: 1 gallon of water with 1 pound of crushed mesquite pods steeped 18 hours got me a specific gravity reading of 1.030, which would make a beer of about 3% alcohol. Specific gravity is a way to measure the sugar content of a liquid, and is measured with a hydrometer.

That's not strong enough to be a syrup, though. Now you need to reduce the liquid to get it to the sweetness you want.

Again, *don't boil it.* I pour the syrup into a pot and heat it to the steaming point, and let that cook *very* gently until it is reduced by half, about 2 hours. Slowly reducing the syrup produces cleaner flavors than you'd get by boiling it down.

▶ The bark of the screwbean mesquite is as tough as the desert it lives in.

And what are those flavors? They are borderline mystical. Seriously. Mesquite bean syrup combines hints of malt, mocha, cinnamon, and vanilla with a definite woody background. It is wonderful stuff you need to taste to fully appreciate.

Once you make the full syrup, it's great added to hot chocolate or coffee, drizzled on ice cream like the Pine Nut Ice Cream (page 174), added to seltzer water for a fizzy soft drink, or drop a glug in a glass and top it with bourbon or whiskey or even an anejo tequila.

Mesquite syrup will keep indefinitely if you cook it down to a specific gravity of 1.3, which will take a while. Or you can simply make the initial brew and add enough sugar to get to that specific gravity. Don't want to bother with all this? You can kinda-sorta cheat by adding a ratio of 1:1 mesquite brew to sugar, shorting the sugar a bit—so if you have, say 4 cups of the brew, add 4 scant cups of sugar, heat to dissolve the sugar, and the result will be stable.

If you keep it light, it will ferment eventually, but should still keep for a week or two in the fridge.

Cholla buds, despined and cooked.

HOW TO EAT CHOLLA BUDS

Properly prepared, cholla buds taste like a fantastical combination of green bean, artichoke heart, and asparagus. They need to be gathered in spring, anywhere from March to early May depending on the species and where you live. Cholla grow in Mexico, as well as the states of California, Nevada, Arizona, Utah, New Mexico, Colorado, and parts of Nebraska, Oklahoma, and Texas.

The plant is a crazy-looking cactus: It starts with a central stalk that eventually gets woody, then grows arms in all directions at once. There seems to be no rhyme or reason to it, although I am certain there must be one in there somewhere. Oh, and cholla are covered in nasty spines. *Covered*. For eating, most people favor the buckhorn, staghorn, and pencil cholla.

Every spring the cactus puts out new arms and an array of flower buds. These of course turn into flowers of many colors. I've seen red, yellow, and lavender-ish ones. After that, it sets fruit very similar to those of the prickly pear—and yes, you can make a cholla fruit syrup with the fruit of the Christmas cholla that is pretty close to my recipe for prickly pear syrup. But in this case, it is the buds before the flowers form that you want.

The Tohono O'Odham of the Sonora pluck the buds off the cactus with wooden chopstick-like things—regular tongs work fine—and then meticulously remove the spines. Use a stick, or wooden paddle, or a thick glove to rough up the buds a bit (don't wail on them, though) to knock the spines off. This will get most of them off. Sadly, most is not all.

Like their cousins the prickly pears, cholla have glochids, too. Glochids are nearly invisible spinelets that feel like like getting fiberglass into your skin. You can pick them off with tweezers, but a better method is to kill them with fire.

Use a little torch to burn off most of the spines. This goes much faster than the tweezer method. No torch? Rotate the buds over the flame of a gas burner.

Then boil them for a minute or two in very salty water. Shock them in cold water to halt the cooking process. They will keep for a week or so in the fridge like this.

My advice: Dehydrate them. Fresh cholla are nice, but they have that same slimy thing going on as do nopales, the pads of the prickly pear. Not my favorite, although if you are into slime get your freak on. I dehydrate them at about 105°F, which keeps them pretty. You can also dry the buds in your oven, set to its lowest setting, or in hot shade.

Dried cholla buds will last until the Second Coming. Keep them in a mason jar, and if you have one of those silicon packets, drop one in; this keeps moisture out of the jar.

To eat cholla buds, rehydrate them overnight in some water, or boil them straight away. Regardless they need to be simmered until tender, which can take anywhere from 30 to 90 minutes. If you want to eat your cholla buds faster, dehydrate, cook, then freeze in a bag: That way you can just take them out of the freezer and pop them into beans or whatever.

How to use them? As a cool accent in any Southwestern dish. My favorite is mixed with beans, especially tepary beans, which are native to the Sonoran Desert. The Tohono O'Odham toss them into a sort of antipasto salad, or sauté with some chile and onions.

▼ The moon rises over a lone yucca in the desert.

SONORA

El Desierto. The desert is what Sonora is known for, but Mexico's second-largest state is so much more than that. Hundreds of miles of coastline on the Sea of Cortez, mountains high enough to see snow, and in the south, some of the richest agricultural land in the Western Hemisphere.

Sonora is where wheat and beef reign supreme. It is widely regarded as home to Mexico's best beef, and indeed a huge amount of Sonoran beef literally walks across the border en route to American feedlots for grain finishing. Sonoran soft wheat is unmatched in its flavor and ability to make delicate tortillas, and has gained a following with artisanal breadmakers far beyond the desert.

Where Nuevo Leon is all about manufacturing, Sonora is deeply agricultural. Even its baseball team—in Sonora, baseball eclipses soccer in popularity—is called the Naranjeros, the orange pickers. The Western ranching tradition that goes well beyond cattle and stretches up into California's Central Valley holds sway throughout Sonora down into neighboring Sinaloa. Think cowboy farmers, not the Midwest.

The food here reflects that tradition. Carne asada is common all over the borderlands, but when it comes to both the dish and the event, most tip their Stetsons to the Sonorans. And their translucent, delicate flour tortillas make a Texas tortilla seem ham-handed by comparison. There's even a giant one called a sobaquera that stretches for two feet or more, yet is still so thin you need to double it up to make the classic burro percherón.

Carne seca and machaca, fried ribeye tacos, mystical cuts of beef unseen even in Arizona, and big beef stews—even the most traditional Sonoran pozole, called gallina pinta, has beef instead of pork.

Lorenzas are a hugely popular snack: it's a corn tortilla covered in cheese set on a grill to crisp, and once the cheese melts, it's normally topped with chopped carne asada. Sort of a tostada meets quesadilla meets carne asada taco.

The sun sets in Ures, Sonora.

But the top snack here is a dogo. Sonoran hot dogs are legendary, and legendarily free form and fun. Almost always wrapped in cheap, thin bacon, the dogs are served nestled in special buns and topped with more or less anything you can think of, from beans and chiles to cheese, carne asada, shrimp, avocado, and a galaxy of salsas.

All this is not to short the state's seafood. Sonora and Baja share the Sea of Cortez, and almost every seafood specialty in Baja can be found in Sonora as well, in places like Puerto Peñasco or Bahia Kino, only 45 minutes from the capital of Hermosillo.

If Monterrey is the Chicago of Mexico, Hermosillo is its Fresno: far smaller, intensely agricultural, hot, diverse, and easy to love. Even the architecture reminds me of Fresno, or as that

They take their flour tortillas seriously in Hermosillo, Sonora.

city's boosters love to call it, Fres-yes! Hermosillo is the center of the state's cuisine.

Sonoran food is simple, its origins farmer food. There are few fancy sauces, and nothing like the moles of Oaxaca. Its position as a Spanish-speaking extension of the American West (although the American West could equally be seen as an English-speaking extension of vaquero culture) squares Sonora with the big bold flavors of both Texas and American Southwestern cuisine: simple chile sauces, open fire cooking, and lots of vegetables orbiting the beef that is central to everything here.

Smoke and char are signatures of Sonora, along with its beloved pepper, the wild chiltepin chile. Dried orbs of fiery goodness, chiltepins show up everywhere in Sonora—as well as in neighboring Arizona. Smoke even permeates the state's iconic sweet snack, the coyota, which is basically a Mexican Pop Tart. Coyotas in Hermosillo are almost always baked in a wood-fired oven, and that flavor carries over into the pastry. Villa de Seris is the mecca for coyotas, with Doña Coyo's coyotas as the insider favorite over the more famous Doña Maria's.

Unlike Chihuahua, which is largely at altitude and gets snow in winter, Sonora is mostly low-lying, and hot. So hot that parts of the south, around Navajoa, reach levels of heat and humidity considered unlivable by the United Nations. The locals call it the calurón, the Big Heat. Every Oxxo convenience store is packed with water, Tecate Light, and Pedialyte: Hydration is serious business in a place that can reach 115°F with 95 percent humidity.

Other than the chilled contents of the Oxxo coolers, bacanora and lechuguilla are what slake a thirst in Sonora. These are their homegrown mezcals, made from the agaves *A. angustifolia* and *A. lechuguilla*, respectively. Lechuguilla, rare in the United States, is, along with Oaxacan tobalá, my absolute favorite mezcal. Floral, smooth, with layers of flavors that reveal themselves only by slow sipping a copita unadorned, lechuguilla is a perfect thing to drink after a proper carne asada.

The company Sotoleros makes a good one available in the US, but both lechuguilla and bacanora are only now coming into American markets, so many more labels will be available as time goes on.

SONORAN ENCHILADAS

PREP TIME: 30 MINUTES | COOK TIME: 20 MINUTES | SERVES 4

Humble, homey, satisfying, these enchiladas are as minimalist as it gets: thick, handmade corn tortitas bathed in a red enchilada sauce and dressed simply, with queso fresco or cotija, shredded lettuce, cilantro, and onions. They make a filling lunch or breakfast, an accompaniment to stews or meaty things, or as a nice vegetarian meal.

I first ate them in Tucson, but really enjoyed them in Nogales and Hermosillo, where an order costs less than $2. You can use the red enchilada sauce on page 37 or the tomato sauce for the chiles rellenos on page 231.

They do not keep well, so make them and eat them. Leftover tortitas get heavy and crumbly.

- 3 cups masa harina
- 1 large russet potato, peeled and diced
- Salt
- 1 heaping tablespoon lard or shortening
- Oil for frying
- 1 recipe Red Enchilada Sauce (page 37)
- 1 recipe Hank's Taco Onions (page 46)
- 1 cup shredded iceberg or romaine lettuce
- 1 cup crumbled queso fresco or cotija cheese

Boil the potato in salted water until soft. Remove and save the water. Let the potato cool while you whip the lard in a large bowl until it's fluffy. When the potato is mostly cool, add it to the bowl, then the masa harina and enough of the potato water to pull everything together; start with 3 tablespoons and add more 1 tablespoon at a time until you get a soft dough. Knead this well.

Form balls about the size of a golf ball or a little larger and pat them by hand into fat disks about ¼ inch thick; these are called tortitas in Spanish. Smooth out any cracks with your fingers. Repeat with the rest of the dough.

Heat the enchilada sauce in a small pot. It need not boil, just steam or simmer a little.

Fry the tortitas in vegetable oil until slightly browned, flipping once or twice.

To serve, bathe the tortitas in the red sauce and set on a plate. Three to five is a good serving. Top with the cheese, onions, and shredded lettuce.

"La paciencia es amarga, pero sus frutos son dulces."

Patience is bitter, but its fruits are sweet.

SONORA HOT DOGS

PREP TIME: 20 MINUTES | COOK TIME: 25 MINUTES | SERVES 6 TO 8

Dogos, as they are called in Sonora, are the most popular cheap late-night food in Hermosillo and Ciudad Obregon. On one trip, my friend Charlie de la Rosa and I ate far more than we thought possible in a plaza right outside the University of Sonora filled with dogo vendors. The best Sonora dogs in the United States are those from El Güero Canelo in Tucson. What makes them special are the thin bacon wrapping on the dog and the special soft buns, which are very close to New England lobster roll buns.

Your best bet is to get an unsplit soft hoagie roll and slice a pocket in the middle: Sonoran dog buns are closed at their ends, and this helps them contain the prodigious toppings, which can range from, well, I've seen dogo stands with 20-plus optional toppings, so anything goes. I offer some suggestions below.

- 6 to 12 beef hot dogs
- 1 or 2 slices of thin bacon per hot dog
- 6 to 12 jalapeños or serranos
- 1 pound white onions, minced
- Soft brioche-style hoagie rolls or large hot dog buns
- Mayonnaise
- 1 recipe Pico de Gallo (page 46)
- Leftover Border Beans (page 265) or Charro Beans (page 167; optional)
- Guacamole (page 272; optional)
- Mustard and hot sauce, Huichol if possible

Turn your oven to 200°F and set a cooling rack over a baking sheet inside to keep your dogs warm.

Wrap the bacon around the hotdogs: Start at one end and wrap at an angle, overlapping each turn. When you get to the end of the dog, tuck the bacon in on itself. This helps prevent it from unraveling. Do this for all the dogs. You can also stretch a piece of bacon on a cutting board and roll a dog up into it; tuck the end in this case, too.

Grill or sear your dogs in a pan over medium heat—nothing too ragingly hot. Turn them often to crisp the bacon. When the bacon is crispy on all sides, set the dogs on the rack in the oven.

Blister the jalapeños and serranos in the bacon fat. You want the skins to be loosened, with some browned bits on the peppers. Set these aside. Add the chopped onion to the bacon fat and brown over medium-high heat. You want the onions well browned.

If your rolls are not already split, slice open a pocket in each one. Wrap them in paper towels and microwave them for about 10 seconds. The buns are steamed in Sonora.

Spread mayo in the bun's pocket, stuff a dogo in there, and add some onions, some pico de gallo, maybe some cooked beans, guacamole, mustard, and hot sauce. Huichol brand is the best hot sauce for a Sonoran dogo, in my opinion.

You eat the blistered chiles alongside the dog: bite of hot dog, bite of chile.

GREEN CHILES RELLENOS

PREP TIME: 1 HOUR | COOK TIME: 20 MINUTES | SERVES 6 TO 8 AS A STARTER

Unless you live in the western half of the borderlands, this is not your typical chile relleno. It's better. It relies on Hatch-style chiles, called chiles verdes in Sonora, and Mennonite cheese from Chihuahua. In Sonora, queso asadero or queso fresco are most common, but I've eaten them with the less melty panela, too.

No chile relleno is easy to make. You need to roast fresh chiles, seed them without destroying the chile, stuff, batter, and fry in the right temperature oil or else they get heavy and greasy. Normally served with a light tomato sauce, these are also absolutely amazing as the filling for a burrito or a Chimichanga (page 209).

You will want to choose peppers that are large and straight, ideally with stems. This will make them easier to roast, clean, and move to the hot oil once battered. For the sauce, I recommend starting with 6 chiltepin or pequin chiles, or 3 árbols—it's supposed to be zippy—adding more if it's not spicy enough for you.

If by chance you have access to the toasted wheat flour of the Tohono O'Odham, or any other style of toasted flour, use that. It adds a lot of flavor.

Save this recipe for a party or a weekend, as it's kind of a production. But your family and friends will love it, either as a starter or a simple vegetarian supper.

Sauce

1 pound tomatoes, chopped

½ cup chopped white onion

2 cloves garlic

1 teaspoon Mexican oregano

Chiltepin or other small hot chiles (see headnote)

Salt

2 tablespoons lard or oil

Relleno

10 to 12 large Anaheim chiles (Hatch style)

1 pound queso asadero, Oaxaca, Chihuahua, or fresco, or mozzarella

5 eggs, separated

4 tablespoons flour, plus more for dusting

Oil for frying

Roast and skin your chiles following the directions on page 32. Broiler should be your last resort on this recipe because you want the chiles to have some firmness in them, and a broiler tends to fully cook the peppers.

Make the sauce: Put everything except the lard in a blender and purée. Thin with water if you need to; it should be the consistency of thin gravy. Heat the lard in a medium pot over medium-high heat and pour the sauce in. It will spatter, so keep stirring it until everything combines. Cook this over very low heat while you make the rellenos.

Carefully make a 4-inch slit in a chile, close to the top. With a sharp paring knife, cut out the core of seeds. Using a small spoon, carefully remove as many seeds inside the chile as you can; a few strays are fine. Repeat with the remaining chiles.

NOTE: If you end up with a chile that tears badly, you'll have to use it in some other recipe. A small tear is salvageable, but you ideally want no extra hole in the pepper.

Cut pieces of cheese and fit one inside each chile. You can use multiple pieces. If you are using a not-so-melty cheese like queso fresco, be careful to not overfill the chile. Melty cheese will fill the interior of the pepper better. Repeat with the remaining chiles.

Beat the egg whites to stiff peaks. Gently fold in the egg yolks, one by one, then mix in the flour.

Set a cooling rack over a baking sheet in the oven and turn the oven to "warm."

Heat oil to a depth of about ½ to 1 inch in a large pan. You're shooting for 350°F.

Dust the chiles in flour. When the oil hits 350°F, hold the stems, cut side up, and dredge the chiles in the batter, making sure they're fully coated. (Do this close to the hot oil.) Lay the peppers gently into the hot oil, cut side up, and spoon hot oil over the tops to set the batter. Fry until golden brown, flipping once.

Set the finished rellenos on the rack in the oven while you do the rest.

Serve atop some of the sauce.

GALLINA PINTA

PREP TIME: 20 MINUTES | COOK TIME: 4 HOURS | SERVES 10 TO 12

Gallina pinta, painted hen in Spanish, is at its core a sort of pozole—a simple stew of hominy (nixtamalized corn) and meat. But unlike most other versions of pozole, this one adds beans. There is a similar stew in Chihuahua called muni-pozole, a specialty of the Tarahumara. Beef is the most common meat in gallina pinta, but I've seen recipes that use venison, and that's what I used here, smoked. Any red meat will do. Interestingly, gallina pinta, despite its name, never uses chicken. Go figure.

This is one of those recipes that is as good or as average as you want to make it. Sure, you can make gallina pinta with canned beans, canned hominy, and even canned meat. People do, and it's perfectly fine to make it this way if you are busy on a worknight. But it will be so much better if you make everything from scratch—even the nixtamal, or hominy.

The corn used in Sonora is always white pozole corn, which means the kernels are big and starchy. You can't use sweet corn here. The gold standard of any pozole is a variety called cacahuazintle. You can buy it online from Masienda. You can also buy nixtamalized, dried corn from Rancho Gordo. As for the beans, simple pinto beans are a fine choice, but I prefer tepary beans which are native to Sonora. They are smaller and meatier than regular pintos. Any yellow, brown, or tan bean will do.

Top your stew with cilantro and onions that you've soaked in some lime juice. You'll also want some dried chiltepin or other small, hot chiles for garnish.

Once made, this stew only gets better in the fridge over the next few days, so make a big batch on a weekend and eat it all week. You can freeze it, too.

- 1 pound dried pozole corn, or 2 pounds canned hominy
- Salt
- 3 pounds venison neck, or shoulder or shank, or oxtail, shin or beef stew meat
- 1 white onion, quartered
- 6 unpeeled cloves garlic
- 2 quarts venison or beef stock
- 2 quarts water
- 1 pound dried pinto or tepary beans, or 2 pounds canned
- 3 to 5 green Hatch or Anaheim chiles, roasted, seeded and chopped coarsely
- ½ cup chopped cilantro, for garnish
- ¼ cup freshly squeezed lime juice
- ½ white onion, minced
- Dried chiltepin chiles, for serving

This assumes you've nixtamalized your corn the previous evening, or are starting with nixtamalized corn. If you are using canned hominy, simply remove it from the can and rinse well. Keep it in a bowl.

If you are smoking your meat before starting the stew, I advise doing this the day before, but regardless, you will want to salt the meat well, then smoke it over low heat, about 200°F, for about 3 hours. The goal is to get it a little smoky. You will definitely need to cut it into hunks of about ¼ to ½ pound.

When you are ready to start the stew, char the cut sides of the quartered onion and the unpeeled garlic cloves on a comal, griddle, or cast iron pan. Peel the garlic, then mince it and the onion. Add these to a large soup pot.

Add the corn and meat and cover with the stock and the water. Bring to a boil, then drop to a gentle simmer. Cook gently, with the pot mostly covered, until the meat wants to fall off the bone, which should take a couple hours.

About 90 minutes into the cooking time, add the dried beans. You'll likely need another hour of gentle simmering. If you are using canned hominy and/or beans now is the time to add them. This is the time to soak the chopped white onion in the lime juice, along with a little salt, in a bowl.

Once the meat, corn, and beans are nicely cooked, add the chopped roasted green chiles. Fish out the meat and discard the bones. Chop the meat against the grain so there are no long strings of meat. Return it all to the pot.

Serve topped with cilantro, the lime-soaked onion, and some hot chiles.

POZOLE BLANCO

PREP TIME: 20 MINUTES | COOK TIME: 4 HOURS | SERVES 10 TO 12

The beauty of pozole blanco is its purity: Nothing can distract you from the broth, which is the star here. Yes, it is designed so you can add green or red salsa to your bowl, making this soup something of a dealer's choice, but I prefer it clear, with lots of dried chiltepin chiles crushed into it.

In a perfect world, you would nixtamalize your own corn, nip off the root end of each kernel, and simmer that with a pig's head. This will get you close to the ancestral dish the way it's been made for centuries. The freshly nixtamalized corn tastes so much better than either canned hominy or dried, nixtamalized corn, but you can use those. Sweet corn is not a substitute.

As for the pig's head, it has meats of varying flavor and color, and there is so much collagen in it that the broth will set up like Jell-o in the fridge; this is a good thing, because that collagen lends heft and body to the broth. You simmer the pig's head with the corn until the meat wants to fall off. You then fish it out and strip the meat off, chopping the weirder bits small and leaving the obviously meaty bits large.

I get it. You may not want to go looking for a pig's head to make pozole blanco. An alternative is to buy pork shoulder plus a couple pig's feet, which are available in many markets. If you can't get pig's feet, the world won't end, but your pozole won't be as good. Like the head, you simmer the feet until tender, fish them out, and mince the meat and skin.

You can make pozole blanco with chicken or any other white meat bird, like pheasants or turkey. If you do, try to get some chicken feet from the market for the collagen. Or go for poultry + pig's feet.

A typical pozole will have onions and garlic, plus bay leaves and Mexican oregano in the broth, and often some allspice berries and black peppercorns. Super simple.

Then, when you serve it, everyone can add whatever they like to their pozole. Common toppings include: limes, shredded cabbage, sliced radishes, avocado, pickled white onion, cilantro, and dried hot chiles.

One other thing. If you want, you can add a cup or more of the Red Enchilada Sauce (page 37) or the Salsa Verde (page 70).

Pozole

- 2 pounds dried field corn or nixtamalized corn, or 2 30-ounce cans of hominy)
- 1 pig's head, (or 4 pounds pork shoulder and 2 pig's feet)
- 1 tablespoon Mexican oregano
- 3 bay leaves
- 10 allspice berries
- 15 whole black peppercorns
- 1 large white onion, chopped
- 8 cloves garlic, thinly sliced
- Salt

Submerge the pig's head in water. If you are using dried corn, add it now. If not, wait a while. Bring this to a simmer, and skim off any froth that accumulates. When the froth subsides, add the remaining pozole ingredients and keep the pot at a simmer. If you are using the pork shoulder and feet, it's the same procedure.

If you are using freshly nixtamalized corn or canned hominy, add it after the pork has been simmering for 1 hour. Continue to simmer everything until the meat wants to fall off, or the shoulder meat can be shredded easily. This will take longer for a head than pork shoulder.

If you are using the head, fish it out and strip off all the meat; discard the skull. If it had its tongue, peel that and chop coarsely. The rule of thumb with a head is to chop recognizable meat coarsely, everything else fine. If you are using the shoulder and feet, fish out the feet and discard the bones, then mince everything fine. Once it's chopped, return all the meat to the pot.

OPTIONAL: Once the head is out of the broth, I try to pick out the bay leaves, allspice berries, and peppercorns. This makes the soup easier to eat later, but if you miss a few, it's not a big deal.

Toppings
6 limes, quartered
¼ head cabbage, shredded
2 avocados, sliced
6 radishes, sliced
½ cup chopped cilantro
Dried hot chiles

Once the meat and corn are tender, you are ready to rock. Lay out all the toppings, and let people mix and match as they like.

NOTE: If you are doing the chicken or other poultry version, you will want the equivalent of 2 chickens, about 5 to 6 pounds of poultry—plus a pound or two of chicken feet or 2 pig's feet.

PICADILLO

PREP TIME: 20 MINUTES | COOK TIME: 20 MINUTES | SERVES 6 TO 8

The difference between Mexican picadillo and Midwestern taco meat is like the difference between sin and syntax: One's fun, the other boring as hell. Picadillo is easy to make, quick, and so much better than ground meat + McCormick's mild taco seasoning. Lots of versions exist, and most are relics from the Renaissance, when sweet-plus-meat was a thing. You see a lot of raisins and sometimes dates, occasionally actual sugar, plus almonds. See the meat mixture in Empanadas de Santa Rita (page 195) for that sort of picadillo.

I first came across this recipe, credited to Balvanera Gonzalez de Cabrera, in a cool little book called *La Cocina Familiar en el Estado de Sonora.* Interestingly, it is originally a venison recipe, but any ground meat works here. I've since read a few other Sonoran picadillo recipes in Spanish, and talked to a few Sonoran friends about how they make picadillo. This is an amalgam of those.

Use picadillo in tacos, as a fantastic empanada filling, mixed with eggs and stale tortillas for chilaquiles, stuffed in a burrito (especially a breakfast burrito), or even as the filling for a tamal. It makes a helluva chile relleno filling, too.

Picadillo will keep in the fridge a week or so. It will freeze OK, but I wouldn't use thawed picadillo for anything other than a filling you won't see, like in an empanada or pasty. The reason is because thawed potatoes get mushy and a little weird. They taste fine, but are not as pretty.

- 3 tablespoons freshly rendered lard, or some other fat
- 2 pounds ground venison or other meat
- 1 large white onion, chopped fine
- 1 carrot, peeled and diced
- 1 cup peeled, diced potato (optional)
- Salt
- Crushed dried chiltepin chiles (or any hot chile)
- 4 cloves garlic, minced
- 1 cup chopped roasted green Hatch, Anaheim, or poblano chiles, (about 4 to 6 chiles)
- 2 to 4 roasted whole tomatoes, crushed by hand
- 10 green olives, chopped
- 2 teaspoons dried oregano, Mexican if possible
- 1 teaspoon ground cumin
- 1 teaspoon ground black pepper
- 2 cups venison stock, or any other stock

Heat the lard over high heat in a large skillet; I use a cast iron frying pan. Add the meat, spreading it out in an even layer. Salt it well. Sear this without touching for 2 to 3 minutes. Then stir well and sear some more. You want the meat to get legitimate browning, not just turning gray. Sometimes this takes 10 minutes or so.

Add the onion, carrot, potato and hot chiles, if using. Mix well and cook these for about 5 minutes, stirring often.

Add all the remaining ingredients and stir to combine. Turn the heat down to medium and let this simmer for maybe 5 to 10 minutes, until it is as soupy or as dry as you like.

Keys to Success

- Picadillo should be finely ground, so use only finely ground meat. This is not a problem if you are buying it, only if you are grinding it yourself. I use a 4.5 mm die.
- If you plan on making burritos, definitely add the potatoes. It helps bulk it up.
- As for the roasted green chiles, you can use canned ones here.
- If you hate olives, skip them. They are not in every version of picadillo.
- Any sort of heat will do if you can't get chiltepins or pequins, from red pepper flakes or cayenne to Thai chiles to serranos or habaneros.

CARNE CON CHILE

PREP TIME: 45 MINUTES | COOK TIME: 3 HOURS | SERVES 6

Carne con chile, meat with chile sauce, is a bedrock recipe not only in Sonora, but also Arizona and parts of New Mexico. Not to be confused with chile con carne, which is basically the long way of saying "chili," carne con chile is a very simple dish of braised meat—beef, lamb, or venison in this case—with a simple chile sauce, served with rice and beans.

But as with anything so simple, ingredients and technique make all the difference. I've eaten this dish many times, and it can range from meh to mesmerizing. Everything on the plate matters.

Let's get the beans and rice out of the way first. Start with my recipe for Red Rice (page 36). The beans should be the Border Beans (page 265) or the Charro Beans (page 127). Use tepary, bayo, pinto, or pinquito beans.

For the meat, use some sort of meat with connective tissue in it. I prefer venison neck, shanks, or venison shoulder. All of those cuts from goats or sheep are perfect, too. With beef, you want shanks, shins, oxtail, brisket, or chuck.

This is not traditional, but I try to smoke my meat first. It adds a ton of flavor, and carne con chile isn't complicated, so each little trick helps. I salt my meat overnight, or even for a couple days, then smoke big pieces at about 185°F for about three hours. Enough to get a nice smoke ring and smoky flavor.

Then braise the meat. While that cooks, you make the chile sauce. The sauce lives or dies on the flavors of smoke and char. Toasted chiles and cumin seeds. Charred onion and garlic. And I use smoked salt to season it. So while it looks like a simple sauce, there's a lot going on.

Serve this with the rice and beans and some flour tortillas. Soak some chopped white onion in lime juice and chop some cilantro to finish it all off.

Once made, the meat will keep, refrigerated in its braising liquid, for a week. The chile sauce will keep for several weeks in the fridge. To serve, you shred the meat coarsely, then toss with some of the warm chile sauce. I recognize that many versions of carne con chile cook the meat in the sauce, but I find that deadens the flavor of the sauce. Whichever you prefer.

Meat

- 3 pounds venison or beef neck, shoulder, or shank
- Salt
- 1 quart venison or beef stock
- 1 quart water
- 4 bay leaves
- 1 avocado leaf (optional)
- 1 onion, quartered
- 3 cloves garlic, smashed

OPTIONAL SMOKING STEP: Salt the venison the night before you plan on smoking it and set in the fridge. The next morning, smoke the meat at 185°F for about three hours. I use mesquite here, but whatever wood you like will do.

Put the meat and all the other ingredients for the meat in a stewpot and bring to a simmer. Cover the pot. You can simmer this on the stovetop or in a 300°F oven.

Meanwhile, make the sauce. Start by toasting the chiles. Heat a comal, flattop, or large, heavy frying pan over medium heat. While the pan heats up, remove the stems and seeds from the dried chiles. Using a metal spatula, toast all the chiles quickly, pressing on them to flatten. They will get pliable quickly. You'll only need about 20 to 30 seconds per side, and you can flip them back and forth if you want. Do not let them char or burn. Move them as you go to a large bowl. When they are all toasted, pour boiling water over them to soak.

Spread the cumin seeds on the hot comal. Let them toast, moving them more or less constantly, until they smell nice, about a minute or two, tops. Move them to a spice grinder and grind to a powder. You can use ground cumin but it won't be as good.

CARNE CON CHILE, continued

Chile Sauce

- 2 to 4 dried chiles moritas (or chipotles from a can)
- 10 to 15 guajillo, New Mexican, California or similar mild red dried chile
- 1 tablespoon cumin seeds
- 1 white onion, cut in quarters
- 5 cloves garlic
- 1 tablespoon Mexican oregano
- 2 tablespoons lard or vegetable oil
- Salt and black pepper (smoked salt if you have it)

Char the garlic and onion on the comal. Set them down on the hot surface and let them sit there until you get some nice blackening. Move the garlic around to char on all sides. When they're ready, peel the garlic, and coarsely chop the onion.

Move the rehydrated chiles (and chipotles), the garlic, cumin, oregano and a healthy pinch of salt to the blender. Add a little of the braising liquid and purée. You want the sauce to have the consistency of heavy cream.

OPTIONAL STEP: Push the sauce through a fine-meshed sieve to remove small bits of chile skin and seeds.

Heat a pot over medium heat and add the lard. When the lard is hot, pour the sauce in and stir, stir, stir until the fat emulsifies. Bring it to a simmer and cook for 20 minutes, then turn off the heat until the meat is ready.

Once the meat is tender, somewhere between 90 minutes and 3 hours or so—you'll know when you can pull it apart fairly easily with two forks—it's time to serve. I like to pull the meat into largish pieces and put it in the sauce pot to bathe for 10 minutes before serving.

> "A desert is a place without expectation."
>
> Nadine Gordimer

DEEP-FRIED RIBEYE TACOS

PREP TIME: 30 MINUTES | COOK TIME: 20 MINUTES | SERVES 6

I ate these at Tacos de Armando in Hermosillo, Sonora, and had to recreate them at home. They're indulgent, crispy, chewy, meaty bits of awesome. Like most tacos in Sonora, they come simply: flour tortilla and the meat. You then dress it up however you like at what is essentially a fixins' bar that has lots of different salsas, limes, pickled serranos, chiltepin chiles, shredded cabbage, and the like.

These should be served on flour tortillas. That said, if you are gluten intolerant or prefer corn tortillas, it'll be fine.

Why ribeye? Ribeye is tender and fatty, so you get that balance between crispy fat and chewy meat without it being so gnarly you're chewing for days. Backstrap is the way to go with wild game.

If you want to go super traditional with ribeye tacos, you'd go with either a Chiltepin Salsa (page 204) or a Fire-Roasted Salsa (page 38), often called salsa tatemada in Sonora. But you'll also see Guacamole (page 272), and its thinner Taquero Avocado Salsa (page 248).

Limes and onions soaked in lime juice are traditional, as is chopped cilantro.

Over in Monterrey and in Texas, chicharron de ribeye is an appetizer, with the meat cut larger and served in a molcajete over guacamole.

- 1 small white onion, minced
- ⅓ cup freshly squeezed lime juice
- 2 pounds ribeye or venison backstrap
- Salt
- 1 quart lard or vegetable oil
- 18 flour tortillas
- Guacamole (page 272; optional)
- Hank's Refried Beans (page 35; optional)
- ½ cup minced cilantro
- Lime wedges to serve
- Salsas of your choice

Soak the minced onion in the lime juice with some salt. Set this aside as you proceed.

Trim all silverskin away from the meat. Cut it into pieces a little larger than you'd want in a taco, so maybe 1 inch square, more or less; they shrink when fried. Salt the pieces well and set in the fridge for 15 minutes while you chop cilantro, slice limes, and get your oil hot.

Put the lard or oil in a heavy pot. If you want to fry everything at once, increase the lard and use a big pot. Heat it to 350°F. As this is happening, put a cooling rack over a baking sheet in the oven and set the oven to "warm."

Take the meat from the fridge and pat it dry. Fry in batches so you don't crowd the pot. Fry, stirring the meat around, for about 5 to 7 minutes, until it's pretty and browned on the outside. Drain and put on the rack in the oven. Let the oil temperature return to 350°F before doing the next batch.

When the meat is done, heat the tortillas and make some tacos! I like starting with guacamole or refried beans—the meat will not roll off this way—then salsa, then the onions and cilantro.

Keys to Success

- Overloading a fryer will drop the temperature too much and it will take longer to brown the meat, and it will overcook. I fried this recipe in four batches.
- Salt the meat and set it in the fridge. This seasons it and keeps it cold so you will have a pink center after frying.
- Pat dry before frying. Water and hot oil don't like each other.
- Let the oil return to temperature before frying the next batch.

PORK WITH WILD GREENS

PREP TIME: 30 MINUTES | COOK TIME: 3 HOURS | SERVES 6 TO 8

Wherever you are along the borderlands, if you see them, always order a dish with quelites, a catch-all term for whatever the wild greens are where you happen to be. This stew is my rendition of the many, many similar ones I've eaten from Tijuana and Sonora to New Mexico and Texas.

This recipe is red, but you could easily use a green tomatillo-based salsa instead. Basically you braise pork shoulder, ribs, or some other tough cut in a flavorful broth, then you remove the bones and chop coarsely, strain the broth, and add the salsa, which gives you that red color. The greens go in during the last 10 minutes or so.

You usually eat this as a plate of food, alongside rice and beans. But you can use it to fill burritos, or even better, Sopes (page 137).

The three most common plants used in these stews are purslane, lambsquarters, and amaranth greens. Orach and New Zealand spinach are great options, as are regular spinach or chard.

Once made, this will keep a week in the fridge. It doesn't freeze well once you put the purslane in it, but the base of meat, broth, and salsa does freeze well, and it can be pressure-canned like any other stew. This is a good trick, because then you can open a jar, heat it up, and toss in fresh greens. Easy peasy.

Braised Pork

3 pounds pork shoulder, cut into large hunks

Salt

3 bay leaves

1 tablespoon Mexican oregano

½ onion, chopped coarsely

4 cloves garlic, smashed

1 sprig epazote (optional)

2 avocado leaves (optional)

Salsa

4 plum tomatoes, halved

1 white onion, quartered

4 unpeeled cloves garlic

2 to 5 guajillo chiles, seeded, stemmed and rehydrated

2 to 5 ancho chiles seeded, stemmed and rehydrated

2 to 5 chiles moritas or chipotles in adobo

¼ pound tomatillos, husked

Salt

3 tablespoons lard or vegetable oil

To Finish

2 pounds purslane or other wild greens (see headnote)

Crema or sour cream to taste

Cover the pork shoulder with water in a large, lidded pot like a Dutch oven. Bring to a boil, then drop to a simmer. Skim off any scum or froth that develops. Add the remaining braise ingredients, cover the pot, turn the heat to low and simmer gently until the pork is tender—anywhere from 90 minutes for store-bought pork to 3 hours for an old wild hog.

Meanwhile, get a comal, griddle, or cast iron pan hot and sear the onion, the cut side of the tomatoes, and the garlic until well blackened. While this is happening, stem and seed the chiles and rehydrate them with hot water.

When the vegetables are well charred, discard the garlic skins. Put the onion, tomatoes, and garlic in the blender, along with the chiles; discard the chile water. Add the tomatillos and a pinch of salt and purée. If you want to, push the salsa through a fine-mesh sieve into a bowl to remove any bits of skin and seed, which are undigestible.

Heat the lard in a sauté pan and pour the salsa in. It will spit and sputter. Stir this constantly until the lard is incorporated, then turn the heat to low and cover the pot.

When the pork is tender, strain the broth and reserve. Slice the pork across the grain into chunks so you don't have long, stringy pieces. Wipe out the pot, then return the pork and the strained broth to it, adding the salsa and the greens. Simmer this for about 10 to 20 minutes, adding salt to taste.

Serve with the crema alongside, with some hot sauce, and tortillas.

Notes

- If you can't find the exact chiles, any combination will do. Other good ones are pasillas, California, and New Mexican chiles. For the spicier moritas, you can usually find canned chipotles in adobo.
- While this is mostly done with pork, venison or any other red meat will work well, and there is a version done with jackrabbit in Sonora. Wild turkey legs would be good, too.
- If you cook this down so it's not quite as stewy, you can use it as a taco filling.

CARNE ASADA

PREP TIME: 45 MINUTES | COOK TIME: 20 MINUTES | SERVES 6 TO 8

Carne asada is the soul of the border. Beef grilled perfectly over wood or charcoal. Every state and region does it, and every region's carne asada is slightly different. But most will agree that if Sonora's is not the best, it is at least among the best. Like barbecue, carne asada is both a noun and a verb, a dish and a happening, a way of life.

Carne asada is the most popular taco filling all over the United States, and along with barbacoa, is the most popular in the borderlands as well. I've eaten it hundreds of times in every state along the border, in restaurants, backyards, roadside stalls, fancy parties.

Variation is encouraged in the world of carne asada. Here are the only rules that I've been able to suss out:

- It's always red meat, usually beef. Venison is a good substitute. Usually several different cuts.
- The meat is usually plain, with only salt and pepper, although marinades start to appear in Baja, especially with arrachera (skirt steak).
- Always cilantro, and usually white onions soaked in lime juice.
- Always some sort of salsa.
- Tortilla choice is personal and regional. But flour is most common.

When it comes to a Sonoran carne asada, there are set-piece standard sides:

- Grilled Cambray green onions, either chopped or served on the side.
- A fiery chiltepin salsa that looks tame . . . but isn't.
- A thin, pourable avocado salsa.
- Shredded cabbage or lettuce, and maybe some sliced cucumbers on the side.

Meat for Carne Asada

Meat cuts should be something you can cook hot and fast, and ideally you'd use a mix because each cut has a slightly different flavor. Good choices include:

- Skirt steak, arrachera. Grilled fast and sliced across the grain, the cut is perfect for tacos.
- Flank steak is almost as good.
- Ribeye, or venison backstrap, or tenderloin.
- I used the spinalis, the chain or ribeye cap, off a nilgai in the pictures. You can sometimes buy beef chain or ribeye cap in markets and it's a perfect cut for carne asada when taken from large animals.
- Flat-iron steak. This is one of my favorite grilling steaks.
- Hanger steak is a great choice if you can find it. Beef and bison are most common, but you can harvest it off elk and moose.
- Sirloin steak is good, too, and you can use any cut that is free of connective tissue.

Grill your meat over a hot fire until it's done to your liking. I prefer medium for tacos, but it's up to you. Toppings are up to you. See mine below.

Taquero Avocado Salsa

5 large tomatillos, husked and sliced in half

½ cup chopped white onion

3 jalapeños, seeded and chopped

1 clove garlic, chopped

1 avocado, halved and pitted

⅓ cup chopped cilantro

½ cup crema, or ⅓ cup sour cream + milk

Salt

Tacos

2 pounds steak, venison, or beef (see headnote for cuts)

Salt and black pepper

Oil for the grill and to slick the meat and onions

1 pound green onions

18 to 24 flour tortillas

½ cup chopped cilantro, for garmish

2 cups shredded cabbage or romaine lettuce

1 large cucumber, sliced (optional)

Limes and the hot salsa of your choice

Taquero Salsa

Put all the ingredients for the salsa except for the salt in a blender and purée. Add enough water to make the salsa pourable, blend again, then salt it to taste. Keep it refrigerated while you get everything else ready.

Tacos

Salt the steak well while you get your grill ready. If you're using a thick steak like a ribeye, leave it out to come to room temperature. If a thin steak like flank, skirt, flat-iron, or hanger, leave it in the fridge. These are so thin that in order to get nice grill marks—that Maillard reaction we all love—you need the meat to be cold; otherwise it will be inedibly well-done before you get them.

Once the coals are ready, scrape any residue off the grates, then wipe them with half of an onion, if you have one. Then dip a paper towel in oil or melted fat (beef fat is ideal), and wipe down the grates. Pat the steaks dry and slick with a little oil. Lay them on the hottest part of the grill.

Slick the green onions with oil, salt them, then grill alongside the meat.

Grill the steaks to the doneness you like; remember you can always cook it more if you're unsure. I prefer to flip only once to get good sear marks. Generally speaking, you'll want thin steaks on the hot part of the grill the whole time, for about 2 to 3 minutes per side. Ribeyes need that, plus more time on the cooler side of the grill.

Move the meat to a cutting board to rest, and grind black pepper over it. Let it rest for 5 to 10 minutes before chopping for tacos. Remember when doing this that you want bits—slices tend to pull out of the tortilla when you're eating them.

To build a proper Sonoran carne asada taco, fill a warm flour tortilla with meat, then add some shredded cabbage and maybe some cilantro, some of the avocado salsa, then some hot salsa. Cucumber slices and the green onions go on the side, to eat between tacos.

Keys to Success

- If you can get it, use mesquite charcoal or wood for this. Mesquite is made for carne asada. Oak is a good alternative, and pecan would be my third choice.
- Have the salsas and the garnishes made before you put the meat on the grill.
- If you are buying your tortillas, go to a Latin market and look in the fridge or freezer: Sometimes they have excellent flour tortillas that will still need to be finished on a comal. These are way better than shelf-stable ones.
- Grind your own pepper. It's a thousand times better than preground. And with meat this simple, you'll notice.
- If for some reason you have leftover meat, it is great chopped small and mixed with melty cheese in fried empanadas.

BURRO PERCHERÓN

If the Juarez burrito is minimalist and spare, Sonora's burro percherón is its opposite. Named for the legendary breed of giant draft horses, the percherón is basically impossible to make in the United States outside of Arizona because to be one, this mega burrito requires a sobaquera, the gigantic yet gossamer flour tortilla so named because they extend from the maker's fingertips to her armpit, her sobaco. This tortilla is doubled over itself and filled with a combination of wondrous things to eat.

Traditionally made with carne asada, chunks of avocado, refried beans, salsa, melty cheese, and crema, a percherón can now be had with basically anything, like any other burrito. The double layer of insanely thin tortilla gives these monster burritos the air of lightness, like a croissant filled with beef bourguignon. But make no mistake, this Hermosillo invention will keep you sated for a very long time.

CANDIED SQUASH

PREP TIME: 20 MINUTES | COOK TIME: 2 TO 3 HOURS | SERVES 8 TO 10 AS A SNACK OR LIGHT DESSERT

Pumpkin or winter squash tends to play more of a sweet role along the border, and nowhere more so than in Sonora. There is a large, native squash there that Indigenous groups have been peeling, spiralizing, and drying for millennia—a practice echoed 1500 miles north among the various tribes of the Great Plains. The Spanish brought sugar and spices, and this candied pumpkin recipe is, like a lot of border food, a beautiful meeting of the cultures.

The pumpkin or squash is nixtamalized—exactly like corn—which hardens it against long cooking. Skip this step and you have a sweet pumpkin mush great as a dessert empanada filling (use the sweet empanada dough on page 195), but not as a standalone dessert.

I've eaten chunks of candied squash all over Baja and Sonora, but the best was in the town of Ures, east of Hermosillo. My friend Charlie de la Rosa and I pulled over to buy some freshly dried chiltepin chiles, and it turned out there were lots of other Sonoran delights at those roadside stalls. This was one of them. You buy it by the chunk, and eat it as-is, sticky sweet and warming with the classic pumpkin spice aromas and flavors.

You will need calcium hydroxide to make this recipe. This is the mineral used to nixtmalize corn, and it's sold as "cal" in every Mexican market. You can buy it online from places like Masienda. I weigh things in metric measurements because it's important to have the exact ratio of squash to cal to water.

Once you make this, it will keep in the fridge a week or more. It does not freeze well.

- 500 grams winter squash, peeled, seeded, and cut into 2-inch chunks
- 20 grams cal
- 1 liter (1 kilogram) water
- 2 cups brown sugar
- 1 teaspoon ground cinnamon
- ¼ teaspoon ground cloves
- ½ teaspoon ground nutmeg
- ½ teaspoon ground ginger (optional)
- 2 teaspoons vanilla extract (optional)

Dissolve the cal in the liter of water. You might need to heat it a little to do this, and if so, let the water return to room temperature before adding the chunks of squash. Submerge the chunks in the solution and let them set overnight.

The next morning, rinse the squash well. Pour another liter or so of water into a pot and add the sugar and spices, except for the vanilla extract. Bring to a boil to dissolve the sugar, then put the squash in. Turn the heat down to get a very gentle simmer, and cook the pumpkin until soft but not falling apart, about 2 hours.

You want the cooking liquid to reduce dramatically during this process, to the point where in the final hour or so, you'll need to partially cover the pot and carefully move the squash around so It stays coated with the syrup. If using, add the vanilla extract at the end and mix gently.

Serve chunks of squash at room temperature or cool. They are outstanding alongside vanilla ice cream.

It will keep a few weeks in the fridge, but does not freeze well.

NOTE: Prep time does not include the overnight soak in the cal solution.

COYOTAS

PREP TIME: 45 MINUTES | COOK TIME: 20 MINUTES | MAKES ABOUT A DOZEN PASTRIES

The signature pastry of Sonora, coyotas are, well . . . a lot like a Mexican Pop Tart. They are round yeasted pastries that enclose a variety of fillings. Most traditional is simply grated piloncillo, the minimally processed brown sugar that comes in cones. Dulce de leche is another common filling, but I've seen pretty much everything in there—much like pop tarts.

The spiritual home of the coyota is Hermosillo. There's a whole neighborhood devoted to them. Queen among the many shops selling coyotas is Coyotas Doña Maria, said to be the birthplace of the pastry, but I prefer the coyotas from Doña Cuyo. Coyotas have since spread all over northern Mexico (I've eaten them in Monterrey), and they are easy to find in Arizona.

I'll provide a sample filling below, but this is your chance to break out your homemade jams, which make for a perfect filling. Apple butter rocks, too.

Once made, coyotas will keep a day or two, but they are best eaten the day they are made.

Dough

- 7 grams active dry yeast, about 2 heaping teaspoons
- 150 milliliters warm water (about ¾ cup)
- 50 grams white sugar (about 4 tablespoons)
- 250 grams lard or vegetable shortening (about ½ pound or 1 cup)
- 500 grams all-purpose flour, about 4 cups
- 5 grams salt (about 1½ teaspoons)

Dissolve the yeast in the warm water with a pinch of the white sugar.

Beat the lard with the rest of the white sugar until fluffy. Mix the salt and flour. Add the flour to the lard mixture and mix well, until it resembles a coarse meal. It's OK to have a few larger lumps. Pour in the yeast and water solution and knead this well until the dough comes together in a cohesive ball. Pinch off balls of about 35 to 40 grams, the size of a walnut. Place these balls in a plastic bag and let them rest for 15 to 30 minutes, or a bit longer if your dough feel dry.

Preheat your oven to 375°F. Line 2 baking sheets with parchment paper.

If you are using the sample filling, mix the sugar and flour together.

Using either a tortilla press or a rolling pin, flatten 2 balls of dough into a disk about ⅛ inch thick, so thicker than a tortilla. They should be roughly 4 to 4½ inches in diameter. If they are not the same size, you can use a pizza or cookie cutter or a small plate to cut them to the exact size. **TIP:** Line only one side of the tortilla press with plastic. The disk will stick to the other, but will peel off easily.

(If you are using a cone of piloncillo, you can soften it in a microwave for about 20 to 40 seconds. This makes it much easier to grate.)

Sprinkle a healthy amount of the brown sugar mixture, roughly 2 tablespoons, using your fingers to squash the pile into a cohesive mound. Leave ½ to 1 inch space around the edges. If using jam, spread a bit on the disk, leaving the same amount of space. Top with the other disk, press down the edges, and crimp with the tines of a fork.

Carefully slice a cross into the center of the top disk, taking care not to slice the bottom disk. Set the coyota on the parchment paper and repeat with the remaining dough and filling. You can also poke steam holes with the tines of a fork.

Filling

300 grams of dark brown sugar or grated piloncillo, (about 1½ cups)

30 grams flour (about 3 heaping tablespoons)

TIP: Make different steam hole patterns for different fillings, so you can tell them apart, for example, a cross for brown sugar, fork tines for jam, a single slash for dulce de leche, etc.

Bake for 20 to 25 minutes, until the edges brown a little. Let them cool a bit before moving to a cooling rack. They can be eaten warm or at room temperature.

Variations

- Add finely chopped nuts to the brown sugar. Pecans would be most traditional.
- Mix equal parts dulce de leche with minced nuts and use that as a filling. You'll see it called cajeta in most of Mexico.
- For a very Baja touch, use pitahaya marmalade as the filling. Any cactus fruit jam is excellent here.
- Membrillo, quince paste, is very traditional.
- Fig paste is another favorite.

"Más vale atole con risas que chocolate con lágrimas."

Porridge with laughter is preferable to chocolate with tears, old Mexican saying

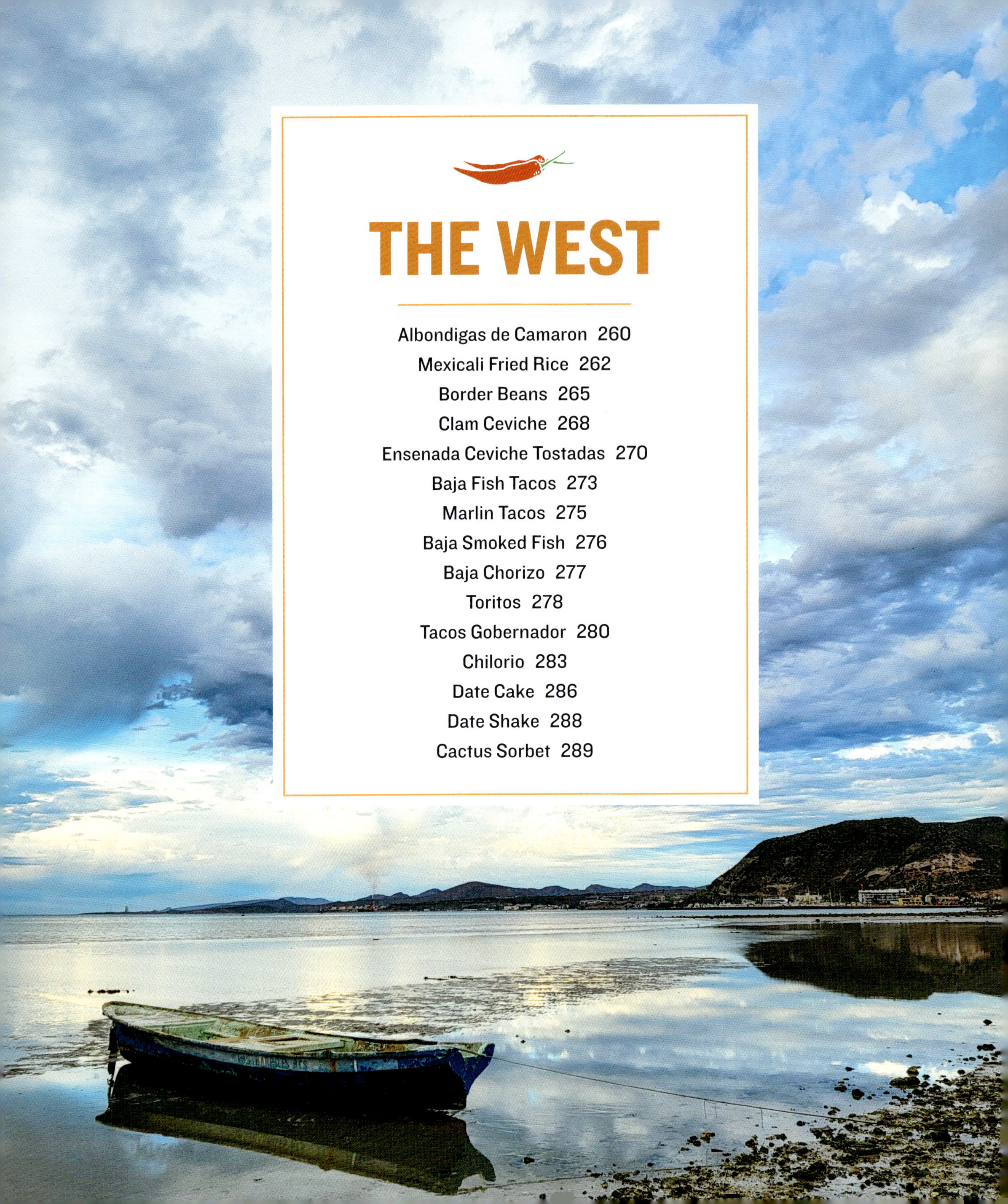

THE WEST

I'll admit it: Even with all the places in Mexico I've been, when I close my eyes and think of that country, my mind takes me immediately to La Paz, in Baja Sur. Although a quarter-million people live there, La Paz feels as its name suggests: peaceful. A city with restaurants, museums, and a university, it's telling that the defining feature of the city is its malecón, a promenade along the bay that stretches for almost two miles. It's the center of social activity there, where the whole city comes out to just . . . chill.

La Paz was the first place I ever visited in Mexico and it helped spark a fire within me that burns to this day. And while La Paz is 838 miles from the border, Baja Sur retains a border-like feel because of Los Cabos: The twin cities of Cabo San Lucas and San José del Cabo are Mexico's fourth-most visited vacation destination, and the American influence there is as strong as it is up the road in Tijuana.

That gringo influence waxes and wanes as you drive north from the cape, through deserts and beaches and over mountain passes high enough to support bishop pines. What always remains is a deep sense of California, summers of suede hills dotted with deep green oaks, springtime a riotous fiesta of greens and yellows, punctuated by the cadmium-hued flowers of the California poppy. I lived in Sacramento for 19 years. Cali blood flows in my veins even now. I can tell you, having driven Baja, eaten its food, chatted up its residents, soaked in the landscape, fished, gathered and yes partied all along the peninsula, that California is California. The main effect of the border is merely to switch the dominant language from English to Spanish: Californios son Californios.

California, Alta and Baja together, is a vibe more than anything else. And that vibe is a curious combination of entrepreneurial spirit with chill. Run a booming ceviche stand in Ensenada or Chula Vista six days a week, surf on Sunday. The flow of people, cuisine, and culture through the San Ysidro port of entry—the busiest border crossing in the Western Hemisphere—feels seamless. I've had Uber drivers from Tijuana drop me off at taquerias in San Diego and have been served excellent craft beer by a lovely woman from Coronado at a bar in Tijuana.

Playa Balandra in Baja Sur is considered one of the most beautiful in Mexico.

All of this makes perfect sense.

The Mexican state of Alta California encompassed what is now the American state of California, plus all of Utah and Nevada, plus northern Arizona and parts of Colorado and Wyoming. El Camino Real, the royal road, stretched from a few miles north of San Francisco nearly 1600 miles southward to Los Cabos. The interplay between the two states, made three in 1974 when Baja Sur became a state, has always been tight, and usually friendly.

This extends into the cuisine. In all my years of visiting San Diego and Baja, the food is essentially the same on either side. Initial white settlement from Texas to Arizona was from the American South. Not so in San Diego, so you won't see things

Clockwise: The mural in the back room of Caesar's in Tijuana, birthplace of the Caesar salad; spider crabs called marcianos, Martians, in Popotla, Baja; salsas at Casamarte in La Paz, Baja Sur.

like green chile grits there, unless it's some nouveau chef having fun. Cal-Ital, the fresh, light, bright fusion of California ingredients with Italian and Mediterranean cuisine, shines as strong in the Valle de Guadalupe, La Paz, and Ensenada as it does in San Diego, Los Angeles, and San Jose.

Even the wine culture crosses boundaries. Baja's Valle de Guadalupe is Mexico's only world-class wine region, and touring the vineyards and wineries there feels exactly like a Spanish language version of wandering around Central California's Paso Robles or the Sierra Foothills or Sonoma. And to be honest, most everyone there speaks English, too.

Like along the rest of the border, carne asada is king. But only when it comes to land-based meats. Sonora is a state of beef, with seafood. The West is made up of states of seafood, with beef. But this is all fluid. You can eat shockingly good carne asada tacos in Tijuana, Mexicali, and Chula Vista the same way you can get memorable seafood in Hermosillo.

For the most part, this chapter is about fish and seafood. Standing tall above all other dishes is the fish taco, claimed equally by San Diego and Ensenada. Hard to say who came up with it first, but it is believed to have developed its current form in the beginning of the 20th century, when a wave of Japanese immigrants brought with them tempura—which in turn had been brought to Japan by the Portuguese in the 1500s. The current fish batter used today is a slightly heavier tempura.

Ceviche, a dish originally from Peru, is universal, and can be had in myriad forms, as is aguachile, which is essentially ceviche without the marination. The raw clams are epic, some of the best in the world. If you haven't eaten chocolata clams or the cockle pata de mula, or *oh!* callos de hacha, a sort of mega scallop, have you really been to Baja?

Baja's long isolation from the rest of Mexico created a "fish-ification" of a great many traditional Mexican favorites. Machaca made not only with shredded beef jerky, but with salted, dried fish, notably skates and rays. This machaca de mantarraya is strong tasting, but makes a fantastic quesadilla. My favorite example of this is chorizo made with clams or abalone, and indeed you can use the Baja chorizo recipe on page 277 and sub in tough quahogs, butter or horseneck clams, or geoducks in the grinder.

Smoked fish replaces smoked meats all over the peninsula. Usually big pelagic fish like tuna, yellowtail, amberjack, swordfish, and marlin, you can buy hunks of smoked fish for tacos, quesadillas, and burritos. Side note: The customs agent didn't bat an eye when I brought a couple pounds across the border. "We see that a lot," he said.

Like Texas, New Mexico, and Sonora, whole books could be written about the cuisine of the Californias, Alta and Baja. What follows are what I think are the greatest hits, the dishes I've returned to every time I visit.

Low tide in San Felipe, Baja, California.

ALBONDIGAS DE CAMARON

PREP TIME: 1 HOUR | COOK TIME: 20 MINUTES | SERVES 6

Albondigas de camaron are Mexican shrimp balls, simmered gently in a tomato-chile sauce. They're easy to put together and make a great appetizer. I've eaten them numerous times in La Paz, where they are a specialty, but you'll see renditions all along the Sea of Cortez.

Any shrimp will work here, but my advice is to buy frozen, shell-on, medium-sized Gulf shrimp—you'll want to make a quick shrimp stock with the shells. And keep in mind this recipe works with fish, too.

The general idea is to make the shrimp balls (the mix can be refrigerated for a few hours in advance), then make the sauce while you are letting the mixture rest. The sauce can also be made in advance. Typically you'd serve these as one course in a multicourse meal, but I've served them with rice and called it good.

Once cooked, the shrimp balls will keep a few days in the fridge before they get overly fishy. You can also freeze them, but I would cook them first in salty water, then cool, then freeze. Reheat frozen shrimp balls directly from the freezer.

Shrimp Balls

- 1 pound shrimp, with shells
- ½ teaspoon salt
- ½ teaspoon black pepper
- ½ teaspoon cayenne or other chile powder
- ½ teaspoon Mexican oregano
- 1 tablespoon minced fresh epazote or ½ teaspoon dried
- ⅛ teaspoon baking powder
- 3 tablespoon masa harina. or fine cornmeal
- 1 egg, lightly beaten

Sauce

- 6 cups shrimp stock, fish or crab stock, or clam juice
- ½ pound Roma tomatoes, or 1 cup crushed tomatoes
- 2 tablespoons olive oil
- ½ white onion, minced
- 1 ancho chile, stemmed, seeded, and rehydrated
- Salt
- Freshly squeezed lime juice
- Mexican oregano or cilantro, for garnish

Shrimp Balls

Shell the shrimp and save the shells for the stock. Either grind the shrimp coarsely in a meat grinder, pulse in a food processor, or chop them fine. I prefer the meat grinder.

Mix all the ingredients together well in a bowl. It might be loose at first, but give it 20 minutes in the fridge before you add more masa harina. You will need to be able to form balls of this mix, but since masa takes time to absorb moisture, you won't know if it's too loose immediately. Once you're good with the mix, make it into balls. I like to go with ¼ cup and make them large, but a tablespoon is also a nice size.

Sauce

While the shrimp ball mixture is hydrating in the fridge, make the sauce. Start by covering the shells with 6 cups water, bring it to a simmer and add salt to taste. Let this cook gently while you make the shrimp balls. Once the shells have simmered 20 to 30 minutes (all this can be done ahead), strain it and set it aside.

While the stock is simmering, sauté the onion in the olive oil until it's soft, but not browned. Add this to a blender. Add the ancho chile, the tomatoes, salt, and some of the stock to the blender and purée. Add the rest of the stock and mix well. Adjust the salt.

To Finish

Bring the sauce to a simmer and gently drop in the shrimp balls. Let them simmer gently for 10 to 15 minutes. Add lime juice to taste, and serve with the sauce, garnished with Mexican oregano or cilantro.

Keys to Success

- Bonus Step: Char the onion and the tomatoes on a griddle until blackened, then purée. This is a nice step I do often. If you do this, skip the olive oil.
- You can add garlic to the sauce if you want. Or you can make it hotter by using other dried chiles, like guajillo or pasilla, or by adding a few árbol chiles to the mix.

MEXICALI FRIED RICE

PREP TIME: 15 MINUTES | COOK TIME: 10 MINUTES | SERVES 4

I ate this at The Dragon in Mexicali, and it is a perfect example of the Chinese-Mexican fusion of that town. I've only ever seen this fusion in Baja, although it's likely being done elsewhere—it's too good.

Use this recipe as a template, not dogma. Feel free to mix and match ingredients. It's an excellent use of leftover carne asada, too. If you're using it, add it when you'd add the shrimp. For the avocado, try to find a slightly underripe one.

- 1 tablespoon lard or peanut oil
- 6 ounces Mexican chorizo, loose, not cased
- 3 green onions, chopped, white and green parts separate
- 3 cloves garlic, chopped
- 1 or 2 serranos, seeded and minced
- 2 carrots, peeled and diced small
- 1 cup peas, fresh or thawed
- ½ pound small shrimp, peeled
- 3 cups cooked, cooled rice
- 2 eggs, lightly beaten
- 1 avocado, diced
- 2 tablespoons soy sauce
- 1 tablespoon sesame oil

Get a wok or large frying pan very hot over a strong burner. Add the lard or peanut oil, and the moment it begins to smoke, add the chorizo. Stir-fry this until the chorizo is cooked, 2 to 4 minutes. Add the garlic, chiles, and the white part of the green onions. Stir-fry about 30 seconds.

Add the rice, shrimp, carrots, and peas and stir-fry 2 minutes. Push everything to one side of the wok or pan and pour in the beaten eggs. Swirl it with a chopstick or somesuch until it sets, then stir-fry it into the rest of the rice. This helps keep it in largish, recognizable pieces.

Let the stir-fry sit for 1 minute without touching it. You want to develop some browning and crispiness on the bottom. After the minute has elapsed, pour the soy sauce in around the edges of the rice, then mix well. Turn off the heat and drizzle the sesame oil over it. Toss with the avocado and serve.

MEXICALI CHINESE FOOD

Mexicali, sister city to Calexico, California, is the center of Chinese food in both Mexico and the 1951-mile-long border. After the US Congress passed the Chinese Exclusion Act of 1882, thousands of Chinese living in the US fled across the border. Another wave came in the 1930s, after many Mexican states, including Sonora, barred Chinese people from living there. Many settled in Mexicali, and to this day it remains a haven for Chinese immigrants.

One day, while eating at a prestigious Mexicali restaurant called The Dragon, we asked our waiter about this. Turns out he had left China only a few years before, and went straight to Mexicali, where he had relatives. His Spanish was excellent, and so was the food. While you can find plenty of superb Cantonese food there, Mexicali is also home to a fantastic fusion of border and China: arrachera stir fries, chorizo and avocado in fried rice, roasted chiles everywhere.

CARNE ASADA FRIES

There may be no more iconic San Diego dish than the brothers that are carne asada fries and a California burrito. They are, in a way, the same thing eaten in different forms. Carne asada fries are what you think they are: French fries topped with grilled beef, guacamole, pico de gallo, sometimes pickled jalapeños (or fresh), sour cream, and either melty cheese or cotija. If this sounds like nachos but with fries, you are correct. The California burrito is all that stuffed into a burrito with refried beans and red rice.

It works, and it's great. To make this at home, however, you'll need to have a bunch of other dishes on hand, ready to go:

- Pico de gallo (page 46)
- Refried beans are optional, but if you want them they're on page 35.
- Guacamole (page 262)
- Carne Asada (page 246) or Fajitas (page 122), chopped

This is why it's mostly a restaurant dish, or a party dish. You can of course shortcut the process and use canned refried beans and salsa, but if you're going to go for it, go for it.

The shortcut I do recommend is to get par-cooked frozen fries. Shoestring are best. Making your own fries from scratch, plus all the other ingredients in carne asada fries, makes this humble dish more complex than a Oaxacan mole.

Once you have fries and everything else ready, arrange the fries in a platter, top with the carne asada, then some refried beans, any chiles you're using, pico de gallo, then lots of melty cheese, such as Oaxaca, asadero, Chihuahua, or mozzarella. This would also be a good place for that "Mexican blend" you see in supermarkets. Put everything under a broiler until the cheese melts, then serve with sour cream.

For the California burrito, add red rice to the mix, and fold everything up in a large flour burrito tortilla. It's a gigantic meal, so wait that obligatory hour before getting in the water. Surf's up!

BORDER BEANS

PREP TIME: 20 MINUTES | COOK TIME: 2 HOURS | SERVES 8

Frijoles fronterizos is a Western variant on the charro beans of the east. It's basically a hot bean salad, with cooked beans, chopped crispy bacon, chopped tomatoes and herbs, chiles, onions, and garlic. It's not soupy like charro beans.

Most often made with pinto beans, I prefer to use tepary beans, which are native to the Sonoran Desert. You can buy them online, and they grow easily and prolifically if you live in a hot, dry climate. Teparies come in various colors, but they are all small, firm, and meaty; they do take longer to cook than pintos, however.

Serve your border beans as a side dish or on tortillas, or mixed into or alongside simple rice.

- 1 sprig epazote
- 4 slices bacon
- ½ pound Mexican chorizo, loose, not cased
- 1 small white onion, chopped
- 2 cloves garlic, chopped
- 1 Anaheim chile, roasted, skinned, seeded, and coarsely chopped
- 4 cups cooked beans
- 2 to 4 Roma tomatoes, chopped
- ½ cup queso fresco or cotija cheese, crumbled
- Salt and pepper
- Crushed chiltepin chiles, (optional)

Generally you will need 2 cups dry beans to get around 4 cups, but it's not an exact science. Cook them in lots of water at a slow simmer. After about 90 minutes, add the epazote, if using. When the beans are reasonably soft, about 2 hours, add salt. This can all be done up to a couple days ahead of time. If you do cook them ahead of time, store them in their cooking liquid in the fridge.

When you are ready, cook the bacon in a large frying pan over medium heat until crispy. Remove and chop.

Add the chorizo, onions, and garlic to the pan and cook over medium-high heat until the chorizo is nicely browned. Add the chopped Anaheim, the cooked beans, and a little of the cooking water. Mix well and let this cook gently for 10 to 20 minutes. Don't let the beans stick to the bottom of the pot. Keep adding cooking liquid, stock, or water as needed. You want it a little wet, but not soupy.

Mix in the chopped tomatoes and let this cook a couple minutes, then remove from the heat. Add the cheese and serve with the bacon on top. I like to crush a bunch of dried chiltepin chiles over everything, too.

SHELLFISH PARADISE

Southern California and Baja are a seafood lover's paradise. Spiny lobsters, sea urchin, crabs of many varieties—including monstrous spider crabs nicknamed marcianos, Martians—blue shrimp, oysters, both farmed and wild, geoduck clams, Pismo clams, chocolate clams, pata do mula cockles, and perhaps the king of them all, the callo de hacha, a gigantic pen shell whose main muscle looks like the world's largest scallop.

I was more or less weaned on New England clams, and have yet to meet a tasty bivalve I didn't like. Patas de mula are a black cockle, also called a blood clam. They're chewy, briny, and meaty—yes, there's a touch of copper penny going on, too—and always served raw. Chocolatas, so called because of their milk chocolate–colored shells, and pismo clams, called queen clams in Spanish, are usually served raw, but you can get them cooked in any number of ways. The most fun may be in Loreto, where they will bury clams hinge side down in the sand, cover them all with driftwood and brush, set it on fire, then lift the clams out of the sand to eat simply, with hot sauce.

Spiny lobsters are legendary along the whole coast, and in season are on all the menus in San Diego down to Los Cabos. They are not cheap, often costing more than a Maine lobster in New England, but they are tasty and worth trying if you've never had the pleasure. Lobster tacos are my favorite.

Above all, however, are those callos de hacha, *Atrina maura*. Native to the Sea of Cortez, their shells can reach a foot long or more, and the center muscle, the scallop, can be 3 inches across and 2 inches tall. They are so revered fancy restaurants as far away as Monterrey or Mexico City will fly them in and charge hefty prices for a portion. Mostly served seared, or raw in ceviche or aguachile, they are a princely bite and equal to the best scallops in the world.

CLAM CEVICHE

PREP TIME: 15 MINUTES | MARINATING TIME: 30 MINUTES | SERVES 4 TO 6

Clam ceviche is common all over Baja California, but you'll see this style of ceviche most often around Ensenada, although I've eaten it in La Paz as well. Mostly it's made with chocolata clams, which are a signature of Baja. They are a lot like pismo clams in California.

Any species of clam will do, however, even the giant horseneck and butter clams of the Pacific Northwest. If you're in the East, cherrystones are perfect: big enough to chop, not so giant that they're like rubber, as the big chowder clams are. You could coarsely grind the feet of chowder clams for this. Skip the stomachs on the big clams.

Marinate the clams in the juice along with red onion or shallot and some small hot chiles. I prefer fresh chiltepin chiles in season, but any small hot red pepper will do. Thai peppers are great. Leave this for 30 minutes to an hour, then add cilantro, maybe a little minced garlic, and something else crunchy. It could be sliced raw asparagus, green beans, or celery.

I used sea beans, which I gathered near where I dug the clams for this ceviche. I also seasoned everything with green salt, which is made from powdered sea beans. These are nice touches if you have the products available.

Try to eat your clam ceviche the day it's made. You can keep it in the fridge for a day, but it won't be as nice. This recipe works with fish or shrimp, too.

- 1 5-ounce can V8 Spicy Hot (or tomato juice)
- ¼ cup freshly squeezed lime juice
- ¼ cup clam juice
- 1 tablespoon Worcestershire sauce
- A few dashes of Maggi seasoning (optional)
- 1 cup minced red onion or shallot
- 1 pound minced clams
- Minced small, hot chiles, to taste
- 1 tablespoon minced fresh Mexican oregano, or 1 teaspoon dried
- ¼ cup minced cilantro
- ½ cup chopped sea beans (optional)
- 1 tablespoon extra-virgin olive oil (optional)

Mix together the V8 or tomato juice, lime juice, clam juice, Worcestershire sauce, and Maggi, if using. Mix in the minced onion and clams, chiles to taste, and the oregano. Let this steep in the fridge for 30 minutes.

Mix in the remaining ingredients and serve with tortilla chips or on tostadas.

GREEN SALT

Powdered, dried salicornia—sea beans, saltwort, sea asparagus, and chicken feet are among the plant's names—has been an important source of salt among Indigenous peoples wherever it grows. But the term "green salt" was made popular by the Noriega family of Ensenada, Baja, which was the first commercial source of this product. Its briny flavor is perfect for seasoning fish and seafood. You can find it online and in some swanky supermarkets.

Or make it. Salicornia lives on every seacoast, and some species even live along alkali lakes inland. Harvest the tender stems of salicornia while it's vibrantly green, generally late spring through early fall. Older parts of the plant have a silica-strengthened center that isn't fun to eat. Dehydrate your harvest in a dehydrator, about 120°F, or in hot shade, until completely brittle and dry. Then use a coffee grinder to grind it to a powder, sifting out any stubborn chunky bits. It will keep for years this way.

ENSENADA CEVICHE TOSTADAS

PREP TIME: 30 MINUTES | COOK TIME: 15 MINUTES | SERVES 6

"Ceviche tostadas" is almost redundant on the border: It's the most common way you see the dish served. But there's a trick so your tostadas don't shatter on the first bite, dumping all your toppings into your lap. The best tostadas are made from corn tortillas made from masa harina that was a bit more coarsely ground than normal. Homemade ones are perfect for this. If you are buying tortillas, look for stone-ground ones, or any that look a bit thicker and coarser than usual.

Unless you have a known and trusted brand of premade tostadas, I do not recommend buying pre-fried ones because they almost always seem to shatter. Something about frying your own seems to help them hold together better. When you fry tortillas for tostadas, make sure the oil is hot and the tortillas fry until most of the bubbles die down. Flip them a couple times, and use tongs to press down on any spots where the tortilla balloons up.

And you don't have to fry ceviche tostadas. You can also cook the tortillas directly on the burner, or toast them on a comal or griddle. The comal method works much better with stale corn tortillas. Toasting over a grill is great, too.

You'll notice that the fish in this ceviche is cut really small. It's a cool style I've eaten in Ensenada, where you run the fish through a meat grinder fitted with a coarse die. While that sounds like you'd get a mush, you don't if the fish is cold enough. It's a great method.

The guacamole on the bottom is important. It serves as a tasty "glue" for whatever is on top—not just ceviche—so it doesn't slide all over the place when you try to eat it.

I use mahi mahi here, but any fish will work. Be sure to freeze your fish first for food safety, especially freshwater fish. No one likes to eat parasites.

Ceviche

- 1½ pounds skinless, boneless mahi mahi (or other fish)
- Salt
- 1 cup freshly squeezed lime juice
- 1 medium white onion, minced
- 1 to 4 serrano chiles, minced
- 1 yellow or orange bell pepper, diced small
- 1 teaspoon dried Mexican oregano (optional)
- 4 to 6 Roma tomatoes, diced small
- ½ cup chopped cilantro, or more if you want
- Sliced radishes, for garnish

To make the ceviche, chop the fish small, or run it through a meat grinder with a coarse die, about 6.5 mm if you have a choice. Put it in a bowl and mix in the lime juice, Mexican oregano, minced onion, bell pepper, and serranos. Sprinkle some salt over everything and set this in the fridge for at least 30 minutes.

Meanwhile, make the guacamole. If you have a molcajete, use that. If not, use a regular mortar and pestle. If you don't have that, use a food processor or a fork. Start by adding the onion and serrano and some salt. Pound or grind that together into a paste. Add the lime juice and cilantro and grind that in, then pound and grind in the avocado. Adjust the seasoning with salt and lime if needed. If you only have a food processor, toss everything in at once.

After you've done that, toast or fry the tortillas to make tostadas. If they are stale, you can toast them on a comal or griddle until they are crispy, turning them from time to time. You want to do this over high heat. You can also fry them in a little vegetable oil or lard. Get the oil hot, about 350°F, and fry the tortillas, turning them a few times, until the bubbles die down, about 5 minutes. Use tongs to press down any spots that balloon up.

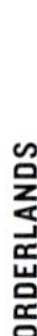

Guacamole

Salt

¼ cup minced white onion

1 serrano, minced

3 tablespoons lime juice

2 tablespoons minced cilantro (optional)

2 or 3 avocados

Tostadas

12 to 18 corn tortillas

If your tortillas are not stale, the best way to make tostadas is to set them directly over a gas burner or charcoal grill that's hot but not blazing. Turn them frequently until they are crispy. Some spots may catch fire. Blow them out.

When you are getting ready to serve, mix the tomatoes and cilantro into the ceviche.

To finish, spread some guacamole on the tostadas, top with the ceviche—drain it with a slotted spoon—and garnish with the radishes. Oh, and that leftover marinade? Fantastic as a shot mixed with equal parts silver tequila or mezcal.

BAJA FISH TACOS

PREP TIME: 30 MINUTES | COOK TIME: 30 MINUTES | SERVES 6 TO 8

By far the most famous taco of the West, a Baja fish taco is as iconic as carne asada taco. You can find masterful examples of them from Los Cabos to San Diego, all playing off the same riff: beer-battered fish, corn tortilla, creamy sauce, shredded cabbage, salsa of your choice. Batter, fish, and tortilla are the keys here: All contribute to the magic. I've eaten hundreds of fish tacos, and this is how I make them at home.

If you can't have alcohol, use a nonalcoholic lager beer. Athletic Brewing's Cerveza Athletica is a good option.

Fish

- 2 pounds of your favorite fish
- Salt
- 1 teaspoon garlic powder
- 1 teaspoon dried Mexican oregano
- 1 teaspoon baking powder
- 1½ cups cake or all-purpose flour, plus more for dusting
- ½ cup cornstarch, or potato starch
- 1 heaping tablespoon yellow mustard
- 1 12-ounce bottle Mexican lager, ideally Pacifico or Tecate
- Oil for frying

To Finish

- 12 to 18 corn tortillas
- ¼ head of cabbage, sliced very thin
- Avocado-Tomatillo Salsa (page 43)
- Hank's Pico de Gallo (page 46)
- 2 to 4 quartered limes

Optional Crema

- ⅓ cup mayonnaise
- ½ cup Mexican crema
- 1 to 2 tablespoons adobo from a can of chipotles in adobo
- Juice of a lime
- Salt

If you're making the crema, mix all the ingredients together in a bowl and add salt to taste. If you can't find Mexican crema, thin sour cream with a little whole milk. If you have a squeeze bottle, put the sauce in it. If not, you can spoon it on later.

Cut the fish into pieces fit for a taco. They should be as long as your tortillas, and no more than about 1½ inches wide. Salt them.

In a bowl, mix the garlic powder, oregano, ½ teaspoon salt, the baking powder, flour, and cornstarch. Take care to crush the Mexican oregano to a powder as you put it in the bowl.

Get everything ready to make tacos. Set a cooling rack over a baking sheet and put that in the oven, and turn the oven to "warm." Pour oil to a depth of about 1 to 2 inches into a heavy frying pan. Heat it to 350°F to 365°F.

As the oil heats up, add the mustard, then the beer in with the dry ingredients. You want a consistency like house paint or slightly thinner. Add ice water or more beer if you need to.

Pat the fish dry with paper towels then dust in the extra flour. When the oil is hot, dredge a few pieces of fish through the batter and fry until golden brown, turning as needed. This should take between 4 and 6 minutes. Do this in batches so you don't crowd the pan, and be sure to let the oil return to at least 350°F before adding another batch.

Set the finished pieces of fish on the cooling rack in the oven.

To finish, heat up the corn tortillas, add a piece of fish, then top with a salsa or two, some of the crema, and some shredded cabbage. Squeeze some lime over it all for added acidity.

MARLIN TACOS

PREP TIME: 20 MINUTES | COOK TIME: 45 MINUTES | SERVES 6 TO 8

The fundamental ingredient in this taco is smoked marlin (recipe follows). In Baja, smoked marlin is primarily obtained when sport anglers kill a marlin—when the fish swallows a hook or fights so hard it can't be released. Smoked yellowtail or tuna are typical alternatives in Mexico, and literally any smoked fish will work with this recipe. Some excellent choices would be smoked shad, smoked whitefish, smoked salmon, smoked lake trout, smoked mullet or catfish, or smoked bluefish or mackerel.

Tacos de marlin are usually a sort of quesadilla, a folded-over taco cemented with melty cheese, either queso Chihuahua or queso Oaxaca. I've seen marlin tacos done on flour tortillas, but corn is the norm. The filling is essentially a mish-mash of the marlin, roasted green chiles, tomatoes, onions and garlic, and herbs, cooked in a little butter.

You can make the filling up to a day or two ahead, then heat corn tortillas to make them pliable, set some shredded cheese down, top with the filling, fold over and sear on a comal or griddle until you get a little char. Sometimes the tortillas break, but since you have a layer of melted cheese, it's all good.

Another option for the marlin filling is to use it in the Empanadas (page 195).

- 2 tablespoons butter or olive oil
- 1 cup minced white onion
- 3 jalapeños, minced
- 3 cloves garlic, minced
- 2 poblano or Anaheim chiles, roasted, seeded and chopped coarsely
- 4 plum tomatoes, seeded and diced
- 1 pound smoked marlin or other fish, flaked out
- 1 teaspoon Mexican oregano
- Salt
- 12–16 corn tortillas
- ½ pound Oaxaca cheese, mozzarella, or Chihuahua cheese, grated

Heat the butter in a large sauté pan over medium high heat. Add the onion and jalapeños and cook, stirring often, until the onions brown a little, about 8 minutes. Add the garlic, roasted chiles, tomatoes, smoked fish, and the oregano and stir to combine. Taste for salt and add some if needed. Drop the heat to low.

Heat up corn tortillas on a comal or griddle and keep them in a tortillero or wrap them in a kitchen towel to keep them warm.

To build the tacos, spread the cheese across a tortilla, add some filling and fold over. Set the taco on the hot comal or griddle and press down with a spatula until the cheese melts. Cook each side until you get a little char. Repeat with the remaining tacos.

You can keep the finished tacos hot by putting them on a rack set over a baking sheet in a 200°F oven.

BAJA SMOKED FISH

PREP TIME: 5 MINUTES | COOK TIME: 3 HOURS | SERVES 6 TO 10

Smoked swordfish, marlin, sturgeon, cobia, or really any big meaty fish is a fantastic way to eat these big chunks of meat. It's almost beefy in a way, and if done right, the fish stays juicy. I learned this method at Ahumadora Pacifico in Ensenada. Every day they smoke fish out back over embers of manzanita or mesquite wood. Almost all their inventory sells out each day for tacos, tostadas, empanadas, or just to gnaw on.

Mesquite is the best wood here, but oak or a fruitwood are OK. If you have access to manzanita wood, use it.

Keep the temperatures low, below 200°F, and smoke for several hours. I prefer to go a full 4 hours, and if you can keep the temperature below 170°F, you can go as long as 5 or 6 hours. The Mexican smoked marlin is very smoky.

Use your fish in any Mexican dish calling for smoked marlin, or slice it and eat it on a cracker or by itself. I also like eating it hot, right out of the smoker, over a green salad. Once made, the smoked fish will keep a week in the fridge, and it freezes well.

2 pounds marlin, swordfish or other firm, meaty fish

Salt

Heavily salt your fish; you can even bury it in salt. I use kosher or sea salt for this. Put it in the fridge for 1 hour per pound of fish, for example if it's a 2-pound piece, 2 hours; a half-pound piece, 30 minutes.

Briefly rinse the fish and pat it dry. Let it sit on a rack in a cool place for at least 1 hour or up to overnight in the fridge. At room temperature, put a fan on the fish to speed drying and to keep bugs away.

Get your smoker to a steady, cool temperature. I use a Traeger, so I set it at 175°F or even 165°F. You need to keep your smoker below 200°F if possible. Wood choice is yours, but for a Mexican flavor use mesquite. Oak, maple, or apple are other great options.

Smoke the fish for at least 2 hours, and up to 6. The lower the temperature, the longer you can smoke it for. Four hours at 175°F is a nice compromise. Serve the smoked fish hot right away, or let it cool and use it for other dishes.

Ahumadora Pacifica in Ensenada, Baja.

BAJA CHORIZO

PREP TIME: 1 HOUR | MAKES 2 KILOS, ABOUT 4 ½ POUNDS

Chorizo varies depending on where it is made, and in Baja it's normally a duller red than the lurid versions laced with achiote paste. This is a very simple rendition of chorizo that can be done with all beef, all pork, or a combination of pork fat plus pretty much any other meat; I make mine with venison and pork fat. This is a loose sausage, so no need to case it.

The chiles should be mild, such as colorado, dried red Hatch chiles, or guajillo. If you want to add some zip, include up to 60 grams (2 ounces) hot chiles, such as dried chipotle (morita or meco), puya, or if you're brave, chiltepin, or árbol.

- 1.5 kilos lean meat, beef, pork, etc, 3 ⅓ pounds
- 0.5 kilos pork or beef fat, about 1 pound
- 35 grams sea salt, about 6 teaspoons
- 175 grams dried red chiles, stemmed seeded, and ground
- 40 grams garlic powder, about 2 tablespoons
- 5 grams ground cumin, about 1 teaspoon
- 6 grams dried Mexican oregano, about 1 tablespoon
- 2 grams ground coriander, about 1 teaspoon
- 6 grams ground black pepper, about 2 teaspoons
- 1 cup white or cider vinegar
- ½ cup water

Grind your dried chiles into a powder. You can also use a premade chile powder—not chili powder, which has other ingredients in it. Paprika is a decent substitute. Or you can rehydrate your chiles in the water and vinegar, purée that in a blender, and add the purée to the ground meat mixture later.

Make sure your meat and fat are cold, around 34°F. Cut them into chunks that will fit in your grinder, and mix well with the chiles and all the remaining ingredients, except the vinegar and water. Grind through a fine die, 4.5 mm. If your meat and fat are full of sinew, grind first through a medium die, rechill the mixture until it's cold again, then grind a second time through the fine die.

Add the vinegar and water and mix well with clean hands until the whole mixture can be picked up in one glob. This will keep a week in the fridge and it freezes nicely.

TORITOS

PREP TIME: 45 MINUTES | COOK TIME: 20 MINUTES | SERVES 6 TO 8 AS A STARTER

Another excellent use of smoked fish, toritos are unique to Baja and the coast of Sonora. They are a sort of chile relleno, a fish- or seafood-stuffed pepper, almost always a chile güero, which is more or less the pale Hungarian wax pepper you see in most supermarkets.

You remove their tough skins, hollow them out, stuff with smoked fish, minced shrimp, or crab, and top with cheese. A quick trip under the broiler and they're done! Any smoked fish works here, and if you can't find the pale green chiles, use big jalapeños.

12 to 16 chiles güeros

Oil for frying (see below)

4 or 5 slices bacon

½ pound smoked fish or minced, cooked shrimp

½ red onion, minced

1 serrano chile, seeded and minced

1 Roma tomato, seeded and minced

1 clove garlic, minced

¼ cup minced cilantro or parsley

½ pound melty cheese, such as Oaxaca, asadero or mozzarella

Sauce

1 cup soy sauce

¼ cup freshly squeezed lime juice

Hot sauce to taste

The easiest way to peel these chiles is to fry them. But be warned: They will pop and spatter. Have a spatter guard or a lid handy. The skins will bubble and separate from the pepper. Let them cool a little and peel while still warm.

Slice a T shape in each peeled chile: The short axis of the T is just below the stem, the long goes down the center of the pepper, leaving about ½ inch before the end. With a paring knife, carefully slice out the seed ball in the pepper, then use a little spoon or butter knife to remove as many seeds as you can; it's OK if a few are still in there. This can be done up to 2 days in advance.

Fry the bacon crispy, drain, and chop.

In a bowl, mix the smoked fish or minced shrimp and the chopped bacon, the red onion, serrano chile, tomato and garlic, along with half the minced cilantro or parsley.

Stuff the peppers with this mixture. Set them side by side in a broiler pan and top with the cheese. Broil until the cheese melts and browns a little.

To make the sauce, simply mix all the ingredients and serve underneath the toritos.

DRIED FISH AND SEAFOOD

Fish, skates, rays, and seafood have been dried for future use as long as there have been people in Baja, as well as the coastline of California, Sonora, and Sinaloa. A huge variety of seafood substitutes for land-based meats exist there, none more popular than fish-based machaca. Machaca is pounded beef or venison jerky. Fish and especially skates and rays get this treatment in Baja. You will see machaca de mantarraya all over the peninsula. It's an old-timers' favorite, not unlike lutefisk in Minnesota. Strong tasting, salty, and chewy, it takes some getting used to, but I find that if you make it yourself and keep it cold, it's way less stinky-fishy.

You can salt and dry any fish, but lean ones are best. Simply bury them in salt for a day or three, then brush the salt off and hang to dry in a cool, breezy place or the fridge until the fish is as hard as a rock. It will then keep indefinitely. Refresh by soaking in water for a day, changing the water from time to time.

Shred and use in recipes like the marlin tacos, or as an empanada filling.

TACOS GOBERNADOR

PREP TIME: 45 MINUTES | COOK TIME: 20 MINUTES | SERVES 4 TO 6

Like chilorio, tacos gobernador, governor's tacos, came to Baja from Sinaloa, and there are variations of this dish all over the Pacific coast; I've had great ones in San Diego. Legend has it that in 1987, the chefs at Los Arcos in Mazatlan invented these tacos to impress the governor of Sinaloa, who was visiting them.

But even searching for the original recipe from Los Arcos turns up variations. Some versions claiming to be the original include celery and, oddly, machaca, which is finely shredded dried beef. Most do not, however, and I suspect this could be a mix-up in conversations between cooks: Machaca de camaron is a term in Pacific Mexico for chopped shrimp. I've seen cooks from other parts of Mexico miss this and add the dried beef.

Here are the constants:

- Shrimp. Usually medium or large shrimp, cut into pieces.
- Cheese. Always melty cheese, usually queso Chihuahua or asadero or Oaxaca. Most are easily available in Latin markets, but mozzarella is a very good substitute.
- Always onions, usually white. Sliced or chopped.
- A bit of chopped garlic.
- Chiles. I've seen chipotles in adobo, but mostly I see roasted, skinned, and seeded Anaheims or poblanos, cut into strips. Poblanos are a decent substitute.
- Often dried Mexican oregano and/or fresh chopped cilantro.
- Sometimes tomato, sometimes not. Apparently not at Los Arcos.
- Butter is the fat, although I prefer lard and I've seen olive oil.
- Corn tortillas are traditional, but I've seen tacos gobernador served on flour tortillas in Baja.

Regardless of the exact combination you choose, it'll be a good one. The cheese adds heft to the taco, and the little edges that brown or even burn are one of the highlights. Even with all that, tacos gobernador are still light enough to make a half dozen disappear.

Like the marlin tacos on page 275, making these is a bit more like making a quesadilla than a traditional taco. You warm the tortillas, then add some cheese, and once it starts melting, add the remaining filling and fold the taco over to get it to stick.

Be warned: Tacos gobernador are as messy as they are delicious. Eat with plenty of beer, napkins, and some hot sauce.

IMPORTED BEER - BREWED IN

- 2 Anaheim or poblano chiles,
- 2 tablespoons butter, lard, or olive oil
- 1 white onion, thinly sliced
- 2 cloves garlic, minced
- 4 small, hot chiles, chopped (optional)
- 2 Roma tomatoes, seeded and diced
- 1 pound peeled shrimp, cut into bite-sized pieces
- Salt
- ½ teaspoon Mexican oregano (optional)
- 2 tablespoons chopped cilantro
- ½ pound shredded melty cheese (see the list on page 280 for options)
- 8 to 12 corn tortillas

Roast the chiles and set them in a plastic bag to steam the skins off. Skin, then remove the tops and all the seeds. Slice them into strips crosswise. You can dice them if you prefer.

Heat the butter in a large pan over medium-high heat. Add the onions and sauté until wilted, about 3 to 5 minutes. Add the garlic, chiles if using, diced tomato, shrimp, oregano, and salt and toss to combine. Sauté until the shrimp turns pink, about 3 to 4 minutes. Mix in the cilantro and turn off the heat.

Heat tortillas on a comal, griddle, or large frying pan, or on a grill. Set the tortilla down, then add a generous portion of shredded cheese on it. As soon as the cheese starts to melt, spoon some filling into the center and fold the taco over. Press down with a spatula to set the taco, let it char a bit on that first side, then flip to brown the other side. Serve at once.

CHILORIO

PREP TIME: 30 MINUTES | COOK TIME: 2 HOURS | SERVES 6 TO 8

Whenever I am in Baja Sur, I always stop at El Comal on the highway between Los Cabos and La Paz. It is a fantastic open-air rest stop full of culinary delights. I've never had a bad meal there. But my favorite thing on their menu is the chilorio. Chilorio was originally a Sinaloan dish, but the connections between Sinaloa and Baja Sur are strong; a ferry service links them.

The soul of chilorio is the combination of shredded pork, chiles, cumin, and something acidic, usually vinegar. This sets it apart from a similar dish from Sonora, Carne Con Chile (page 240), which is less acidic and the meat is often in larger pieces. I've seen chicken versions of chilorio, too. Pork, wild or farmed, javelina, chicken, pheasant, chukars, grouse, or rabbits would all work.

Chilorio is always shredded, because it is intended to be used in tacos, burritos, tortas (Mexican sandwiches), or alongside rice and beans. I've seen it served in Sopes (page 137), too. It is fantastic as a filling for the Empanada dough on page 195.

The salsa is pretty standard: Char onions and garlic, toast the cumin and dried chiles if you want to, then put it all in a blender with Mexican oregano, water, and salt and purée. That goes into the searing meat and gets cooked by the lard, and, after a bit, you smash it all together to get a pan of shredded amazingness.

Once made, chilorio keeps for a few days in the fridge, and reheats well.

- 2 to 3 pounds pork shoulder
- 1 large white onion, sliced in quarters
- 8 unpeeled cloves garlic
- 2 to 5 bay leaves
- Salt
- 4 guajillo chiles
- 4 pasilla or ancho chiles
- 4 chipotle chiles
- 1 tablespoon cumin seeds, or 2 teaspoons ground
- 2 teaspoons coriander seeds, or 1 teaspoon ground
- 1 tablespon oregano, Mexican if possible
- ½ cup apple cider vinegar, or more to taste
- ⅓ cup lard or oil

Cut the pork into large chunks about 3 inches across. Put them into a large, lidded pot and cover with water by 1 inch. Bring to a boil and skim any froth off. Lower the heat to a simmer and add one quarter of the onion, 2 garlic cloves, and the bay leaves. Salt to taste and cook until the pork is tender.

Remove the seeds and stems of all the chiles. It's OK if a few seeds get stuck.

Meanwhile, make the salsa.

Heat a comal or griddle or heavy frying pan over high heat and char the rest of the onion and garlic cloves. While the vegetables are charring, bring a medium pot of water to a boil. While that is heating, quickly toast the chiles on the hot comal—about 30 seconds total, flipping a couple times. You want the dried chiles to blister a little, but not blacken. When they are toasted and the pot of water hits a boil, put the chiles in the water and turn off the heat.

If you want, toast the cumin and coriander seeds in a hot, dry pan until they smell nice. Put them in a spice grinder or a blender and grind. This step does add a lot of flavor.

When the onions and garlic are nicely charred and the chiles soft, put them in a blender with the oregano and spices, salt, vinegar and enough water to make a sauce with the consistency of cream. Purée.

NOTE: The timing reflects farmed pork or a young wild hog. Older animals might take longer to get tender.

Once the pork is tender, drain the broth and discard it or use in another recipe; it's great as a broth to cook the Barbacoa (page 87) or the Carne con Chile (page 240). Wipe out the pot and add the lard. When it's hot, add the chunks of pork and sear hard on one side—you want a combination of crispy and soft.

When you have achieved that, pour in the salsa and mix well. Turn the heat to a simmer and cook for 10 to 20 minutes, then smash everything with a potato masher or two forks before serving.

Variations

- The chile mix determines the heat level. Skip the chipotles if you want to keep it mild, and for a redder sauce, use only guajillos, or New Mexican red chiles or California chiles, which are dried red Anaheims.
- If you hate vinegar, use lots of lime juice.

> "The desert lies beneath and soars beyond any possible human qualification."
>
> Edward Abbey

DATE CAKE

PREP TIME: 40 MINUTES | COOK TIME: 40 MINUTES | SERVES 6 TO 8

Various forms of date cakes pop up during the holiday months around Calexico and in Baja California, where you can often see "pan de datil" or "pastel de datil" signs on the side of the roads; dates are grown throughout the region, into California and Arizona. If you see one of these signs in your travels, stop and buy a cake. They're dark, rich, and slightly sticky. The texture is spongy and moist, and you really taste the date flavor. Not all date cakes have nuts, but I prefer them with pecans, walnuts, or hickory nuts.

The addition of mayonnaise in the cake may seem strange, but it is a well-established cake addition. The first reference to mayo being in a cake is in a recipe printed in a 1927 edition of the Oakland Tribune newspaper—and that cake had dates in it, oddly enough.

My recipe is loosely based off one in the little book *Cocina Familiar en el Estado de Baja California*, which also uses mayonnaise.

1½ cups finely chopped dates
2 cups cake flour
½ teaspoon baking soda
½ teaspoon baking powder
½ teaspoon salt
1 cup chopped pecans
1 heaping cup mayonnaise
2 teaspoons vanilla extract
¾ cup dark brown sugar or grated piloncillo
Powdered sugar for dusting

Set the chopped dates in a bowl and pour 1 cup boiling water over them. Cover the bowl and let this sit for 30 minutes.

Preheat the oven to 350°F. Grease a 9-inch cake pan with butter, then dust it with flour.

Mix the cake flour, baking powder, baking soda, and salt in a bowl.

Purée the dates with their water, along with the vanilla extract and brown sugar.

Pour this into the bowl with the dry ingredients, then mix in the chopped nuts and the mayo. Mix well into a batter. Pour the batter into the prepared cake pan and bake uncovered for 40 to 45 minutes.

Set the cake, still in the pan, on a cooling rack and let it cool for about 15 minutes. If the cake seems stuck in the pan, run a thin knife around the edge of the pan to free it. Put a plate over the cake and invert the pan to remove the cake. Put another plate over the cake, turn it right side up, and dust with powdered sugar. This cake is best eaten slightly warm, but it's great at room temperature, too.

It'll keep, covered, at room temperature for a few days. It does not freeze well.

DATE SHAKE

PREP TIME: 5 MINUTES | SERVES 2, CAN BE DOUBLED

Date shakes are insanely good when drunk where dates grow, which is to say Southern California, Baja, and Arizona. I first drank one in Calexico, California, and it was creamy heaven. The combination of dates, milk, and vanilla ice cream is perfect for those 115°F days in, say, Yuma or Mexicali or, well, Dateland. Yes, there's a Dateland in Arizona (see page 213).

You can adjust the thickness with more or less ice cream, but for the real deal, you should be able to drink this through a straw.

- 8 medjool dates, pitted and chopped
- A tiny pinch of salt
- 3 cups cold milk
- 2 cups vanilla ice cream

Put the dates, salt, and 1 cup of the milk in the blender and purée furiously. This can take a minute or more. You really want the dates to be fully incorporated into the milk, or the particles will fall to the bottom of your glass. Check the temp of this mixture because sometimes this process can warm up the milk substantially. If it's not ice cold anymore, you can refrigerate the mix until it's cold again.

When you are ready, add the remaining ingredients and blend until frothy. Pour into glasses and enjoy!

OPTIONS: You could add ¼ teaspoon of ground cinnamon if you'd like. Another option is to toss a handful of ice cubes into the blender when you are ready to finish the shake. That will drop the temperature enough to keep things cold.

CACTUS SORBET

PREP TIME: 15 MINUTES | CHILL TIME: 1 HOUR | MAKES 1 QUART

This is my rendition of a sorbet, a nieve, you can find all over Baja. There it's made with the puréed fruit of the pitahaya cactus, but those are almost impossible to get in the United States. Tunas, the fruit of the prickly pear, are far more common. I have instructions on making the base prickly pear juice on page 58. If you can't find nice red tunas, you can buy prickly pear syrup online. Thin this with some water until it's right at your sweetness tolerance, then add the lime juice, liquor, and salt.

The liquor is there to add flavor, and to prevent the sorbet from freezing solid. If you don't drink alcohol, you can leave it out.

- 4 cups prickly pear juice
- 1½ cups sugar or honey
- ¼ cup freshly squeezed lime juice
- 1 or 2 tablespoons silver tequila, bacanora, or sotol
- Pinch of salt

Mix all the ingredients well until the sugar and salt have completely dissolved. If everything isn't already cold, chill the mixture to at least 40°F before putting into your ice cream maker. Follow your ice cream maker's directions and store in the freezer.

▼ Pitahaya fruit vendor in Popotla, Baja, Mexico.

A cow skull stands vigil in a ranch near Muzquiz, Coahuila, Mexico.

SOURCES

Your local Latin market will have most of what you need to cook through this book. And in all but a very few places in the United States and Canada, there will likely be one within 20 miles of you. But if not, the following online and mail order sources will help.

RANCHO GORDO

(ranchogordo.com)
An excellent mail order source for quality beans, excellent Mexican oregano, dried hominy for pozole and gallina pinta, some nice dried chiles, and New Mexican chile powder—which is to say powdered mild red chiles, not the chili powder in supermarkets, which has lots of other things in it. Their Xoxoc Project, a cooperative with small Mexican producers, is a godsend. You can get pinole and rare beans there, as well as sal mixteca, which is a natural salt-bicarbonate mixture that makes the best beans!

MASIENDA

(masienda.com)
The single best source for high-quality masa harina there is. They have lots of colors, but for a borderlands cook you really only need white and blue. They sell bayo beans, as well as other varieties. Masienda also makes the best molcajete and best tortilla press I've ever used, and their comal is excellent, too. You could do worse than shop Masienda before cooking anything from this book: It'll set you up right.

RAMONA FARMS

(ramonafarms.com)
A fantastic purveyor of dried goods, notably chicos corn, tepary beans, stone-ground wheat, and heirloom desert corn.

LOS CHILEROS

(loschileros.com)
A great place to just shop around for Southwestern ingredients: dried chiles, herbs and spices, pozole corn, pinole, a sopapilla mix, and chile powders.

HAYDEN FLOUR MILLS

(haydenflourmills.com)
The best source for real Sonoran wheat flour, which is the gold standard for flour tortillas. They also sell a tortilla flour that is a cooperation with Masienda: It's 50-50 corn and wheat flour, and makes a very interesting tortilla.

YOLI TORTILLERIA

(eatyoli.com)
Makes the finest Sonoran flour tortillas you can buy outside of Arizona or Sonora. They sell mail order in refrigerated cases, so the tortillas arrive in great shape, and can be frozen. Their corn tortillas are excellent, too.

BROKEN ARROW

(brokernarrowranch.com)
The nation's best purveyor for wild venison, nilgai, and wild boar. Based at a gigantic ranch in Texas, they are the only company that combines sharpshooters and a mobile USDA processing truck to provide a real "wild" product. Their animals are technically livestock, but are left to roam free and eat what they can. Broken Arrow also sells high-quality quail.

CAPPADONA RANCH

(cappadonaranch.com)
A great source for mesquite flour.

TOHONO O'ODHAM SAN XAVIER CO-OP

(sanxaviercoop.com)
No online orders, but if you live around Tuscon, their products are top notch, from tepary beans to toasted Sonoran wheat flour, cholla buds and even saguaro cactus syrup!

CHERI'S DESERT HARVEST

(cherisdesertharvest.com)
The best source for prickly pear syrup, jam, and jelly.

NATIVE SEED SEARCH

(nativeseeds.org)
Not only can you buy all the seeds from all the varieties you'd ever want to grow for a borderlands kitchen garden, they also sell Indigenous basketry and art, as well as a wide array of Sonoran pantry items, such as beans, corn, wheat, dried chiles, honey, herbs, smoked salt, and more.

SOUTHWEST DISK

(southwestdisk.com)
Makes high-quality discos for discada. Veteran-owned and based in New Mexico, they also sell burners for them, which can be convenient because the shape of a disco sometimes doesn't lend itself to regular burners.

ACKNOWLEDGMENTS

The gratitude I feel for the dozens and dozens of people who helped me write the book humbles me. Every day, sometimes every hour, I spend along the border I learn something new, whether it's from a friend, a colleague, a stranger—or from Nature herself. More than any other book I've written, I feel more like a vessel than the captain. The content of *Borderlands* reflects my experiences, wide and weird and varied as they are. That is a direct result of adventures planned and unplanned, quests and happenstance, and chance conversations with a guy at the bar or an Uber driver or a clerk at a gas station. There was even a Sinaloan dude with a flat tire I helped fix on a lonely road in Arizona, who told me all about chilorio. They all deserve thanks.

I do want to name some folks, however. Starting with my ex, Holly Heyser, who first showed me how good Mexican food can be, decades ago; she photographed a great many photos in this book, and edited all of them. To Patricio Wise and Cinthia Martinez, who set me on this path and helped me with my Spanish—sometimes in hilarious ways.

Then there are the chefs: Hector Palacios of La Paz, Javier Plascencia and David Hussong of Ensenada, Christian Duthoy of Chihuahua, Maria Mazón of Tucson and Sonora, Guillermo Gonzalez Beristain of Monterrey. I'm not going to leave out Beto Pedrosky of Chihuahua just because he's not a chef; his knowledge of northern Mexican agave spirits is unmatched.

Another set of individuals who have dedicated their lives to the gastronomy of their regions deserve mention, too: Cuitláhuac "Don Piquino" Córdova in Tamaulipas; Gualberto "Weber" Elizondo of Nuevo Leon; Melissa Guerra of South Texas; Ana Rosa Beltrán of Chihuahua; and Elsa Olivares Duarte of Sonora. Fellow author Pati Jinich and my friend Maggie Unzueta of Mama Maggie's Kitchen have also been invaluable.

A tip of the hat to my travel companions: Charlie de la Rosa, Abe Sanchez, Sarah Hart, Mike Ortiz, Jonathan O'Dell, Sharon Lashway, and Jesse Deubel.

The team who put together this book is second to none: my sister Laura Shaw, who has designed my last four books; Lisa Ekus, Jeff Barker, Beth Schatz Kaylor, Chris Niskanen, and Suzanne Fass, my critical readers and editors; and Holly for her photos, which are all the best ones.

Finally, to my amazing, fantastic, and loyal readers of both Hunter Angler Gardener Cook and To the Bone. When I asked for recipe testers, more than 400 of you answered the call! That was far more than I could handle, but I am grateful for every one of you. And to those of you who got a recipe to test? Here you go:

Saul Gomez Acosta, Tim Akimoff, Troy Allison, Max Bittle, Jen Bowden, Duncan Boyd, J. Brandon, Don Burleson, Troy Burns, Dan Capshaw, Robyn Cardwell, Kristina Cool, Sean Corrigan, Kim Walker Daniels, Adam Davis, Mike Desjarlais, Cole Devine, Dale Dishman, Drew Dittmer, Dan Dutton, Russell Edwards, Trudy Ellingsen, Greg Fletcher, Anne Hansen, Tricia Oshant Hawkins, Dave Hedlund, Josh Hoffman, Cathy Hovde, Dorothy Howe, Brad Huffman, Ted Jones, Joe Keough, Callie Koch, Daniel Kozlak, Josh Kuhn, Gail Lafosse, Matthew Lewis, Sharon Loomis, Mark McAdoo, Carol Ann McDaniel, Heather McDevitt, Dale McIntyre, Nick Myers, Danielle Neibling, Cheryl Olman, Cory Ondrejka, Nathan Osborn, Matt Parks, Christine Peterson, Jacob Pickett, Jed Portman, Gena Pressley, Steve Rosenstock, Barb Sargent, Nick Spinelli, Ed Standefer, Yaroslav Stepanov, Gary Strickland, Brendan Volk, David Weber, Jaydene Welzmiller, J.R. Young, Kelly Zamudio, Tyler Zander, and Dave Zehnder.

◀ The author stirs a chacales stew in Coahuila, Mexico.

REFERENCES

Abundis, Ana Rosa Beltrán del Rio, *La Milpa Rarámuri en Las Gorditas Chihuahuenses*, UNAM, Mexico City, 2021.

Aguilar, Karla Bernal, *Verbo Gusto*, Conaculta, Mexico City, 2021.

Aguilar-Rincón, Víctor Heber, *Los Chiles de México y su Distribución*, SINAREFI, Colegio de Postgraduados, Texcoco, Estado de México, 2010.

Aldana, Josefina Rayas, *Recetario Exótico de Sinaloa*, Conaculta, Mexico City, 2004.

Alpers, Jackie, *Taste of Tucson*, West Margin Press, Berkeley, CA, 2020.

Anderson, M. Kat, *Tending the Wild: Native American Knowledge and the Management of California's Natural Resources*, University of California Press, Berkeley, CA, 2005.

Bayless, Rick, *Authentic Mexican*, William Morrow, New York, 2007.

Bayless, Rick, *Mexico One Plate at a Time*, Scribner, New York, 2000.

Bayless, Rick, *Rick Bayless' Mexican Kitchen*, Scribner, New York, 1996.

Bean, Lowell John, *Temalpakh: Cahuila Indian Knowledge and Usage of Plants*, Malki Museum Press, Banning, CA, 1972.

Buechner, Emajean Jordan, *Mexican Cooking: Estilo Auténtico de Sonora*, Thunderbird Press, Metarie, LA, 1982.

Buitimea, Rosa Yocupicio, *Recetario Indígena de Sonora*, Conaculta, Mexico City, 2000.

Cameron, Sheila McNiven, *The Best from New Mexico Kitchens*, New Mexico Magazine, Santa Fe, NM, 1978.

Campuzano, Guillermo Moraga, *Comida Tradicional del Desierto de Altar*, Conaculta, Mexico City, 2016.

Cárdenas, Juan Ramon, *La Senda del Cabrito*, Larousse, Mexico City, 2020.

Casey, Clyde, *Red or Green: New Mexico Cuisine*, University of New Mexico Press, Albuquerque, NM, 2007.

Chapa, Martha, *Cocina Regia*, Gobierno del Estado de Nuevo León, Monterrey, Nuevo León, 1986.

Chávez, Julio Cesar Osuna, *Recetario Tradicional Sudcaliforniano*, Conaculta, Mexico City, 2016.

Conaculta Océano, La Cocina Familiar en el estado de Baja California, author, Mexico City, 1988.

Conaculta Océano, La Cocina Familiar en el estado de Sinaloa, author, Mexico City, 1988.

Conaculta Océano, La Cocina Familiar en el estado de Baja California Sur, author, Mexico City, 1988.

Conaculta Océano, La Cocina Familiar en el estado de Sonora, author, Mexico City, 1988.

Conaculta Océano, La Cocina Familiar en el estado de Chihuahua, author, Mexico City, 1988.

Conaculta Océano, La Cocina Familiar en el estado de Tamaulipas, author, Mexico City, 1988.

Conaculta Océano, La Cocina Familiar en el estado de Coahuila, author, Mexico City, 1988.

Conaculta Océano, La Cocina Familiar en el estado de Nuevo León, author, Mexico City, 1988.

Connoley, Rob, *Acorns and Cattails: A Modern Foraging Cookbook of Forest*, Farm & Field, Skyhorse Publishing, New York, 2016.

Consume Chihuahua, government of Chihuahua publication, unknown date.

Cordero-Cordell, Teresa, *Aprovecho: A Mexican-American Cookbook*, Hippocrene Books, NY, 2004.

Córdova, Cuitláhuac ed., *Sabor a Tamaulipas*, unknown publisher, 2023.

Desert Harvesters, *Eat Mesquite and More: A Cookbook for Sonoran Desert Foods and Living*, Desert Harvesters, Tucson, AZ, 2018.

Duarte, Elsa Olivares, *El Sabor de Sonora*, Editorial Imagines de Sonora, Hermosillo, Sonora, 2013.

Dunmire, William, *Wild Plants of the Pueblo Province*, University of New Mexico Press, Santa Fe, 1995.

Dunmire, William, *Wild Plants and Native Peoples of the Four Corners*, University of New Mexico Press, Santa Fe, 1997.

Emilia, Katherine Esther, *Recetario Menonita de Chihuahua*, Conaculta, Mexico City, 2004.

Felger, Richard, *People of the Desert and Sea: Ethnobotany of the Seri Indians*, Univ. of Arizona Press, Tucson, AZ, 1985.

Flores, Iraís Piñón, *Recetario Indígena de Baja California*, Conaculta, Mexico City, 2000.

Frank, Lois Ellen, *Foods of the Southwest Indian Nations*, Ten Speed Press, Berkeley, CA, 2002.

Gálvez, Alyshia, *Eating NAFTA: Trade, Food Policies and the Destruction of Mexico*, University of California Press, Berkeley, CA, 2018.

Gardiner, Michael, *Cali-Baja Cuisine*, Rizzoli, NY, 2023.

Garza, Lucy, South Texas Mexican Cookbook, Eakin Press, Fort Worth, TX, 1982.

Garza, Mario Horacio Mena, *Recetario de Pescados y Mariscos de Sonora*, Conaculta, Mexico City, 2004.

Gencarelli, Marisa Tapia, *Sonora*, Independently Published, Kansas City, MO, 2021.

Glueck, Rachel, *The Native Mexican Kitchen*, Skyhorse Publishing, New York, 2020.

Godoy, Sergio A. Sandoval, *Gente de Carne y Trigo*, Clave Editorial, Mexico City, 2015.

González, Víctor Manuel Jiménez, *Baja California: Guía para Descubrir los Encantos del Estado*, Océano, Madrid, 2009.

Guzmán, Gonzalo, *Nopalito*, Ten Speed Press, Emeryville, CA, 2017.

Harelik, Tiffany, *The Big Bend Cookbook*, American Palate, Charleston, SC, 2014.

Healy, Ernesto Camou, *Cocina Sonorense*, DR Instituto Sonorense de Cultura, Hermosillo, Sonora, 2007.

Heritage Cookbook: A Round Up of Wild and Regional Foods, Museum of South Texas History, Edinburg, TX, 2017.

Hernandez-Rodriguez, Rafael, *Food Cultures of Mexico*, Greenwood, Santa Barbara, CA, 2021.

Hodgson, Wendy, Food Plants of the Sonoran Desert, University of Arizona Press, Tucson, AZ, 2001.

Holtz, Déborah, *Tacopedia*, Phaidon, New York, 2015.

Hussong, David Castro, *The Baja California Cookbook*, Ten Speed Press, Emeryville, CA, 2020.

Jamison, Cheryl Alters, *The Border Cookbook*, Harvard Common Press, Boston, 1995.

Jáquez Rosas, María del Roció, *Patrimonio Gastronómico de Chihuahua*, Instituto Chihuahuense de la Cultura, Chihuahua, 2016.

Jinich, Pati, *Treasures of the Mexican Table*, Houghton Mifflin Harcourt, Boston, 2021.

Kane, Charles, *Sonoran Desert Food Plants*, Lincoln Town Press, Oracle, AZ, 2011.

Kavena, Juanita Tiger, *Hopi Cookery*, Univ. of Arizona Press, Tucson, AZ, 1980.

Kerr, W. Park, *The El Paso Chile Company's Texas Border Cookbook*, William Morrow & Co., New York 1992.

LaTorre, Dolores, *Cooking and Curing with Mexican Herbs*, The Encino Press, Austin, TX, 1977.

Lawton, Cappy, *Enchiladas: Aztec to Tex-Mex*, Trinity University Press, San Antonio, TX, 2015.

Linares, Edelmira, *Quelites: Sabores y Saberes*, UNAM, Mexico City, 2020.

Losón de Fábregas, Maria, ed., *Tamaulipas: Aromas y Sabores*, Gobierno de Estado de Tamaulipas, Mexico City, 2002.

Manning, Wayne, "The Genus Carya in Mexico," *Journal of the Arnold Arboretum*, vol. 30, no. 4, 1949, pp. 425–432.

Martinez, Liddy, *The Chile Line: Historic Northern New Mexican Recipes*, Pajarito Press, Los Alamos, New Mexico, 2019.

Martinez, Mely, *The Mexican Home Kitchen*, Rock Point, NY, 2020.

Martinez, Zarela, *Food from My Heart*, MacMillan, New York, 1992.

McNamee, Gregory, *Tortillas, Tiswin and T-Bones: A Food History of the Southwest*, University of New Mexico Press, Albuquerque, NM, 2017.

Medrano, Adán, *Truly Texas Mexican*, Texas Tech University Press, Lubbock, TX, 2014.

Moral, Paulina del, *Recetario Mascogo de Coahuila*, Conaculta, Mexico City, 2000.

Nabhan, Gary Paul, *Gathering the Desert*, University of Arizona Press, Tucson, AZ, 1985.

Nabhan, Gary Paul, *Mesquite: An Arboreal Love Affair*, Chelsea Green, White River Junction, VT, 2018.

Neithammer, Carolyn, *The Tumbleweed Gourmet*, University of Arizona Press, Tucson, AZ, 1987.

Neithammer, Carolyn, *A Desert Feast*, University of Arizona Press, Tucson, AZ, 2020.

Olvera, Enrique, *Tu Casa Mi Casa*, Phaidon, New York, 2019.

Olvera, Enrique, *Mexico from the Inside Out*, Phaidon, New York, 2015.

Ortiz, Félix Cantú, *Diario de Cocina de mi Abuela*, Palibrio LLC, Bloomington, IN, 2014.

Pain, Alfonso, *Western Mexican Cook Book*, Booksmith, Tucson, AZ, 1971.

Peyton, James W., *El Norte: The Cuisine of Northern Mexico*, Red Crane Books, Santa Fe, NM, 1995.

Pijoan, Paula, *Plantas Nativas Comestibles de Baja California*, Culinary Art School, Tijuana, Baja, 2018.

Pilcher, Jeffrey, *Que Vivan Los Tamales: Food and the Making of Mexican Identity*, University of New Mexico Press, Albuquerque, NM, 1999.

Plascencia, Javier, *The Soul of Baja*, Grupo Expansión, Mexico City, 2017.

Ralat, José, *American Tacos: A History and Guide*, Univversity of Texas Press, Austin, TX, 2020.

Ramos-Prieto, Tania Paola, *Los Sabores de mi Tierra*, independently published, 2020.

Rea, Amadeo, At the Desert's Green Edge: An Ethnobotany of the Gila River Pima, University of Arizona Press, Tucson, AZ, 1997.

Rivas, Heriberto García, *Cocina Prehispánica Mexicana*, Panorama, Mexico City, 2016.

Romero, Philomena, *New Mexican Dishes*, Independently published, Los Alamos, NM, 1970.

Ronstadt, Linda, *Feels Like Home: A Song for the Sonoran Badlands*, Heyday, Berkeley, CA, 2022.

Ruta Gastronomía: Nuevo Leon, Coahuila, Durango y Sonora, government publication, no date.

Salmon, Enrique, *Eating the Landscape*, University of Arizona Press, Tucson, AZ, 2012.

Sánchez, Edith Yesenia Pena, *Cocina Tradicional Neoleonesa*, Conaculta, Mexico City, 2017.

Seasoned with Sun: Recipes from the Southwest, Junior League of El Paso, El Paso, TX, 1974.

Slattery, John, *Southwest Foraging*, Timber Press, Portland, OR, 2016.

Some Like It Hot: The Climate, Culture and Cuisine of South Texas, Junior League of McAllen, TX, 1992.

Sonora, María Luisa Villareal, *Cocina Silvestre: Venado, Jabalí y Tepezcuintle*, independently published, 2020.

Swentzell, Roxanne, and Patricia Perea, eds., *The Pueblo Food Experience Cookbook*, University of New Mexico Press, Santa Fe, NM, 2016.

Téllez, Lesley, *Eat Mexico*, Kyle Books, Lanham, MD, 2015.

Trías, Albino Maras, *Comida de los Tarahumaras*, Conaculta, Mexico City, 1999.

Tull, Delena, *Edible and Useful Plants of Texas and the Southwest*, University of Texas Press, Austin, TX, 1987.

Vega, Josefina Rivas, *Recetario Tepehuano de Chihuahua y Durango*, Conaculta, Mexico City, 2004.

Wilkin-Robertson, Michael, *Kumeyaay Ethnobotany*, Sunbelt Publications, San Diego, 2018.

Yescas, Carlos, *Quesos Mexicanos*, Larousse, Mexico City, 2013.

Yetman, David, *Sonora: An Intimate Geography*, University of New Mexico Press, Santa Fe, 1996.

Yetman, David, *Mayo Ethnobotany*, University of California Press, Berkeley, CA, 2002.

Zazueta, Karla, *Norteña: Authentic Family Recipes from the North of Mexico*, Pavilion, London, 2024.

Zurita, Ricardo Muñoz, *Larousse Diccionario Enciclopédico de la Gastronomía Mexicana*, Larousse, Mexico City, 2012.

Zurita, Ricardo Muñoz, *Los Chiles Rellenos en Mexico: Antología de Recetas*, UNAM, Mexico City, 2020.

This juniper near the Chihuahuan Desert Nature Center in Fort Davis, Texas, could easily have been a seedling before European contact with the New World in 1492.

INDEX

Los Tres Gallos
CORSICA
RVCA